Discourse Perspectives on Organizational Communication

Discourse Perspectives on Organizational Communication

Edited by

Jolanta Aritz and Robyn C. Walker

FAIRLEIGH DICKINSON UNIVERSITY PRESS
Madison • Teaneck

Published by Fairleigh Dickinson University Press
Co-published with The Rowman & Littlefield Publishing Group, Inc.
4501 Forbes Boulevard, Suite 200, Lanham, Maryland 20706
www.rowmanlittlefield.com

Estover Road, Plymouth PL6 7PY, United Kingdom

British Library Cataloguing in Publication Information Available

Library of Congress Cataloging-in-Publication Data

Discourse perspectives on organizational communication / edited by Jolanta Aritz and Robyn C. Walker.

p. cm. — (The Fairleigh Dickinson University Press series in communication studies)

ISBN 978-1-61147-437-4 (cloth : alk. paper) — ISBN 978-1-61147-438-1 (ebook)

1. Communication in organizations. I. Aritz, Jolanta, 1968– II. Walker, Robyn.

HD30.3.D56 2012

302.3'5—dc23

2011035437

∞™ The paper used in this publication meets the minimum requirements of American National Standard for Information Sciences—Permanence of Paper for Printed Library Materials, ANSI/NISO Z39.48-1992.

Printed in the United States of America

Contents

Introduction

Jolanta Aritz and Robyn C. Walker

Management and organizational scholarship is a young science, still under construction, and borrowing from more established disciplines such as economics, sociology, psychology, and history. An even more recent turn to communication has provided the field with new alliances and produced new offshoots of research. Sillince and Suddaby (2008) single out two factors that have facilitated this interaction between management and communication. One factor is the increasingly interdisciplinary focus of management scholars reaching out to social sciences and humanities as a way of understanding organizations. The second factor is a growing adoption of social constructionist perspectives by management scholars that highlights the importance of language as a means of analyzing organizations. This "linguistic turn" has produced research that focuses on language as social action. The new linguistic emphasis in management and organizational communication is driven by the idea that "language use does not simply mirror reality out there but rather creates or constitutes it" (Kärreman and Alvesson 2008, 323); in other words, discourse practices are foundational in the creation of social reality.

A major focus of social constructionism is to uncover the ways in which individuals and groups participate in the creation of their perceived social reality. It involves looking at the ways *social phenomena* are created, institutionalized, and eventually, at a societal level, made into *tradition* by humans. Berger and Luckmann (1966) argue that all knowledge, including the most basic, taken-for-granted, commonsense knowledge of everyday reality, is derived from and maintained by *social interactions*. When people interact, they do so with the understanding that their respective perceptions of reality are related, and as they act upon this understanding, their common knowledge of reality becomes reinforced. Since people negotiate this commonsense knowledge, human typifications, significations, and institutions come to be presented as part of shared reality. It is in this sense that it can be said that reality is socially constructed.

According to Berger and Luckmann (1966), actors interacting together form, over time, *typifications* or mental representations of each other's actions, and that these typifications eventually become *habitualized* into reciprocal *roles* played by the actors in relation to each other. When these reciprocal roles become routinized, the typified reciprocal interactions are said to be *institutionalized*. In the process of this institutionalization, *meaning* is embedded and institutionalized into individuals and society—knowledge and people's conception of (and therefore belief regarding) what reality "is"—becomes embedded into the institutional fabric and structure of society, and social reality is therefore said to be socially constructed. This process occurs at every level of society, including the organizational level.

It is this seemingly "invisible" process that discursive approaches to organizational studies can help to illuminate. The realization that meaning is embedded and institutionalized—even inscribed—on individuals, society, and its various entities brings us to an emphasis on language, discourse, or communication, as it is variously referred to by different disciplines, all of which, in various ways, study the same phenomenon. Extending this observation from our discursive perspective, we see that institutions are not just social constructions but social constructions constituted through discourse (Kress 1995; Parker 1992).

Research approaches that focus on language and its use thus may differ from much of the extant research in management and organizations that may take what might be called a positivist approach, which assumes that there is a reality "out there" that can be objectively apprehended and described. "Despite this connection between institutions and language, most institutional theory has been dominated by realist investigations in which the examination of organizational practices has been disconnected from the discursive practices that constitute them" (Philips et al. 2004, 635). Such "realist" approaches may not question how that reality came into being and is reproduced but may instead look at its effects—the institutions, behaviors, and individuals that are a product of this linguistic process. As Zucker (1991) notes, the actual process of institutionalization thus largely remains a "black box"; we know it works, we just don't know how.

It is this seemingly "invisible" phenomenon of reality creation on which discourse perspectives hope to shed more light. More specifically, the appeal of such analysis for management scholarship is its theoretical focus on rhetoric or discourse as a way to analyze organizations and as a practical mode to intervene in organizational structures, to analyze organizational order and to challenge that order, and to understand organizational discourses as a way of organizing (Hartelius and Browning 2008). One outcome of this trend is the emergence of the field of "organizational" or "business" discourse studies, as it is variously referred to by different authors and researchers. This emergence has been marked by research, special conferences, and loose organizational affiliations and publications devoted to exploring and defining studies of organizational or business discourse. This is particularly true of the existing books that address the field (Grant, Hardy, Oswick, and Putnam 2004; Bargiela-Chiappini, Nickerson, and Planken 2007; and Bargiela-Chiappini 2009).

Although similar in their general focus on language, the two terms, *organizational discourse* and *business discourse*, have differing origins. The term *organizational discourse* is generally used by scholars in the fields of management and communication working in the tradition of North American organizational communication; although, one can also come across the term *organizational rhetoric* used in more management-oriented scholarship. Based on the way the two terms are used, we conclude that the rhetorical emphasis, heightened by the use of the term *organizational rhetoric*, is subsumed under *organizational discourse* as one of four domains of discourse that constitute texts for analysis. The other three domains include conversation and dialogue, narratives and stories, and tropes or metaphors (Grant et al. 2004).

In contrast to organizational discourse that has its origins in the North American tradition of communication, the field of business discourse has European roots and has been developed by scholars with training in applied linguistics and sociolinguistics (Bargiela-Chiappini 2009). The two traditions, business discourse and organizational discourse, have much in common and seem to be separated more by their discipline of origin rather than their focus of study.

Business discourse refers to authentic language interaction, talk and writing in a corporate setting, and is "founded on the twin notions of discourse as *situated action* and of *language as work*" (Bargiela-Chiappini and Nickerson 2002, 277, emphasis original). It is a language-based approach of looking at individuals who engage in interaction in a corporate setting that is motivated by a concern to understand how they communicate strategically in an organizational context (Bargiela-Chiappini, Nickerson, and Planken 2007). The variety of methodologies used to conduct such analysis include conversation analysis, pragmatics, corpus linguistics, genre analysis, and rhetorical analysis. In identifying new directions for this approach, though, Nickerson & Planken (2009) also foresee a possible convergence with the organizational discourse research done in North America. They predict an increased focus on the new types of media that are used in business, the influence of multimodality in business communication, and an increased interest in critical research to analyze discourses of inequalities in the business environment. The latter development seems to intersect more closely with some of the organizational discourse research done in North America.

Despite the fact that organizational discourse and business discourse share a common interest in language as the vehicle of analysis of matters pertinent to organizational settings, there has been little overlap of cited works, and each discipline has generated its own body of research looking at communication practices in the workplace. This somewhat artificial divide is best illustrated by the fact that each field has produced its own handbook, *The SAGE Handbook of Organizational Discourse* (Grant et al. 2004) and *The Handbook of Business Discourse* (Bargiela-Chiappini 2009).

Organizational discourse theorists have recently made a distinction between two approaches to organizational discourse, little *d* discourse and big *D* discourse, that may be helpful in better understanding the distinctions between these two camps (Alvesson and Kärreman 2000; Kärreman and Alvesson 2008; Jian et al. 2008). Little *d d*iscourse refers to "talk and text in situational organizational contexts . . . [and] often examines the processes in which organizational actors [engage *d*iscourse to] construct emotion, attitude, identity and various aspects of organizational reality, accomplish work tasks and orderliness, and manage contradictions and work relationships through moment-to-moment talk-in-interaction and creation of local texts" (Jian et al. 2008, 304). In most cases these studies adopt a linguistic approach and use conversational analysis, ethnomethodology, pragmatics, speech act theory, and other methodologies that are grounded in linguistic theory. In this manner, little *d d*iscourse seems to overlap in its focus with the scholarship of business discourse.

In contrast, big *D D*iscourse refers to "culturally standardized interpretive frames historically rooted in systems of power and knowledge." As such, "organizational *D*iscourse studies are interested in showing how *D*iscourse constitutes workers' subjectivities, establishes and naturalizes managerial control, and disciplines the productive body" (Jian et al. 2008, 306). It is grounded in the traditions of critical/cultural studies of media, rhetorical studies, and organizational communication, particularly those extending the work of Foucault.

Jian et al. (2008) note a significant growth of the interplay of these two approaches, yet, so far, there has been less emphasis on little *d* discourse in the field of organizational discourse. This slow embrace of little *d* is not surprising given the challenges that such a union presents: different disciplines of origin, academic traditions, methodologies, geographical location of scholars, academic affiliations and schools, and desired publication outlets. Yet, we find this distinction crucial and see the conversation between so-called little *d* and big *D* discourse instrumental in moving forward and bringing together the two fields in meaningful ways.

This collection of articles is intended to give a collective voice to studies that would otherwise be placed in different categories, some within organizational discourse and some within business discourse. This attempt is grounded in the commonality of interest that both approaches share, their focus on discourse and how it organizes and shapes organizations and their social actors, and a potential interplay between the two that may inform each other and produce new, more complex ways of looking at organizational phenomena. The book is intentionally called *Discourse Perspectives on Organizational Communication* to create a shared space for studies that are grounded in different traditions and to encourage a conversation between them that we hope will contribute to the cross-pollination of the two traditions. After all, social science and linguistic traditions may have more in common than we are willing to acknowledge. It was Dell Hymes who wrote, "The communicative event . . . [is] central. In terms of language proper, the statement means that the linguistic code is displaced by the speech act as focus of attention" (1964, 21).

This book also differs from previous books that have largely focused on explaining the different epistemological and methodological approaches used in the field of organizational and business discourse in a continuing attempt to define the field (Grant et al. 2004; Bargiela-Chiappini, Nickerson, and Planken 2007; and Bargiela-Chiappini 2009). Instead, it provides a sampling of the research being done in each area. In addition to bringing the two traditions of discourse studies together, this collection of articles illustrates two characteristics of the field: 1) the variety of organizational phenomena that might be studied using discourse methods, and 2) the range of epistemological and methodological approaches that might be used in such studies. As such, the field of organizational/business discourse is one of the first to emerge that successfully incorporates a truly interdisciplinary approach, with researchers from both the social sciences and humanities, from communication, linguistics, women's studies, psychology, business and management, sociology, composition and rhetoric, among others.

The first chapter of this volume by Loizos Heracleous, the presentation of an enhanced view of the process of the discursive construction of social reality, is intended to improve the clarity of the theoretical exposition of the field of organizational discourse. Its potential goal is to lead to more structured, cumulative, and theoretically complementary research in the field.

In chapter 2, John McClellan and Stanley Deetz develop a politically attentive relational constructionist (PARC) perspective on organizational communication and examine discourses associated with collaborative conversations about change and environmental sustainability. While many discursive approaches focus on strategic forms of communication to address contemporary social and business issues, they offer a critically inspired, interpretive approach to the study of organizational discourse. Their aim is to examine the practice of free and open forms of communication among a wide range of stakeholders to promote healthy decision-making practices.

In chapter 3, Francesca Bargiela-Chiappini argues that Asian Business Discourses (ABDs) is an enterprise with Western antecedents but with increasingly localized expressions, which reflect the concerns and expectations of specific geopolitical and socioeconomic *locales*. The chapter opens with a selective historiography of "business discourse" and concludes with a reflection on essentialist discourses and the dangers of using homogenizing labels such as "Asian." In between these two bookends, and within the limits of a short essay, Bargiela-Chiappini sketches out some of the issues raised by business discourse research in general, and ABDs in particular. The examples of research work by Eastern Asian scholars is indicative of a growing interest in the application of ethnographic and discourse analytic approaches to the interpretation of verbal and written communication in the workplace. Some of them also interrogate the ideological import of corporate language policy and the continuing gap between work practices and business communication pedagogy.

In chapter 4, Misa Fujio and Hiromasa Tanaka follow on Bargiela-Chiappini's call for analysis of localized discourses (specifically, Japanese business discourses) to apply an epistemological framework based on concepts developed by Japanese scholars. This chapter seeks to bridge the gap between business discourse analysis and the study of organizations in Japan by setting the analysis of the meeting data against current business practices as shaped by native management theories.

In chapter 5, Gail Fann Thomas and Kimberlie Stephens use text analysis techniques as a means to rethink theories of policy making. Using a contemporary case in the United States, the authors will show how an attention to discourse can reframe the political space and help public managers reimagine avenues for policy development.

In chapter 6, Torsten Oliver Salge and Michael Ian Barrett look at the rhetorical strategies through which organizational exploration and exploitation initiatives are being legitimated in a public hospital. Using a two-by-two cell design, the study draws on rich observational, interview, and archival data to identify within-group commonalities as well as cross-group differences in discursive legitimation strategies.

In chapter 7, Miguel F. Ruiz-Garrido, Immaculada Fortanet-Gómez, and Juan Carlos Palmer-Silveira replicate and update Skulskad's studies (1992, 1993) of Chairman's Statements in two languages, English and Spanish, paying special attention to the discourse elements used by the authors of these documents to establish a friendly and open relationship with the reader.

In chapter 8, Donald L. Anderson draws upon discourse excerpts taken from a yearlong study of a project team at Techco, a high-tech organization, to look at organizational identity in the United States. For the Techco team, organizational identity was negotiated and made meaningful to participants during discussions of benchmarking, or explanations of other organizations' forecasting practices. While members explicitly pointed to benchmarking as a method for understanding others (the surface rationale also provided by management literatures), it also served an important identity function as it created a shared organizational identity that Techco team members would later draw upon.

In chapter 9, John M. Conley, Lissa L. Broome, and Kimberly D. Krawiec present the results of an interview-based study of the discourse of diversity in a particular business setting: the corporate boardroom. They explore the narratives (or, synonymously, stories or accounts) that are produced by board members, executives, government officials, and others when they are asked to explain whether and why diversity matters on corporate boards.

In chapter 10, Daphne A. Jameson and Judi Brownell explore how organizations try to create shared meanings and collective commitment to environmental values in written texts, in particular through narrative and symbolism, and how contradictions and discrepancies undermine texts' persuasiveness. In a narratological analysis of environmental texts from the lodging industry, they explore the rhetoric of "greenness," showing how patterns of narrative structure established relationships among organizations and the constituencies whom they wanted to influence. They discuss how the resulting story lines affect organizational ethos: identity built on demonstrated credibility and deeply held values.

In the conclusion, the editors reflect on the contributions made in this collection to the study of business and organizational discourse and discuss how discourse methods and approaches can complement and enhance our current understandings and study of organizations with a particular focus on organizational change and identity.

REFERENCES

Alvesson, Mats, and Dan Kärreman. 2000. Taking the Linguistic Turn in Organizational Research. *Journal of Applied Behavioral Science* 36: 136–58.

Bargiela-Chiappini, Francesca. 2009. *The Handbook of Business Discourse.* Edinburg: Edinburgh University Press.

Bargiela-Chiappini, Francesca, and Catherine Nickerson. 2002. Business Discourse: Old Debates, New Horizons. *International Review of Applied Linguistics in Language Teaching, (IRAL)* 40: 273–381.

Bargiela-Chiappini, Francesca, Catherine Nickerson, and Brigitte Planken. 2007. *Business Discourse*. New York, NY: Palgrave Macmillan.

Berger, P., and T. Luckmann. 1966. *The Social Construction of Reality: A Treatise in the Sociology of Knowledge.* London: Penguin Books.

Grant, David, Cynthia Hardy, Clifford Oswick, and Linda Putnam. 2004. *The SAGE Handbook of Organizational Discourse.* London: Sage.

Hartelius E. J., and L. D. Browning. 2008. The Application of Rhetorical Theory in Managerial Research: A Literature Review. *Management Communication Quarterly* 22: 13–40.

Hymes, D. 1964. Towards Ethnographies of Communication: The Analysis of Communicative Events. In *Language and Social Context: Selected Readings,* ed. P. P. Giglioli, 21–45. Harmondsworth: Penguin Books.

Jian, G., A. M. Schmisseur, and Gail T. Fairhurst. 2008. Organizational Discourse and Communication: The Progeny of Proteus. *Discourse and Communication* 2: 299–320.

Kärreman, Dan, and Mats Alvesson. 2008. The Communicative Constitution of What? A Response to Jian et al. *Discourse and Communication* 2: 321–25.

Kress, G. 1995. The Social Production of Language: History and Structures of Domination. In *Discourse in Society: Systemic Functional Perspectives,* eds. P. Fries and M. Gregory, 169–91. Norwood, NJ: Ablex.

Nickerson, Catherine, and Brigette Planken. 2009. Europe: State of the Field. In *The Handbook of Business Discourse,* ed. Francesca Bargiela-Chiappini. Edinburg: Edinburgh University Press.

Parker, I. 1992. *Discourse Dynamics: Critical Analysis for Social and Individual Psychology.* London: Routledge.

Philips, N., T. B. Lawrence, and Cynthia Hardy. 2004. Discourse and Institutions. *Academy of Management Review* 29: 635–52.

Sillince, J. A. A., and R. Suddaby. 2008. Organizational Rhetoric: Bridging Management and Communication Scholarship. *Management Communication Quarterly* 22: 5–13.

Zucker, L. G. 1991. The Role of Institutionalization in Cultural Persistence. In *The New Institutionalism in Organizational Analysis,* eds. W. W. Powell and P. J. DiMaggio, 83–107. Chicago: University of Chicago Press.

1

Four Propositions toward an Interpretive Theory of the Process of Discursive Reality Construction

Loizos Heracleous

Over the last decade the field of organizational discourse has developed from being a nascent, unstructured, and emergent field toward maturity, characterized by established specialist conferences, creation of research centers, publishing of special issues in leading journals, and a vibrant international community of scholars contributing to this field. Various definitions of discourse have been adopted, influenced by the paradigmatic standpoint and research goals of their authors (see, for example, Grant et al. 2004; Heracleous 2006a; Phillips and Hardy 2002). In this chapter I define discourses as collections of texts, both verbal and textual, that are patterned and underlied by certain structural features that lend both coherence (at the structural level) as well as patterned variation (at the communicative level) to them. Language is the raw material that constitutes texts, collections of which in turn constitute discourses that exist in a mutually constitutive relationship with actors' interpretations and actions (Heracleous and Barrett 2001; Heracleous and Hendry 2000).

The view that discourse does not merely function as a conduit for the transfer of communicative messages, in a merely representative, functional fashion, but is constructive of social and organizational reality is an accepted assumption of a wide spectrum of theoretical fields. Social constructionism, for example, holds that individuals, through social interaction, construct "semantic fields" or "zones of meaning" within which they conduct their daily affairs (Berger and Luckmann 1966, 55). Rhetorical studies, in addition, aim to uncover how speeches or texts gain persuasive force that can shift audiences' or readers' perceptions of reality on pressing social issues (Gill and Whedbee 1997; Charland 1987; Gronbeck 1973). Critical theory and critical discourse analysis focus on unmasking what they see as the surreptitious effects of discourse in constructing particular subject identities and particular versions of the "truth" that skew power relations in the interests of the already powerful, with the explicit aim of delegitimating these constructions and inducing social change (van Dijk 1993; Mumby and Stohl 1991).

Indeed, one of the key contributions of organizational discourse to organization theory is to argue for, and aid a deeper, more nuanced understanding of, the social construction of reality (Grant, Keenoy, and Oswick 2001). As organizational communication theorists have argued, organization and communication are co-constitutive, conversations are sites of organizing processes, and texts are reflections of sense making and interpretive processes within particular communities of practice (Taylor and Robichaud 2004; Taylor and Van Every 2000). Despite the widespread acceptance of the constructive role of discourse (Hardy 2001), however, discussions of discourse more broadly, and understandings of the process of discursive reality construction more specifically, remain unclear (Chia 2000) and fragmented (Alvesson and Kärreman 2000). In this chapter I draw from speech act theory, rhetoric, ethnography of communication, social constructionism, social cognition, symbolic interactionism, and critical discourse analysis to advance four propositions toward an interpretive theory intended to aid further understanding of the process of discursive construction of reality within an integrative framework.

Responding to its complex nature and to the multidisciplinary antecedents of discourse (Grant, Keenoy, and Oswick 2001; Heracleous 2004, 2006a; Oswick, Keenoy, and Grant 2000), and following Ashby's (1960) notion of requisite variety, the four propositions build on a broad array of theoretical domains that are not thoroughly distinct but overlapping in their aims and concerns. As used here, these domains share key tenets of the interpretive paradigm (Burrell and Morgan 1979).[1] The four propositions can help to address the research challenge of improving the clarity of theoretical exposition in the field of organizational discourse, addressing interrelated levels of analysis, and potentially leading to more cumulative and integrative research in this field.

THE FOUR PROPOSITIONS

The four propositions are:

1. Discourse can fruitfully be seen as situated symbolic action
2. Discourse and cognition are mutually constituted
3. Social reality is constructed through discursive symbolic interaction
4. Discursive reality construction is hegemonic, biased in favor of dominant interests

Proposition 1 relates to the ontology of discourse. It underlies and informs the other three propositions and is located at a metatheoretical level. Proposition 2 outlines the basic assumption on the relationship of discourse to agents' thinking, which in turn can diffuse and become institutionalized through discursive symbolic interaction (proposition 3). Proposition 4 introduces the elemental dimension of power, in effect helping to explain why understanding the relationship between discourse and social reality construction is a worthwhile endeavor. Taken together, these propositions shed light on the process of discursive reality construction.

Proposition 1: Discourse Can Fruitfully Be Seen as Situated Symbolic Action

The three components of this proposition (situated nature; symbolic nature; and action dimension), function at multiple levels of analysis. Situational contexts, for example, are nested within broader organizational and institutional contexts. Viewing discourse as action, moreover, is a valid perspective at the micro, meso, and institutional levels. At the micro level of individual action, for example, analysis can examine an actor's employment of specific communicative actions with intent to achieve certain goals. Communicative actions also occur within social interaction, where meso-level analysis can examine other agents' interpretations of intended meanings based on their own understandings and concerns and the interplay of communicative actions within groups and organizations. Lastly, (communicative) actions can be seen as substantive manifestations as well as constitutive elements of institutional structures (Giddens 1984; Searle 1995), including discursive deep structures (Heracleous 2006b; Heracleous and Barrett 2001). Thus, analysis of macro-level institutional arrangements and institutionalized meanings can be informed by examination of communicative actions and agents' first-order meanings (Searle 1995; Suddaby and Greenwood 2005). Below I discuss in more detail the three dimensions of the view of discourse as situated symbolic action, in each case drawing from relevant theoretical antecedents.

Discourse as* action *(proposition 1a).[2] Speech act theory (Austin 1962) helped to propel language from the domain of communication to the domain of action by challenging the traditional assumption of the philosophy of language, that "to say something . . . is always and simply to *state* something" that has truth value, suggesting instead that "to *say* something is to *do* something" (1962, 12, emphases in original). Austin (1962) distinguished among the act of saying something (locutionary act), the intent in saying something (illocutionary act), and the effects of acts on the audience (perlocutionary acts). He referred to utterances that do things as "performatives" (1962, 6) and the contextual circumstances that could hinder this performance "infelicities" (1962, 14). Searle (1975) developed more elaborate typologies of illocutionary acts, specified further their felicity conditions, and introduced the notion of indirect speech acts in which the link between intended meaning and utterance is unclear.

Despite the foundational nature of speech act theory in offering a conception of language as action, the focus is on the micro-level utterances, a level not naturally suited to the analysis of broader collections of texts (which constitute discourses). In order to understand "macro" speech acts (van Dijk 1977), or the effects at the action level of "grand" or "mega" discourses (Alvesson and Kärreman 2000), another approach is needed that can engage with these levels, such as rhetorical analysis.

There are a variety of definitions of rhetoric, but most definitions view rhetoric as discourse that attempts to persuade and move individuals to action, emphasizing its instrumental and pragmatic concerns. In Suddaby and Greenwood's words, "persuasive language, or rhetorical strategy, is a significant tool by which shifts in a dominant logic can be achieved" (2005, 41). In terms of classical rhetoric, persuasive power could be achieved through *ethos*, or the character of the speaker; appeal to *pathos*, or emotion; and finally through *logos* or logical argument (Aristotle 1991). Burke's (1969) work introduced, in addition to persuasion, the concept of identification between rhetor and audience as a key rhetorical process. Rhetoric thus allows a holistic exploration of situation, audience, rhetor, and textual features such as structure and temporality, enthymemes, metaphor, and iconicity to shed light on how discourse can influence actors' understandings, values, and beliefs by espousing particular views of the world (Gill and Whedbee 1997).

The classical rhetorical situation tends to focus on a single orator, a single text such as a speech delivered at a certain point to a largely homogeneous audience, with emphasis on rhetorical techniques and with the aim of persuading the audience, usually within a political context. Contemporary rhetorical analyses have shifted away from this traditional situation and mode of analysis to a more pluralist, constructive (rather than functional) approach that encompasses texts from a group of actors (for example, a stakeholder group or an organization, rather than an individual rhetor), and groups of texts (discourses) as opposed to individual texts such as single speeches. These texts may occur at multiple points, in a variety of contexts, and may be addressed to and produced by heterogeneous audiences (a variety of stakeholders with potentially incompatible interests). Analyses here tend to examine structural properties of such collections of texts, aiming to gain insights in their role in processes of social construction. Examples of empirical applications of rhetorical analysis to societal or organizational discourses with structural level, constructive concerns include Charland (1987), Gronbeck (1973), Heracleous (2006b), Heracleous and Barrett (2001), and Suddaby and Greenwood (2005).

Discourse as* situated *action (proposition 1b). The linkage between text and context is important to a number of fields, including rhetoric, ethnography of communication, critical discourse analysis, discourse pragmatics, and frame analysis. We draw in this section further from rhetoric and from the field of ethnography of communication to draw attention to the situational elements of discourse, which influence both the generation and interpretation of discourse.

Further to the discussion above, rhetoric aims to explore the "dynamic interaction of a rhetorical text with its context" (Gill and Whedbee 1997, 159). The important influence of the context or situation on what should and could be said, as well as the rhetor's competence, were highlighted by Aristotle's definition of rhetoric as "an ability, in each particular case, to see the available means of persuasion" (1991, 36). This definition illustrates the goal-directed and contextual orientation of this field, as does Bryant's (1974, 211) view that "the rhetorical function is the function of adjusting ideas to people and people to ideas." Bitzer (1968) argued that beyond being a necessary condition of rhetorical discourse, the situation offers exigencies that both shape and are addressed by rhetorical discourse. There is thus a mutually constitutive relationship between rhetorical discourse and the situation.

Ethnographic studies of communication (Hymes 1964) have shown that communication cannot be adequately understood as distinct from its context. Frake (1964), for example, has shown how discourse is divided in distinct stages in the "drinking talk" of the Eastern Subanun tribe in the Philippines, where each discourse stage accomplishes different speech acts and has its own logic of appropriateness. "Drinking talk" is simultaneously social interaction, entertainment, and the de facto governance institution of this social group, where leaders are determined based on their skill at "talking from the straw," both in terms of rational as well as aesthetic discourse (1964, 132). Basso (1970), moreover, has shown that not only talk but also silence has different meanings depending on its context of use by identifying several distinct situations where silence is used by Western Apache Indians. Elements of context were synthesized in Hymes's (1972) SPEAKING framework. This refers to S (setting, scene); P (participants); E (ends); A (act sequence); K (key); I (instrumentalities); N (norms of interaction and interpretation); and G (genre). The embeddedness of discourse in its context extends beyond the immediate situation, being nested in wider social and cultural systems: "aspects of meaning and interpretation are determined by culture-specific activities and practices . . . [which] are interconnected in turn with the larger sociopolitical systems that govern and are in part constituted by them" (Gumperz and Levinson 1991, 614).

Discourse as* symbolic *action (proposition 1c). Berger and Luckmann (1966), in their influential statement of social constructionism, suggested that individuals know social reality in terms of symbolic universes constructed through social interaction. They viewed language as the "most important sign system of human society" (1966, 51), the primary means through which "objectivation," the manifestation of subjective meanings through actions, proceeds. Language makes subjective meanings "real" and at the same time typifies these meanings through creating "semantic fields or zones of meaning" (1966, 55), within which daily routines proceed.

Language (as the building block of texts that make up discourses) at a basic semantic level as a system of signs is symbolic, inasmuch as signs have a meaning beyond themselves. From a social construction perspective, however, through its symbolic character, discourse also evokes mental frames that are "metacommunicative" (Bateson 1972, 188), simultaneously highlighting certain meanings and excluding others. A frame can be triggered and represented by a few words or phrases (often metaphorical) that can evoke powerful emotional reactions subconsciously linked to a story line (a fuller representation of the frame) that then shape agents' reasoning and decision making (Marshak and Heracleous 2009).

The framing process evokes particular typifications and associations through connotation as well as displaying the speakers' attitudes and beliefs (Xu 1992). Language, in this perspective, does not simply mirror social reality through (constructed) correspondences between signs and things but constitutes it through its symbolic power, creating conditioned rationalities as widespread ways of thinking within particular social systems (Gergen and Thatchenkery 1996). Such conditioned rationalities were empirically illustrated, for example, by Heracleous and Barrett (2001) and Heracleous (2006a) through application of rhetorical analysis, represented via enthymemes that operated as structural features of the organizational discourses studied. The taken-for-granted premises of these enthymemes not only provided shared understandings but also exerted normative force, legitimizing or challenging agents' interpretations and actions as well as organizational initiatives.

An application of the framework of discourse as situated symbolic action. Heracleous and Marshak (2004) apply the lens of discourse as situated symbolic action to analyze an episode of negotiated order, a meeting of senior managers of Systech, a major IT organization where a new business model for the organization's advanced consulting division was debated. The recently hired group president aimed to implement a model that entailed a move from the more traditional, functionally based, distributed model of client engagement used at the division to a "principal-centered" consulting model involving principals who "owned" clients and were responsible for all aspects of the client engagement. This move would lead to substantial reallocation of power, status, and influence within the division and was hotly contested. At a pivotal moment in the meeting, the chief advocate of the "principal-centered" model acknowledged that things were different in Systech and therefore some responsibilities could be shared rather than fully led by the relevant principal. This led to a more co-operative, productive discussion in which a new integrative model was developed, labeled by the participants as "The Advanced Services Division Business Model." When the output was given to the group president, who had not attended the meeting, he added "(Principal-Led)" in the name, reaffirming his desire for a business model with most of the power and status accruing to principals.

This episode was analyzed firstly through a view of discourse as *action*, examining what the participants said and what they may have intended to achieve through their communicative actions in the meeting. For example, at the locutionary level, the meeting was opened without mention of its purpose and by referring to "customers first" as a superordinate goal. At the illocutionary level this may have been an attempt to start off the meeting smoothly and to encourage group unity in the context of deeply divergent political interests and views bubbling under the surface.

Secondly, it was analyzed through a view of discourse as *situated* action, examining the added value that arises from a knowledge of the different levels of context (interactional, organizational, and industry) in discourse analysis. For example, information about the previous career of the new group president, which was spent in a big 5/4 accounting firm and about his subsequent acquisition of part of Consultco, which was operating through this principal-led model, helps to shed light on his commitment and determination to implement this model in the face of fierce resistance by most Systech actors. Further, a knowledge of the professional background and organizational position of the participants of the meeting (for example, whether they were part of the acquired consulting firm or veterans of Systech) helps to put in context their utterances with respect to the "principal-centered" and distributed models.

Lastly, it was analyzed through a view of discourse as situated *symbolic* action, adding a sensitivity to deeper considerations of how discourse frames, constructs, and represents issues in particular ways. For example, discursive interactions that on the surface appear simply as an exchange of information can mirror considerations of power and archetypal struggles for control and dominance; in this case between the old-timers, representing the distributed way of operating, and the newcomers, representing the principal-led way of operating. Further, the acknowledgement by the newcomer and advocate of the principal-centered model, Grant, that things were done differently in Systech and maybe some responsibilities should be shared, was more than an acknowledgement—it was a symbolic affirmation of his acceptance of the legitimacy of the existing, distributed model and that parts of the distributed model could be integrated in the new model.

Heracleous and Marshak (2004) illustrated that each of these perspectives is both nested in the broader conception of discourse as situated symbolic action but also is additive, in terms of offering a different piece of the puzzle to understanding what went on in the episode through the analysis of discourse. The analysis illustrates how a label ("principal-centered") means much more than its denotational content, being imbued with substantial sociopolitical connotations, and how interactions are much more than merely information transfer among parties but also symbolic statements of agentive positions. Finally, the final actions of the group president illustrate how power can not only be symbolized but also exercised through language.

Proposition 2: Discourse and Cognition Are Mutually Constituted

Our cognitive schemata are shaped and elaborated not only through the effects of our bodily, material existence (Heracleous and Jacobs 2008), but also, importantly, through discursive social interaction. At the individual level, cognition and action are interrelated (Gioia 1986; Thomas and Thomas 1970); what we believe shapes our actions, and vice versa, in a process influenced by our mental maps, our perceived interests, as well as efforts to avoid the uncomfortable effects of cognitive dissonance (Festinger 1959). At the group level, shared cognitions can be seen as "social representations" (Moscovici 1981), or as the deeper aspects of culture, the values and shared assumptions of a group (Schein 2004) that are shaped by and in turn influence discursive social interaction.

Van Dijk (1993, 251) has referred to cognition as the "missing link" between discourse and action. Cognition can be operationalized in terms of the concept of "schema," a central construct of cognitive psychology (Condor and Antaki 1997; Rumelhart 1984). A schema is "a cognitive structure that consists in part of the representation of some stimulus domain. The schema contains general knowledge about that domain, including a specification of the relationships among its attributes as well as specific examples or instances of the stimulus domain" (Taylor and Crocker 1981, 91). As Weick (1977, 277) noted, schemata are "networks of causal sequences" or "causal maps" that are in a mutually constitutive relationship with processes of enactment (see also Weick 1979).

Interpretive schemes and discourse are mutually constituted in a process of continuous interaction, where "understanding is accomplished and communicated mainly by means of symbols (most notably in the form of metaphorical language) that are then retained in a structured or schematic form via scripts. The scripts subsequently serve as a basis for action that further facilitates the meaning construction and sense-making processes" (Gioia 1986, 50; scripts are types of schemata). Cognitive structures are not static; they can be affirmed, elaborated, or challenged when discourse is both interpreted and produced through them (Eoyang 1983, 113), a process that in effect enables discourse to alter individual mental maps, influencing discursive social interaction, and as structuration theory (Giddens 1984) suggests, through the idea of the duality of structure, ultimately the institutionalization of meaning.

Proposition 3: Social Reality Is Constructed through Discursive Symbolic Interaction

Language, as constitutive of texts and discourse, is the primary building block of mental maps or cognitive schemata, is inherent to social interaction and enshrines meanings that over time become institutionalized, affirmed, or challenged through social interaction. According to van Dijk (1990, 165), "Social representations are largely acquired, used and changed through text and talk." More generally, "All concepts, categories, complex representations, as well as the processes of their manipulation, are acquired and used mostly in social contexts of perception, interpretation and interaction" (van Dijk 1988, 134).

Interpretive sociology holds that discursive social interaction is central to the construction of social reality and to agents' actions based on this reality (Berger and Luckmann 1966; Moscovici 1981). As Gioia (1986) observed, action arises out of interpretive schemes, and new experiences or reflections influence interpretive schemes and therefore subsequent action. This interactive view between cognition and discursive action emphasizes the relatively malleable nature of interpretive schemes, which can progressively be redefined through the addition or attrition of concepts, the transformation of perceived causal associations, or the altered salience of concepts (Eoyang 1983).

Symbolic interactionism (Blumer 1969) can inform further our understanding of this process. Even though its origins lie in a reaction to the dominant positivist paradigm in sociology, many of its core premises have over time been accepted in mainstream research (Fine 1993). Symbolic interactionism assumes that individual action arises out of the meanings that situations have for people (Thomas and Thomas 1970); that meanings arise through social interaction with others; and that individuals modify meanings in the process of thinking through issues and interacting further with others (Blumer 1969, 2).

Symbolic interactionism, therefore, has a dual focus on social interaction and on the meanings involved in interaction (Prasad 1993). George H. Mead, the intellectual father of symbolic interactionism, was particularly concerned with the nature of the self, which he conceptualized as a social object arising out of a process of social interaction (Mead 1912, 1913) and primarily through "vocal gesture" or talk, suggesting that "the 'me' is a man's reply to his own talk" (1912, 405). The self becomes a social object when it "assumes . . . the attitudes of generalized others" (1925, 275). For Mead, not only self but mind was also discursively constituted. When individuals talk to themselves as they talk to others, "in keeping up this conversation in the inner forum constitutes the field . . . of mind" (Mead 1922, 160).

Through discursive symbolic interaction, therefore, meanings can become institutionalized or "objectified" (Berger and Luckmann 1966), acquiring a longer-term solidity and reification. Institutionalized meanings have their discursive correlates in the form of discursive deep structures that are intertextual, persist in the long term, are constructive as opposed to merely communicative, transcend individual situations, and are implicit, residing in actors' practical consciousness (Heracleous and Barrett 2001; Heracleous and Hendry 2000).

The linkage of discourse and cognition can enable analysts to access the ideational worlds of groups through discourse analysis and to explore the nature of the interrelations among different discourses corresponding to these ideational worlds (for example, Heracleous 2006b). Further, discourse analysis approaches aiming to understand the ideational world of groups that can be applied to other domains than language; for example, material constructions or "embodied metaphors" constructed by particular groups (Heracleous and Jacobs 2008). From an analytical perspective, embodied metaphors can help researchers gain access to social representations. From a practice perspective, the process of constructing embodied metaphors can help group members create shared understandings of situations (Jacobs and Heracleous 2006) as well as to surface and debate key features of their organizations and competitive contexts (Heracleous and Jacobs 2008).

An illustration of propositions 2 and 3. Heracleous (2006b) studied the organizational discourses operating in a human resources consulting firm and how these discourses influenced actors' ways of thinking and acting in the context of a strategic change program. Further, the study explored how discursive deep structures were diffused and reaffirmed through social interaction and through their manifestation and operationalization in organizational processes and systems. One key finding was that discursive deep structures, such as root metaphors and enthymemes (versus surface communicative actions), are highly influential in shaping mental maps and subsequent actions, reaffirming the links among discourse, cognition, and action. These structural discursive features transcend individual texts and manifest in a variety of situations and at different times, often being taken for granted and implicit rather than explicitly stated (Heracleous and Hendry 2000).

In this organization, the dominant discourse was constituted and patterned by an enthymeme structure that posed financial success as the ultimate objective, higher sales to clients as a means to achieve this objective, and then subordinated other initiatives such as the strategic change program to the dominant discourse (in this case undertaking strategic change as a way of increasing sales to clients). The dominant discourse was an overarching structure that appropriated (or opposed) other discourses operating in this organization. For any actor advocating a course of action or an investment to be taken seriously, they had to frame their arguments in terms of the dominant discourse, in terms of the particular constructions of the central themes of this discourse as well as in terms of its vocabulary and style.

The dominant discourse also shaped how actors interpreted situations and acted based on their interpretations; for example, with respect to the various stakeholders involved in the change program. Consultants, the actors who were seen as making the highest contribution toward increasing sales, received priority in terms of the issues they raised being addressed by the change program; other stakeholders not as explicitly linked to higher sales to clients had lower priority. Other areas where discursive structures manifested included the internal consulting market and the reward and evaluation system. The importance of clients and achieving higher sales to them to reach financial success led to an active internal market, where consultants had to develop their personal networks and their personal positioning as service providers to their colleagues who sold and directed client projects so that they could be invited to participate on projects. In this context, client relationships were a source of power and were zealously developed and guarded. Finally, despite the fact that the reward and evaluation system was formally based on a variety of factors, including developmental and mentoring considerations, consultants believed, in line with the dominant discourse, that the factor that mattered most was personally meeting their sales targets (achieving higher sales to clients).

This study illustrated that discursive structures and constructions persist in the longer term and reside in actors' practical consciousness (Giddens 1984), in effect exhibiting a link between discourse and cognition. Discursive central themes and their constructions take on the properties of normative devices for orienting action, where action is itself a symbolic affirmation (or potentially a challenge) of the importance of these themes (proposition 2). Internal documents produced by consultants exhibited the discursive central themes, many consultants' conversations were structured through these themes, and consultants frequently accounted for their actions or inactions by making reference to them. Further, discursive structures and constructions (which in this case acted as implicit premises in organizational enthymemes) were inculcated to agents through socialization processes such as interaction with other consultants, rituals such as Christmas parties, symbolic factors, and experiences in particular contexts (for example, in the internal consulting market and in consulting engagements, proposition 3).

Other illustrations of the social construction of reality (seen as creating shared understandings or shared representations, to use Moscovici's 1981 term) through discursive symbolic interaction can be found in Heracleous and Jacobs (2008) and Jacobs and Heracleous (2006). These studies illustrated how groups of managers, using the medium of construction toy materials in facilitated workshops, developed shared understandings of their organizational or task identities and work group challenges.

Figure 1.1 below illustrates the above concepts and their levels of application. This figure is not intended to be an illustration of process, but rather

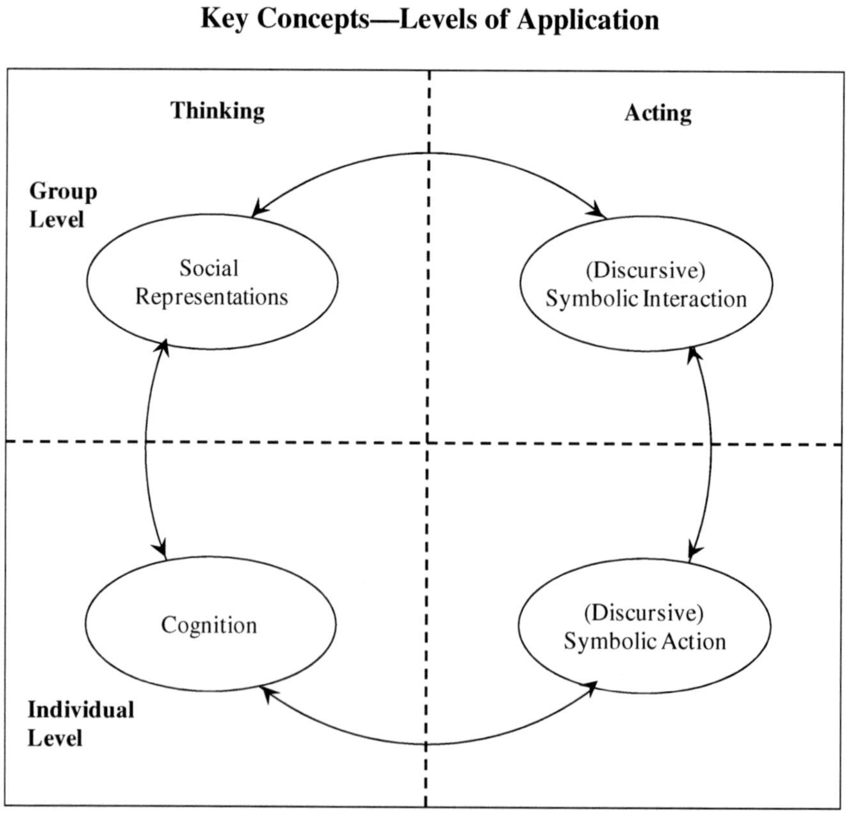

Figure 1.1. Key concepts and their level of application.

an illustration of the positioning of the concepts addressed above in terms of the theoretical levels or distinctions between individual/group and thinking/acting. It also aims to relate the concepts presented above to each other by virtue of their positioning. For example, proposition 2 refers to the mutual constitution of cognition and discourse, and these two concepts are positioned in the lower half of the figure; cognition at the bottom left and discourse at the bottom right. Proposition 3 suggests that social reality is constructed through discursive symbolic interaction. Social reality (seen as social representations) is positioned at the top left-hand side of the figure, and discursive social interaction at the top right-hand side. The view of discourse as situated symbolic action (proposition 1) is represented in the two quadrants on the right-hand side of the figure.

Proposition 4: Discursive Reality Construction Is Hegemonic

Critical discourse analysis aims to demonstrate that discourses, far from being merely representational and neutral, and beyond being constructive (or perhaps through their constructive role), mask and perpetuate unequal and unfair power relations and social practices. This is accomplished by presenting socially constructed situations as natural (the way things should be) and subtly influencing the construction of identities, roles, and "truth," what can be discussed, how, and who has legitimacy to raise and debate issues.

As Giddens (1984) has observed, symbolic universes function not only as communicational and sensemaking mechanisms but also as legitimating ones, where power and domination are inherent elements of structurational processes of social reproduction. Critical discourse analysis views discourses not as neutral or unbiased but as "sites of power" (Mumby and Stohl 1991, 316), often as entrenched "social practices" themselves (Fairclough and Wodak 1997, 258) that produce particular sorts of subjectivity and identity (du Gay and Salaman 1992) in the interests of the powerful.

The theoretical antecedents of critical discourse analysis lay in social theory, in particular the work of Gramsci (1971), Althusser (1971), Foucault (1980), and others (see Blommaert and Bulcaen 2000; Fairclough and Wodak 1997). Foucault's work, especially his genealogical writings (1980) focusing on the intimate links between discourse and power, have been a potent inspiration. Fairclough (1992) has offered a broad organizing framework for critical discourse analysts through his tripartite distinction of discourse as text, discourse as discursive practice, and finally discourse as social practice. The three elements move progressively from text to context and from discourse to practice.

Consistent with our earlier propositions, critical discourse analysis assumes that social realities are principally constituted through discourse, or in van Dijk's (1993, 254) words, that "managing the mind of others is essentially a function of text and talk." Discourses are thus seen as imbued with ideological hegemony, the process by which dominant classes attempt to construct and perpetuate belief systems that support their own interests and make the status quo appear commonsensical and natural (Barthes 1993; Gramsci 1971).

Critical discourse analysis is interventionist; going beyond mere analysis, it is ethically committed to unmasking the processes of domination through which discourses promote social arrangements that support and perpetuate the interests of dominant groups (Barthes 1993; Gramsci 1971; Fairclough and Wodak 1997; Wodak 1990).

In terms of methodology, critical discourse analysts use a variety of interpretively oriented discourse analysis approaches often supplemented by historical analyses, with attention to context, especially discursive and social practices and how these link with the texts under analysis. The foci of study include social problems such as racism, gender relations, ethnic tensions, or literacy, not only as an academic effort but also as a committed form of social intervention (Blommaert and Bulcaen 2000; Fairclough and Wodak 1997; van Dijk 1993; Wodak 1990).

An illustration of the links between discourse and power. Jacobs and Heracleous (2006) used a Foucauldian "archaeological" approach (Foucault 1972), combined with "genealogical" concerns (Foucault 1980), to explore the discourse of German management accounting, or "Controlling Science" as it is referred to. Foucault's (1972) archaeological approach attempts to understand the underlying rules that structure and determine discourses, practices, and subject positions. As Burrell (1988, 229) noted, the archaeologist seeks to uncover "the same in the different"; that is, how the same rules can regulate a variety of discourses and social practices, even as they remain unknown or taken for granted to the agents involved; and suggested that in this type of analysis there is a need to bracket accepted truth so that a more historical, structural, in-depth analytical approach can be achieved.

The authors firstly examined the conceptual foundations of Controlling Science; secondly, identified functional similarities of these conceptions with Taylor's scientific management, shown to be a conceptual ancestor of Controlling Science; and thirdly argued that Panopticism was a common unifying metaphor for both Taylorism and Controlling Science. They found that Panopticism as a disciplinary instrument and as an organizing metaphor could still be discerned in German management accounting, affecting agents' interpretations, actions, and organizational practices. The Panopticon's raison d'etre was surveillance and control of individuals. Its very design operationalized the principle of power as both visible and unverifiable, and its presence enabled hierarchical observation and normalizing sanction. Foucault called Panopticism "a technological invention in the order of power, comparable with the steam engine in the order of production" (Foucault 1976, 71).

Jacobs and Heracleous (2006) analyzed Taylor's scientific management as a conceptual ancestor of Controlling Science and as an operationalization of the Panopticon. The task system as well as the labor office that controls individual workers' performance are in effect representations of hierarchical observation and normalizing sanction, the two cornerstones of the Panopticon. Further, from a genealogical perspective, the authors explored the nature of the Panopticon as a potent metaphor for disciplinary regimes that use hierarchical observation and normalizing sanction and showed that the Panopticon can be seen as a unifying metaphor for both Taylorism and Controlling Science. The authors showed how Panoptical processes within a consulting organization using Controlling Science led to distorted communication, selective reporting of figures, reduction of behavioral options through the assumption of being observed, and the creation of self-discipline along the lines of dominant normalizing sanctions that made the physical presence of an inspector or manager unnecessary.

As an example of critical discourse analysis, Jacobs and Heracleous's (2006) study examines a seemingly innocuous and neutral type of accounting practice, German Controlling Science, and reveals how this practice is bound up with the exercise of power through its embodiment and enablement of the cornerstones of Panopticism: hierarchical observation and normalizing sanction. Controlling Science is revealed not as a neutral record-keeping technology but as a technology of power that subjugates agents by rendering them visible to a system that is simultaneously a domain of accountability and panoptical control. The study also illustrates how agents can manipulate data and communication in order to reduce the impact of the panoptic control system, in an example of Gidden's (1984) concept of the dialectic of control, in the process making it more difficult for the organization to have valid data as a side effect of the panoptic system.

Table 1.1 on the following page portrays the four propositions toward a theory of the process of discursive reality construction.

Four Propositions

Theoretical Propositions	Theoretical Levels	Theoretical Fields	Key Authors Drawn On	Potential Foci For Discourse Analysis
1. Discourse can fruitfully be seen as situated symbolic action	Meta-level conception	As below	As below	As below
1a. Discourse is *action*; it not only says things, but also does things	Multi-level	Speech act theory; Rhetoric	Austin, 1962; Searle, 1975; Aristotle, 1991; Gill & Whedbee, 1997	What does a discourse intend to accomplish, or does accomplish?
1b. Discourse is *situated* action; a figure that assumes meaning in context (the ground), within a dialectical relationship	Multi-level	Rhetoric; Ethnography of communication	Hymes, 1964, 1972; Gumperz & Levinson, 1991	What can a discourse reveal about its context, or vice versa? How do they shape each other?
1c. Discourse is *symbolic* action; it conveys actors' values and beliefs, and constructs or evokes mental frames for interpreting issues	Multi-level	Social constructionism	Berger & Luckmann, 1967; Gergen & Thatchenkery, 1996	What are the constructions conveyed by a discourse, and how are they created by texts?
2. Discourse and cognition are mutually constituted. Discourse arises from, and is interpreted through, mental maps; Mental maps are, in turn, constituted through discourse	Individual/ subjective Process Micro-level	Social cognition	Condor & Antaki, 1997; Gioia, 1986; Taylor & Crocker, 1981	How do discursive constructions shape and/or reflect mental maps? What processes are involved in this mutual constitution?
3. Social reality is constructed through discursive symbolic interaction. This is the principal means through which inter-subjective understandings are created, affirmed or challenged	Group/inter-subjective Process Meso-level	Social Cognition Symbolic interactionism	As above for social cognition Mead, 1912, 1913, 1922, 1925; Blumer, 1969	What constructions are diffused through discursive interaction, and how do they shape social reality? What are the interactive processes involved?
4. Discursive reality construction is hegemonic, biased in favor of dominant interests	Role of power and ideology Macro-level (institutional)	Social theory Critical discourse analysis	Foucault, 1980; Gramsci, 1971 Fairclough & Wodak, 1997; van Dijk, 1993	How does discourse skew social reality in the interests of powerful groups? What interventions can be made to oppose this?

Note: An earlier version of this table appeared in Heracleous and Marshak (2004).

Table 1.1. Four propositions toward a theory of the process of discursive reality construction.

CONCLUSION

Even though discourse is seen as basic to the social construction of reality (Grant, Keenoy, and Oswick 2001) as well as to organizational functioning (Heracleous 2006a; Marshak et al. 2000), understanding of this process remains unclear and fragmented. As a contribution in this direction, in this chapter I suggested four propositions toward a theory of discursive reality construction.

The first proposition concerns a meta-level perspective of the nature of discourse, viewed as *situated symbolic action*. This draws from the basic insight of speech act theory (Austin 1962; Searle 1975) that discourse not only says things but also *does* things. At the same time discourse is *symbolic* in that it conveys actors' values and beliefs and constructs or evokes frames for interpreting the issues at hand, as social constructionism highlights (Berger and Luckmann 1966). Discourse is also *situated* in that discursive interaction takes place within embedded, nested contexts that condition intended and perceived meanings and pose rules of discursive and behavioral appropriateness, as revealed by ethnographies of communication (Hymes 1964; Basso 1970; Frake 1964).

The second proposition relates to individual-level subjective processes (micro level), and draws from the field of social cognition (Condor and Antaki 1997; van Dijk 1990) to suggest that discourse and cognition are mutually constituted. The third proposition then moves to group-level intersubjective processes (meso level), drawing from social cognition and symbolic interactionism (Mead 1912, 1913; Blumer 1969) to state that social reality is constructed through (discursive) symbolic interaction. Meanings can become institutionalized and "objectified" (Berger and Luckmann 1966) through discursive symbolic interaction, which is itself patterned by deep structures of discourse linked to the ideational world of a group (Heracleous 2006b; Heracleous and Barrett 2001). The fourth proposition highlights the role of power and ideology in the functioning of discourse and its social and organizational consequences (institutional, macro level). Based on critical theory and critical discourse analysis (Fairclough and Wodak 1997; Foucault 1980; Gramsci 1971; van Dijk 1993), discursive reality construction is seen as hegemonic, continually biasing or manipulating social reality in the interests of powerful groups.

Figure 1.2 on the following page is a diagrammatic representation of the process of discursive reality construction. It portrays five interlinked social actors within an organizational context. Actors A and B are engaged in discursive symbolic interaction within a particular situational context (proposition 1). There is a dialectical relationship between their own cognition and (communicative) actions (proposition 2). At the same time, they are exchanging

The Discursive Construction of Social Reality

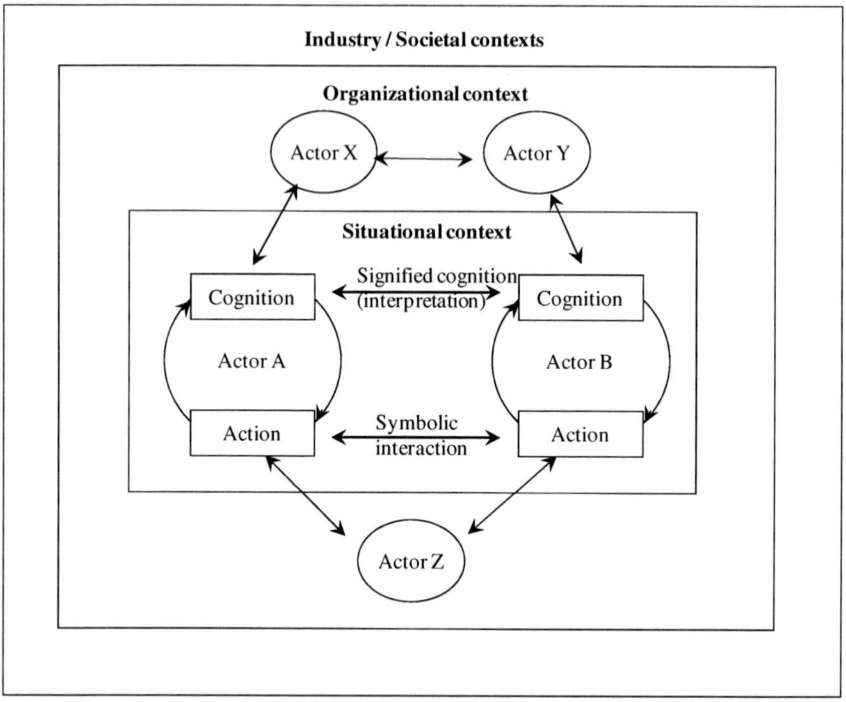

Figure 1.2. A diagrammatic representation of the discursive construction of social reality.

and interpreting discursive meanings through their interpretive schemes, sustaining and objectifying meanings or challenging the status quo (proposition 3). Actors A and B are linked in the same way with other actors, X, Y, and Z. For the sake of clarity of exposition, arrows have not been included from each actor to all other actors, as would be the case in a group context of discursive social interaction.

This whole process is pervaded and infused by issues of power and hegemony as they pertain to the situation, organization, and society these actors are in (proposition 4). Power is not represented pictorially in the diagram in order to highlight that it is not something visible and external to individuals, but deeply embedded in, and constitutive of, social relationships, actions, and cognitions (Foucault 1980). Lastly, actors are situated within nested contexts; the situational context is embedded within the organizational context, itself embedded within industry and broader societal contexts. These contexts are analytically distinct but practically intertwined and inseparable.

These four propositions can contribute toward gaining greater clarity in theoretical exposition and empirical analyses of the process of discursive reality construction, a challenge that characterizes the field of organizational discourse as a whole (Grant, Keenoy, and Oswick 2001). The four propositions offer a systematic way of addressing multiple levels of analysis; firstly, the meta level of the ontology of discourse (the nature of discourse as situated symbolic action, informing the rest of the propositions); secondly, the micro level of single texts, communicative actions, and individual communicative intent and cognition; thirdly, the meso level of discursive interaction and social construction of reality; and finally the macro level of power, social context, and institutionalized meanings.

Importantly, these levels are theoretically interrelated and can be potentially analyzed by multilevel research that collects data at multiple levels of analysis (for example, Donnellon, Gray, and Bougon 1986; Gephart 1993; Heracleous and Barrett 2001). This type of multilevel research can also help to address important research challenges such as exploring both text and its context, or the roles and interrelations of both structure and agency (Hardy 2001). With regard to structure and agency, for example, propositions 2, 3, and 4 move progressively from an agency-centered approach to a structure-centered approach. These propositions are not offered as testable hypotheses (even though testable hypotheses could conceivably be developed to test aspects of their functioning), but rather as principles that could underlie the design of empirical research and aid the interpretation of findings, in the same vein as Giddens (1984, 326–27; 1991, 213), for example, has posed the empirical usefulness of structuration theory.

By providing greater clarity on the different levels of analysis as well as processes involved, the theoretical perspectives that can be drawn on, and potential foci for discourse analysis, these propositions could help in informing and perhaps providing more structure to both conceptualization and empirical research so that a potentially more cumulative body of knowledge in the field of organizational discourse could progressively develop. This could help to address, at least in this domain, a perennial problem of organization theory; being a body of knowledge that bears closer resemblance to a confusing and sometimes incoherent surrealist painting rather than a collection of puzzles with ultimately mutually fitting pieces that will, in good time, form coherent, and perhaps pleasing, pictures.

NOTES

1. Both social constructionism and social cognition research, for example, have become fragmented over time into distinct interpretive and positivist streams (Bowring 2000; Condor and Antaki 1997).

2. The following discussion of discourse as situated symbolic action draws from Heracleous and Marshak (2004), and Heracleous (2004).

REFERENCES

Althusser, L. 1971. *Lenin and Philosophy and Other Essays.* London: New Left Books.

Alvesson, Mats, and D. Kärreman. 2000. Varieties of Discourse: On the Study of Organizations through Discourse Analysis. *Human Relations* 53: 1125–49.

Aristotle. 1991. *On Rhetoric*. (G. A. Kennedy, trans.). New York: Oxford University Press.

Ashby, W. R. 1960. *An Introduction to Cybernetics*. London: Chapman and Hall.

Austin, J. L. 1962. *How to Do Things with Words*. Cambridge, MA: Harvard University Press.

Barthes, R. 1993. *Mythologies*. London: Vintage.

Basso, K. H. 1970. To Give Up on Words: Silence in Western Apache Culture. *Southwestern Journal of Anthropology* 26: 213–30.

Bateson, G. 1972. *Steps to an Ecology of Mind*. London: Intertext.

Berger, P., and T. Luckmann. 1966. *The Social Construction of Reality*. London: Penguin.

Bitzer, L. F. 1968. The Rhetorical Situation. *Philosophy and Rhetoric* 1: 1–14.

Blommaert, J., and C. Bulcaen. 2000. Critical Discourse Analysis. *Annual Review of Anthropology* 29: 447–66.

Blumer, H. 1969. *Symbolic Interactionism: Perspective and Method*. Berkeley, CA: University of California Press.

Bowring, M. A. 2000. De/constructing Theory: A Look at the Institutional Theory That Positivism Built. *Journal of Management Inquiry* 9: 258–70.

Bryant, D. C. 1974. Rhetoric: Its Functions and Its Scope. In *Rhetoric: A Tradition in Transition,* ed. W. R. Fisher, 195–227. Michigan: Michigan State University Press.

Burke, K. 1969. *A Rhetoric of Motives*. Berkeley: University of California Press.

Burrell, G. 1988. Modernism, Postmodernism and Organizational Analysis 2: The Contribution of Michel Foucault. *Organization Studies* 9: 221–35.

Burrell, G., and G. Morgan. 1979. *Sociological Paradigms and Organizational Analysis.* Hants: Gower.

Charland, M. 1987. Constitutive Rhetoric: The Case of the Peuple Quebecois. *Quarterly Journal of Speech* 73: 133–50.

Cheney, G., and D. Lair. 2005. Theorizing about Rhetoric and Organizations: Classical, Interpretive and Critical Aspects. In *Engaging Organizational Communication Theory and Research*, ed. S. May and D. Mumby, 55–84. Thousand Oaks, CA: Sage.

Chia, R. 2000. Discourse Analysis as Organizational Analysis. *Organization* 7: 513–18.

Condor, S., and C. Antaki. 1997. Social Cognition and Discourse. In *Discourse Studies: A Multidisciplinary Introduction*, vol. 1, ed. T. A. van Dijk, 320–47. Beverly Hills: Sage.

Donnellon, A., B. Gray, and M. G. Bougon. 1986. Communication, Meaning, and Organized Action. *Administrative Science Quarterly* 31: 43–55.

du Gay, P., and G. Salaman. 1992. The Cult(ure) of the Customer. *Journal of Management Studies* 29: 615–33.

Eoyang, C. 1983. Symbolic Transformation of Belief Systems. In *Organizational Symbolism*, ed. L. R. Pondy, P. J. Frost, G. Morgan, and T. C. Dandridge, 109–21. Greenwich: JAI Press.

Fairclough, N. 1992. *Discourse and Social Change.* Cambridge, UK: Polity.

Fairclough, N., and R. Wodak. 1997. Critical Discourse Analysis. In *Discourse Studies: A Multidisciplinary Introduction*, vol. 2, ed. T. A. van Dijk, 258–84. Beverly Hills: Sage.

Festinger, L. 1959. *A Theory of Cognitive Dissonance*. London: Tavistock.

Fine, G. A. 1993. The Sad Demise, Mysterious Disappearance, and Glorious Triumph of Symbolic Interactionism. *Annual Review of Sociology* 19: 61–87.

Foucault, M. 1972. *The Archaeology of Knowledge*. London: Routledge.

Foucault, M. 1976. Questions on Geography. In *Power/Knowledge: Selected Interviews and Other Writings 1972–1977,* ed. C. Gordon, 63–77. Pantheon: New York.

Foucault, M. 1980. Power/Knowledge: Selected Interviews and Other Writings, 1972–77. New York: Pantheon.

Frake, C. O. 1964. How to Ask for a Drink in Subanun. *American Anthropologist* 66: 127–32.

Gephart, R. P. 1993. The Textual Approach: Risk and Blame in Disaster Sensemaking. *Academy of Management Journal* 36: 1465–1514.

Gergen, K. J., and T. J. Thatchenkery. 1996. Organization Science as Social Construction: Postmodern Potentials. *Journal of Applied Behavioral Science* 32: 356–77.

Giddens, Anthony. 1984. *The Constitution of Society*. Cambridge: Polity.

Giddens, Anthony. 1991. Structuration Theory: Past, Present and Future. In *Giddens' Theory of Structuration: A Critical Appreciation*, ed. C. Bryant and D. Jary, 201–21. London: Routledge.

Gill, A. M., and K. Whedbee. 1997. Rhetoric. In *Discourse Studies: A Multidisciplinary Introduction*, Vol. 1, ed. T. A. van Dijk, 157–83. Beverly Hills: Sage.

Gioia, D. A. 1986. Symbols, Scripts and Sensemaking: Creating Meaning in the Organizational Experience. In *The Thinking Organization*, ed. H. P. Sims Jr. and D. A. Gioia, 49–74. San Francisco: Jossey-Bass.

Gramsci, A. 1971. *Selections from the Prison Notebooks of Antonio Gramsci*, ed. Q. Hoare and G. Nowell-Smith. London: Lawrence and Wishart.

Grant, D., C. Hardy, L. Putnam, and C. Oswick. 2004. *Sage Handbook of Organizational Discourse*. Beverly Hills: Sage.

Grant, D., T. Keenoy, and C. Oswick. 2001. Organizational Discourse: Key Contributions and Challenges. *International Studies of Management and Organization* 31: 5–24.

Gronbeck, B. E. 1973. The Rhetoric of Social-Institutional Change: Black Action at Michigan. In *Explorations in Rhetorical Criticism*, ed. G. P. Morhmann, C. J. Stewart, and D. J. Ochs, 96–123. Pennsylvania: Pennsylvania State University Press.

Gumperz, J. J., and S. C. Levinson. 1991. Rethinking Linguistic Relativity. *Current Anthropology* 32: 613–23.

Hardy, C. 2001. Researching Organizational Discourse. *International Studies of Management and Organization* 31: 25–47.

Heracleous, L. 2004. Interpretivist Approaches to Organizational Discourse. In *Handbook of Organizational Discourse*, ed. D. Grant, N. Phillips, C. Hardy, L. Putnam, and C. Oswick, 175–92. Beverly Hills: Sage.

Heracleous, L. 2006a. *Discourse, Interpretation, Organization.* Cambridge: Cambridge University Press.

Heracleous, L. 2006b. A Tale of Three Discourses: The Dominant, the Strategic and the Marginalized. *Journal of Management Studies* 43: 1059–87.

Heracleous, L., and M. Barrett. 2001. Organizational Change as Discourse: Communicative Actions and Deep Structures in the Context of Information Technology Implementation. *Academy of Management Journal* 44: 755–78.

Heracleous, L., and J. Hendry. 2000. Discourse and the Study of Organization: Towards a Structurational Perspective. *Human Relations* 53: 1251–86.

Heracleous, L., and C. Jacobs. 2008. Understanding Organizations through Embodied Metaphors. *Organization Studies* 29: 45–78.

Heracleous, L., and R. Marshak. 2004. Conceptualizing Organizational Discourse as Situated Symbolic Action. *Human Relations* 57: 1285–1312.

Hymes, D. 1964. Toward Ethnographies of Communication. *American Anthropologist* 66, part 2: 12–25.

Hymes, D. 1972. Models of the Interaction of Language and Social Life. In *Directions in Sociolinguistics: The Ethnography of Communication*, ed. J. Gumperz and D. Hymes, 35–71. New York: Holt, Rinehart and Winston.

Jacobs, C., and L. Heracleous. 2006. Constructing Shared Understanding—The Role of Embodied Metaphors in Organization Development. *Journal of Applied Behavioral Science* 42: 207–26.

Marshak, R. J., and L. Heracleous. 2009. Evocative Framing: How Discursive Hot Buttons Linked to Implicit Storylines Impact Strategic Decisions. Paper presented at the European Group for Organization Studies conference, Barcelona, July 2–4.

Marshak, R. J., T. Keenoy, C. Oswick, and D. Grant. 2000. From Outer Words to Inner Worlds. *Journal of Applied Behavioral Science* 36: 245–58.

Mead, G. H. 1912. The Mechanism of Social Consciousness. *Journal of Philosophy, Psychology and Scientific Methods* 9: 401–06.

Mead, G. H. 1913. The Social Self. *Journal of Philosophy, Psychology and Scientific Methods* 10: 374–80.

Mead, G. H. 1922. A Behavioristic Account of the Significant Symbol. *Journal of Philosophy* 19: 157–63.

Mead, G. H. 1925. The Genesis of the Self and Social Control. *International Journal of Ethics* 35: 251–77.

Moscovici, S. 1981. On Social Representations. In *Social Cognition: Perspectives on Everyday Understanding*, ed. J. P. Forgas, 181–209. London: Academic Press.

Mumby, D. K., and C. Stohl. 1991. Power and Discourse in Organization Studies: Absence and the Dialectic of Control. *Discourse and Society* 2: 313–32.

Oswick, C., T. Keenoy, and D. Grant. 2000. Organizational Discourse(s): Significations, Stakeholders and Strategy. *Human Relations* 53: 1115–23.

Phillips, N., and C. Hardy. 2002. *Discourse Analysis: Investigating Processes of Social Construction*. Beverly Hills: Sage.

Prasad, P. 1993. Symbolic Processes in the Implementation of Technological Change: A Symbolic Interactionist Study of Work Computerization. *Academy of Management Journal* 36: 1400–29.

Rumelhart, D. E. 1984. Schemata and the Cognitive System. In *Handbook of Social Cognition*, ed. R. S. Wyer Jr. and T. K. Srull, 161–88. Hillsdale, NJ: Erlbaum.

Schein, E. 2004. Organizational Culture and Leadership, 3rd Ed. San Francisco: Jossey-Bass.

Searle, J. 1975. Indirect Speech Acts. In *Syntax and Semantics 3: Speech Acts*, ed. P. Cole and J. Morgan, 59–82. New York: Academic Press.

Searle, J. 1995. *The Construction of Social Reality*. New York: Free Press.

Suddaby, R., and R. Greenwood. 2005. Rhetorical Strategies of Legitimacy. *Administrative Science Quarterly* 50: 35–67.

Taylor, J. R., and D. Robichaud. 2004. Finding the Organization in the Communication: Discourse as Action and Sensemaking. *Organization* 11: 395–413.

Taylor, J. R., and E. Van Every. 2000. *The Emergent Organization: Communication as Its Site and Surface*. Mahwah, NJ: Lawrence Erlbaum Associates.

Taylor, S. E., and J. Crocker. 1981. Schematic Bases of Social Information Processing. In *Social Cognition*, ed. E. T. Higgins, C. P. Herman, and M. P. Zanna, 89–134. Hillsdale, NJ: Erlbaum.

Thomas, W. I., and D. S. Thomas. 1970. Situations Defined as Real Are Real in Their Consequences. In *Social Psychology through Symbolic Interaction*, ed. G. P. Stone and H. A. Faberman, 154–56. Toronto: Xerox College Publishing.

van Dijk, T. A. 1977. *Text and Context: Explorations in the Semantics and Pragmatics of Discourse*. London: Longman.

van Dijk, T. A. 1988. Social Cognition, Social Power and Social Discourse. *Text* 8: 129–57.

van Dijk, T. A. 1990. Social Cognition and Discourse. In *Handbook of Language and Social Psychology*, ed. H. Giles and W. P. Robinson, 163–83. Chichester: Wiley.

van Dijk, T. A. 1993. Principles of Critical Discourse Analysis. *Discourse and Society* 4: 249–83.

Weick, K. 1977. Enactment Processes in Organizations. In *New Directions in Organizational Behavior*, ed. B. M. Staw and G. R. Salancik, 267–300. Chicago: St. Clair Press.

Weick, K. 1979. Cognitive Processes in Organizations. In *Research in Organizational Behavior*, vol. 1, ed. by B. M. Staw, 41–74. Greenwich, CT: JAI Press.
Wodak, R. 1990. Discourse Analysis: Problems, Findings, Perspectives. *Text* 10: 125–32.
Xu, S. 1992. Argumentation, Explanation, and Social Cognition. *Text* 12: 263–91.

2

A Politically Attentive Discursive Analysis of Collaborative Talk

John G. McClellan and Stanley Deetz

A critical focus on discourse directs attention to the politics of meaning making among organizational participants. Recent attention to discourse as a way to understand and engage the complexities of organizational life has spurred interest in the practices and consequences of organizational talk. While much of this work is descriptive or functionalist in nature, involving attempts to understand how meanings emerge in conversation or how talk can help accomplish particular organizational tasks, taking a critical focus on discourse extends analysis a bit further to accomplish additional aims. While the term *critical* has a variety of meanings and is used in many contexts, it typically involves a concern for understanding power relationships within various social practices with a desire to give voice to disenfranchised or otherwise marginalized interests. And while most critical scholars interested in discourse focus on language as the locus of meaning creation and attend to discourse as a means of examining and revealing taken-for-granted understandings of organizational life, much critical work attends solely to large-scale meanings such as ideological formations. In this chapter, however, we focus critical attention on local level discourses that enable some meanings while simultaneously precluding alternative understandings from emerging in talk. This critical attention to discourse attends to the qualities of talk that obscure, devalue, and/or naturalize some interests in relation to others.

As such, we offer a critically inspired investigation of organizational discourse that calls attention to the relational politics of talk during a planning session at ArtCollege, a small college of art and design in the western United States. Specifically, we develop a politically attentive relational constructionist (PARC) perspective and use it as a lens to examine the discourses associated with collaborative conversations about change among participants of this particular organization. We investigate discussions designed to generate options for best using building space in a more environmentally sustainable way and attend to the political qualities of this talk to explore how discourses shape the ways change is understood and enabled. This politically sensitive approach offers a way to engage discourse that directs attention to local, emergent meanings created and recreated among organizational participants in relation to more general understandings of what this organization is and should be.

In this chapter, we review a politically attentive relational constructionist (PARC) perspective of discourse by discussing language as constitutive of social reality and communication as a relational and political practice. We present our methods for engaging in a critically inspired discursive analysis of organizational talk and introduce a collaborative planning meeting at ArtCollege as a particular site for critically exploring organizational discourse. We then present a critical analysis of the discourses associated with change and follow with a discussion of the potential consequences of such analysis for this college of art and design and for scholars interested in critically inspired discursive approaches to change. We conclude this chapter with some reflections on the potential implications for what attention to the relational and political quality of discourse might offer critical approaches for discourse analysis.

A PARC PERSPECTIVE OF DISCOURSE

A politically attentive relational constructionist (PARC) perspective examines talk with the aim of revealing conflicts inherent yet often suppressed in the production of meaning. This perspective directs attention to the relational understandings embedded in language to critique how some meanings are enabled in conversation while others are simultaneously constrained. To help explain this PARC approach, we review what critical perspectives bring to the study of organizational discourse and then direct attention to the relational and political quality of all discourse to reveal how a PARC perspective provides a unique way to critically explore the discourses of organizational life.

Critically Exploring Discourse

Critical perspectives typically focus on the processes and practices of meaning creation to reveal problems in contemporary society that exploit, repress, and misrecognize the interests of some at the expense of others. Critical work is informed by a variety of theoretical perspectives, such as the Frankfurt School's critique of arbitrary authority found within the narratives of modernity (see Horkheimer and Adorno 1947/1972), Habermas's (1984, 1987) critique of instrumental reasoning that usurp other forms of rationality, and Foucault's (1972, 1980) interrelatedness of power/knowledge. These, and other critical perspectives, typically place emphasis on larger-scale meaning formations (such as instrumental rationality, systematic distortions, and knowledge) that become taken for granted and ultimately preclude alternative ways of knowing or being. Critical discourse work typically engages in a broad-based critique of ideological meaning formations that shape the structures that guide social action with an aim of emancipating marginalized groups and/or unmasking unrecognized interests (e.g., Fairclough 1995). For instance, critical discourse analysis (CDA) works to expose ideological meaning formations (functioning as a by-product of social relations) that legitimize power interests within social discourse.

While this type of critical work embraces a concern for revealing hidden power relationships and a focus on language as a way to understand the complexities of organizational practices that marginalize the interests of some groups, it typically does not emphasize local practices of talk. Our critical interest in discourse, however, directly attends to the local and emergent meanings that arise in (or are precluded from) conversation. Consequently, taking such a critical approach to the study of discourse requires attentiveness to what is hidden, obscured, or otherwise treated as natural and normal within conversation. From this perspective, power is not understood as a force "out there" acting upon social participants but as emergent, relational formations arising though local interactions. We call this type of critical approach a political attentive relational constructionist, or PARC, perspective. This approach embraces language as the principle mediator of experience and talk as the process through which all understandings of the world and ourselves are generated, maintained, and changed.

Consequently, this perspective aligns with a critical interest in discourse. While the term *discourse* often refers to the practices of communication or the resulting accomplishments of conversation, its increased use to address a wide range of objectives associates it with most everything and thus risks it meaning nothing (Alvesson 2000). To help focus our attention, we embrace a distinction explicated by Fairhurst and Putnam (2004) between *discourses* conceptualized at the micro level of social action and *Discourses* conceptualized at the macro level as enduring systems of thought. This differentiation is useful to understand how some scholars focus on lowercase *discourse* to engage in descriptive analysis of the meanings emergent from the local practices of talk (e.g., Gergen, Gergen, and Barrett 2004; Murphy 1998) while others attend to the uppercase *Discourse* as a way to understand stable meaning formations that influence ways of understanding the world (e.g., Wodak 1997; van Dijk 1993; Fairclough 1995).

A PARC perspective, however, complicates this simple duality of discourse. Following Boden's (1994) claim that there is no macro/micro distinction of discourse, this approach engages the complexities of organizational talk by attending to the interrelationships among various meanings of organization and understandings of the self as expressed in different contexts and conversations of organizing practice. Additionally, a PARC approach focuses attention on communication as constitutive of social reality while remaining sensitive to the politics of meaning creation. Inspired by those turning to language for understanding social life (e.g., Heidegger 2000; Gadamer 2004), this approach places emphasis on the productive yet inherently indeterminate quality of language and thus attends to the ways in which some meanings become sedimented, naturalized, and treated as normal ways of knowing the world. A PARC perspective thus embraces language not only as central to understanding organization but also as the constructive practice producing all understandings of organizational life.

As such, engaging in a PARC approach for critically investigating discourse attends to language as a relational and political process that constitutes experience. Grounded in the phenomenological perspective that all experiences and things of the world are inseparable from the presubjective, preobjective relationships within the constitutive activities that brought them into being (Berger and Luckmann 1966; Deetz 2003), a PARC perspective recognizes discourse as a practice that calls forth the things of the world. This perspective embraces the notion that experiences and objects of the world are not "out there" as static, stable entities to be named by using language but rather, by using language to name the undetermined "things" of the world, the world becomes constituted through as a set of relational understandings enabled and enacted through discourse. From this perspective, language replaces consciousness as the site of experience production and communication replaces psychology as the focus of attention for understanding organizational life. Thus, a PARC perspective attends to the many relationships that produce meanings among conversational participants and to discourse as a necessarily relational and political activity.

Relational and Political Discourse

Discourse simultaneously produces social realities, relations to those realities, and mechanisms to suppress alternative ways of knowing those realities. As the world becomes defined through discourse, the language used in talk defines the world in a set of relations with other meanings. According to phenomenological perspectives, human experience arises in these relationships among positioned subjects and the not-yet-determined "things" toward which they are directed. Consequently, any meaning of a thing has embedded in it a particular way to relate to that thing—a relational intention. As such, the meanings of the world are defined in terms of a set of relations to the meanings of other things. When language is used to talk about experiences, this process of talk institutionalizes particular sets of relations and subsequently produces the world we know and understand. Recognizing this relational understanding of meaning directs attention to a horizon of other potential ways of knowing, and critical attention can focus on the processes through which particular understandings of the world are created, maintained, and potentially changed. This understanding, therefore, embraces the inherent political processes of language use.

Prior to language use, any number of meanings can emerge. However, the politics inherent in language use results in some meanings being treated as normal and natural while others are excluded as possibilities for conversation. The key is recognizing that any way of understanding the world is not neutral; every understanding of experience pushes forth a particular way to relate to the things of the world. As language sediments particular relational understandings of the world, discourse predefines the world for us. The world is thus called into being through discourse. Critical work therefore seeks to explore the ways in which particular relational understandings become embedded in language. For instance, Foucault (1980) explains this as a process of normalization, Habermas (1984, 1987) considers this as systematically distorted communication, and Laclau and Mouffe (2001) explain how some meanings emerge as dominant through regularity in dispersion across the many institutions and practices of social life. A PARC perspective directs attention, however, to the local practice of talk and the politics of conversation. Thus, it considers activities such as discursive closures or other mechanisms used through conversation that suppress potential conflicts of meaning. All of these critical approaches relate to the notion that organizations are a consequence of naturalized preferential value systems being (re)created through talk. Embracing these ideas reveals discourse as a political process that suppresses the initial tension-filled conditions that created organization and serves to ignore, hide, or treat some understandings of organizational life as self-evident, natural, and unproblematic.

Consequently, this PARC approach embraces the notion that the meanings, knowledge, and values of organization are the result of a temporary arrest of organizing processes generated through discourse, and that talk results in particular relational understandings constituted as consistent and orderly centers in relation to larger discursive articulations (Broadfoot, Deetz, and Anderson 2004). As such, this approach focuses on the interplay among existing understandings of the organization and the self in relation to the organization with the local practices of talk to investigate the politics of meaning creation. Focusing on varieties of meanings enabled through the practice of talk helps to expose the vocabularies of action enacted though conversation as organizational members attempt to create coherent and meaningful understandings of their current and future organizational life. A PARC perspective can thus provide critical insight into the ways discursive formations become articulated, negotiated, and normalized.

Combining the notion that discourse constitutes relational understandings of organizational life and that these relations are political, a PARC perspective focuses on discourse as the principal way for understanding how and why some meanings are expressed and others are not. Additionally, a PARC-inspired analysis focuses on alternative ways to talk that might allow other relationships to come forth through communication. This perspective is sensitive to the political construction of organization and subsequently looks for ways to engage in productive conflicts that might emancipate alternative meanings from dominant, yet hidden, forms of knowledge and understanding. By incorporating interest in the relational politics of meaning construction during local practices of talk, we seek to explore how meanings are (re)created through conversation with others. Performing such analysis of discourse involves engaging in the process of understanding the meanings emergent in language use, critiquing of meanings associated with organizational life, and offering hope for transformation.

ENGAGING IN A PARC-INSPIRED STUDY OF DISCOURSE

In this chapter we explore a moment of discourse consisting of a collaborative planning meeting at ArtCollege in which proposals for the use of a newly available building space are discussed as part of a larger initiative promoting environmental sustainability across the campus. Our analysis seeks to be sensitive to the relational and political construction of meaning during the talk about the potential future of the organization. Using a PARC perspective, we explore the interconnected discourses associated with the organization that generate vocabularies of action as well as resources for the participants of conversation to construct understandings of their future organization. This approach requires looking for nested moments of discursive action through both qualitative and critical methods. While qualitative approaches help to identify and interpret the meanings, beliefs, and knowledge emergent from in-situ moments of talk, critical analysis helps us explore the hidden politics of this talk. This qualitatively informed critical approach facilitates exploration of the relationships among meanings (re)created through discourses associated with talk of change at ArtCollege.

Our PARC-inspired research aims at revealing meanings that become hidden, constrained, or ignored in conversation and thus attends to the meanings emergent in conversation while seeking to expose the interconnected meanings within discourses. To accomplish these objectives, we work to negotiate three important moments of critical analysis: understanding, critique, and transformation (Alvesson and Deetz 2000; Deetz and McClellan 2009). Such an approach attempts to place these moments in conversation in order to explore the complexity of discourse with a focus on the interplay of meanings during moments of organizational talk.

Moments of Critical Analysis

First, we engage in a moment of *understanding*. Inspired by qualitative approaches that seek to develop understandings of organizational events as they occur in "natural" contexts (Lindlof and Taylor 2002), our attention is directed toward understanding the organization as it is known in practice through interviews as well as exploration of organizational events and processes through participant observation. With attention to local practices that connect the lives of real people in actual organizational situations, our aim is to gain an understanding of the meanings constituted by organizational participants and emergent through local interactions. While epistemologically connected to hermeneutics and Foucault's (1972) notion of archaeology, this moment of understanding involves engaging the system of relations that make particular meanings possible at particular moments in particular contexts unique to a particular organization.

The principal methods of gathering data for this moment of analysis consisted of transcriptions of individual interviews, field notes from participant observation, and transcripts of discussions during a collaborative meeting. We used a narrative interview style (Lindlof and Taylor 2002) to elicit stories from nineteen administrators, faculty, and staff of the college about their everyday life as a member of the organization, changes to their organization, and participation in change initiatives. Additionally, participant observation was used to gain understanding of the events and conversations at ArtCollege. Approximately sixteen days were spent on campus for about six to eight hours during each of these days. Following qualitative approaches, field notes were taken that described events and conversations, reactions to the interactions, and interpretations of the organizing practices experienced at ArtCollege. Additionally, using multiple voice recorders, all conversations during a three-hour collaborative planning session among eighteen individuals were used to develop an interpretation of the discourses among the participants. Careful attention to the varied meanings generated during collaborative meetings was taken with the aim of remaining sensitive to the language used as well as the contextual, constitutive, and metaphorical character of the talk about change.

A second moment for analysis negotiated for this study was *critique*. While developing an *understanding* helped to gain an appreciation of the meanings of organizational life as lived, *critique* recognizes that social construction always occurs within relationships of power. A PARC approach focuses on critique through distanciation, or recovery of the suppressed "other." The aim here is to reclaim the indeterminacy within the discourse and consider the always available possibility of conflict in the constitutive process of language use. Critique helps expose the mechanisms through which relations of power are formed, reproduced, and maintained through discourses. Inspired by methods such as Foucault's genealogy (1980) and Derrida's (1976) deconstruction, the aim of critique is to reveal domination of understanding within local discursive practices among organizational participants. The moment of critique explores processes of normalization or moments of closure in discourse as well as opportunities for openings in conversation in which lost conflicts of understanding can be reclaimed (see Deetz, MacDonald, and Heath 2006). As such we seek to identify dominant meanings of organizational life at ArtCollege that are hidden within stable meaning formations that constitute understandings of the organization.

Embracing the notion that all understandings emerge in relation to other meanings, the aim of this moment of critique was to explore understandings of change as expressed during talk and to see how they interrelate with understandings of the organization. Aligned with Hardy and Phillips's (2000) process of discourse analysis, the aim was to understand the meanings constructed in the talk of change at ArtCollege and examine how these constructions relate to the context of change. Thus, the articulations expressed in interviews and a collaborative planning session were placed in conversation to explore the interrelationship among existing organizational meanings (and associated understandings of the self as an organizational participant) with meanings emergent in conversations of change to reveal moments of domination and to potentially expose alternative meanings not expressed, considered, or able to be formulated. Focus was thus placed on what was not said, blocked, or distorted during talk of change, and attention was directed toward contradictions or tensions among various meanings. This moment of critique provided a way to reveal alternative meanings not readily apparent in current discourse by highlighting alternative ways of understanding the organization.

The third moment in need of negotiation is *transformation*. Transformation involves reclaiming alternative meanings that have been marginalized by dominant, taken-for-granted ways of knowing an organization. The aim of this moment is to complicate the discourse and encourage discussion of alternative relational understandings in conversation. Inspired by the notion of creative euphemisms (Bourdieu 1991) and alternative articulations (Laclau and Mouffe 2001; Angus 1992), the aim of this moment is to promote alternative discourses among organizational participants that might inspire new ideas, values, concepts, practices, or ways of knowing to emerge as possibilities for future action. Engaging in transformation generates discourses that inspire alternative meanings and allows organizational participants to invent alternative ways of knowing. Overall, our approach of negotiating these three moments of analysis alters the aim of our research from the traditional discursive approaches, focused on developing deep insight or authoritative knowledge of the organization, toward reclaiming conflicts inherent in meaning construction that are treated as natural and invisible in organizational life to then finding ways of working with organizational members to engender alternative forms of interaction that might produce more productive and useful futures.

A Site for Critically Engaging Discourse

This study was conducted at a four-year accredited private college of art and design located in the western United States, referred to as ArtCollege. The change initiatives at ArtCollege included attempts to increase enrollment and enhance campus facilities to accommodate a larger student population while also promoting environmental sustainability across campus. The approach to change at ArtCollege involved collaborative sessions implemented to design and develop the change programs at the college. These sessions involved workshop-type brainstorming discussions among a variety of stakeholders as a means of contributing to an overall change plan. The aim of these collaborative meetings at ArtCollege was to bring together administrators, faculty, and staff to identify objectives, discuss key obstacles, and initiate plans for sustainable growth and development.

This study explores one collaborative session at ArtCollege to understand how change is potentially enacted (or precluded) as various stakeholders talk about potential futures. Participants in the session assessed for this study included representatives of the college's administration and faculty, such as the college president, various administrative vice presidents, the dean of students, directors of college divisions, and faculty chairs, and other staff members, such as the manager of campus facilities. This three-hour collaborative meeting explored potential ways to use space within three buildings currently owned by the college yet leased to other organizations. With the leases expected to expire in the near future, discussion during the collaborative focused on finding ways to best allocate available building space to best meet the requirements of each department and college while accommodating a growing student population. This collaborative session, as well as interviews and time spent on campus meeting with the administration, faculty, and staff of the college, provided data for this PARC-inspired study of organizational discourse.

THE EMERGENT POLITICS OF DISCOURSE

Following a PARC approach, all interview transcripts, field notes, and collaborative session transcripts were treated symmetrically to identify and put into conversation any emergent discursive themes, practices, resources and to illuminate instances of ambiguity, absence or silence, diversity and stabilization, as well as patterns of fragmentation and integration, destabilization, fixation, and orchestration (Alvesson and Deetz 2000). Placing these moments of analysis in conversation helped to identify and assess the ways in which contestable, relational understandings are put into play. As such, this section contains two main points of analyses. The first reviews meanings of the organization emergent in talk among participants. These meanings represent relational configurations by which the participants know the organization and their relationship with the organization. The second focuses on discursive analysis of the collaborative session with an interest in revealing the interrelatedness among the relational constitution of organization and self with potential proposals for change emergent in the conversation. This analysis reveals the interplay among the discourses and reflects how some talk of change is enabled while other possibilities are not discussed.

Discourses of Organization

Attention was first directed toward the ways in which participants of ArtCollege put into play understandings of the organization that co-constitutes knowledge of the organization and a sense of self as an organizational participant. Four common ways of understanding the organization emerged from the analysis of interviews and field notes. The organization was talked about in terms of being a place for art, for education, for community, and for business. Each way of talking about the organization constitutes a relational understanding of what the organization is as well as a way to know the self in relation to the organization.

First, organizational participants talked of the organization as a place for and about art. This way of talking about ArtCollege provided a specific vocabulary for knowing and subsequently relating to the organization that revealed a relational understanding that art and artists are valued and appreciated as an important part of what it means to participate in the organizing practices of ArtCollege. For instance, when describing the best thing about the college, Russ stated that the most important things about ArtCollege are "the art students, and the artists, and the designers, and the visiting artists. It's the passion and excitement." This way of talking about the organization as a place for art puts into play a particular way to understand the organization and one's relationship with it. For instance, Kellie explains, "I love when we have visiting artists. I'll just sneak out of my office and go to lectures. Where else can you work and do that?" Additionally, this talk produces subject positions that relate the self as one who is an artist. For instance, Alan explained that "I have been trained as a graphic designer," Leslie stated that "I'm a designer," and Russ expressed, "I am an artist. I am still a practicing artist." Talking about oneself as an artist or a designer aligns meanings of the self with particular meanings of the organization.

Second, the organization was talked about as a place for education. This way of talking provided a relational understanding that relates the self as attentive to student learning. For example, Kristen explained that the most important thing about ArtCollege is "the quality of the education and experiences for the students." Additionally, Jim articulated his desire to deliver "good training and development of artists and developing the critical thought, the creativity, as well as the skill sets." Kellie similarly claimed that "this place is about, I think, helping people realize their creativity and training them." This type of talk puts into play subject positions that relate the self to the organization as that of teacher. For example, Alan explained, "Teaching has always been a passion" and Leslie explained, "Ultimately, that is why I'm here. It is to make sure that we turn out the best graduates that we possibly can." And Jim said, "Principally, I see myself as a teacher here." These ways of making sense unite understandings of self with a way of knowing the organization as a place for education.

A third emergent way of talking about the organization is that of a close-knit community. This type of talk revealed meaning embedded in the ways participants enjoyed working closely with others. For example, as Leslie talked about the organization, she explained, "We are really a weird little family . . . that's what makes this place really unique." Similarly, Brian explained, "What attracted me is the college philosophy is one of a very personal atmosphere. It's small, everybody knew each other, the instructors were all professional instructors and it felt very familiar, it had a familiar feeling to it." This familiar feeling extended to talk of congeniality. Sally, for instance, expressed that she enjoyed the "sense of smallness and ready interchange across all groups of people here." This way of talking generates meaning of the organization that privileges a respectful way of interacting with others. For instance, Jim explained that "there's just a sweetness here." This type of talk calls forth a relational understanding that the organization is a unique community in which individuals like Jim enjoy working with "a great team of people."

A fourth way of understanding the organization that emerged from the study was talk of ArtCollege as a business. This type of talk provided a way of understanding the organization as a profit-driven institution that in turn privileged particular activities such as making money and displaying expertise of business techniques and tools. Brian, for instance, talked about the organization as a business as he explained the outcome of a challenging instance as "well, it's our business and we'll decide." Similarly, Alan talked about how faculty chairs at the college function at "the sort of middle-management level." Talking about the college and roles within the college in business terms provides a particular way to engage the organization and others in the organization. This can be seen when Michelle explained that they could do a better job at "documenting, holding people to deadlines and following up." This talk also generates a sense of self as a business person. For instance, Michelle talked about herself as "being someone who's more of a strategist and an analyst." This sense of self relates to the discourse of business and aligns knowledge of the self with the logics embedded in the talk of business, including efficiency, effectiveness, and profit motive. And this kind of talk reveals that participants like Michelle prefer understanding ArtCollege as a business to understanding ArtCollege in terms of a discourse of art, education, or a close-knit community.

Each of these ways of understanding the organization is important as each emerges as a predefined way to know the organization and the self in relation to the organization. Thus, when participants talk about the organization in each of these ways they put into play particular relational understandings. However, these discourses were shared across the organization, by different types of participants at various roles within the organization. Additionally, individual participants often relied on multiple discourses to make sense of the organization and their relationship to it. For instance, some described the college in terms of a place for art and for education and the self as simultaneously an artist and a teacher. An alignment of meaning was also not the only ways these discourses related. Often the meanings expressed contradicted or were in tension with other meanings. For example, a few expressed an inability to know the organization as a business and a close-knit community, which emerged as a tension among ways of knowing the self as a good business person and as a member of the close-knit community.

Overall, each ways of talking about the college establishes an intricate relationship among meanings embedded in discourses that provide a way to know how to act as a participant of the organization. Each relational understanding is also political in the sense that each way of talking about the organization preferences one way of knowing the organization over others. As such, when talk of change occurs, these predefined political and relational meaning formations serve as the tacit backdrop of understanding that bolsters proposals for change. In other words, proposals for changes to the organization are made in relation to these understandings of the organization and can thus serve to enable or preclude possibility for change.

Discourses of Change

After gaining an understanding of predominant ways the organization and self are understood among organizational participants, attention was directed toward the discourse of change during one collaborative session. During the session, talk focused on making proposals for future changes to the organization. Specifically, in this meeting discussion involved developing plans and coordinating among departments for potential future uses of new building space in ways that might accommodate a growing student population while being considerate of ways the campus can become more environmentally friendly. The findings of this analysis reveal how each proposal calls into place predefined relational understandings embedded in the various discourses of organization. As such, the meanings emergent from conversation are those already associated with existing understandings of what the organization is or should be (as well as the sense of self related to these understandings). To illustrate this, we explore three moments of conversation during the collaborative session. The first two show moments when relational understandings of organization and self enable particular proposals for change. The third is a moment of conversation when an alternative proposal for change is closed from conversation, precluding opportunities to talk about the future of the organization in an alternative way.

During the meeting, two breakout sessions occurred, each with nine participants. The participants of each session included a mix of administrators, faculty, and staff. The objective of the breakout sessions was to engage in small group discussion to generate proposals for using potential available building space. During the breakout sessions, two main types of proposals emerged from the conversations. The first included proposals to enhance the student experiences, and the second was a proposal for promoting collaborative spaces for interaction and socialization. Consider, for instance, the following excerpt of conversation from the first breakout group:

Amanda: Yeah, so we have no lecture room in [MainBuilding] whatsoever, and we've got to come up. We hope and pray and go across campus and look for another spot to give our lecture. But also at that same station where we were able to get the lecterns, students were able to check e-mail and stuff like that, and that is also gone now, too. So where in the heck that will be, I have no idea, but we need a lectern.

Renee: We need to talk about that.

Amanda: Yeah.

Jim: Are you at the rooftop unit in [MainBuilding]?

Alan: Well, we want to put them on the roof. They might be out in the back on the ground.

Jim: So then the mechanical is in there?

Renee: Yes.

Alan: We're trying real hard to do that, because that could be our lecture room.

Amanda: Yeah, which would be good.

Alan: But we have no computer access points for students. In the whole building.

Renee: In the whole building?

Alan: In the whole building.

Renee: Correct.

Alan: So we bring them into our office, we put them online, hook it up on desktop, and we . . .

Amanda: Our "Show PowerPoints" or anything like that. Have you got it?

Renee: No.

Jim: In fall, my classes, I had to crowd my students into the office behind me, and we would look at the monitor. That's about as good as it gets right now.

Alan: I think since we've talked about moving, the [pottery] wheel has been there, we've been, if we move the wheels from there, we have to get a mechanical room.

Mark: A mechanical room, yeah.

Matt: We talked about it at . . .

Renee: Yeah. OK. So that is happening at the end of summer.

Amanda: Now, one good upshot, I think, from moving that room from being a lecture room is it is now kind of the multipurpose room. So we had wheel showing in the fall, and now we have a student studio in a quarter of the space, and we are having the papermaking now in there, where the wheels used to be. So that's nice because we just had the wheels stored in it.

Renee: Right.

Amanda: So that's one good thing that did come of that. I will say also that when [Matt] worked so hard at revamping the new wood shop space inside a week, we lost a lot of work space for the students, and that's a big thing that I never . . . But when we start looking forward, having sculpture studios that are adjacent to or close enough to the wood shop and the kiln is really important because the work gets damaged if you are not close enough to the kiln to bring it over right.

Renee: Oh, gosh.

Amanda: Even walking it across campus will put a crack in it such that it will damage the piece. And then also I feel like that is also limiting the scale of work that the students feel able to make.

Renee: I bet. Sure.

Amanda: Because they don't have a space where they can leave the hundred-pound thing and then come back to it, they are only going to make a fifteen-pound thing that they have to then pick up and walk to their car across campus.

Renee: OK, good, and let's address some of those when we talk about the future.

This brief excerpt reveals four specific proposals to enhance teaching. First, Amanda explained the need for a lecture room ("we have no lecture room in [MainBuilding]"). Second, Jim expressed a need for computer access for students ("I had to crowd my students into the office behind me and we would look at the monitor"). Third, Amanda called for a place to store equipment such as pottery wheels ("we have to get a mechanical room"). Fourth, Amanda expressed a need for proximity to particular equipment ("studios that are adjacent to or close enough to the wood shop and the kiln") so students do not need to carry heavy objects across campus. Each of these proposals is offered as a way to enhance the teaching and student learning experiences on campus. What is tacit, or assumed, in this talk, however, is that each proposal might enhance the overall educational experiences for students. There did not appear to be any explanation as to why these were valuable options. All participants seemed to agree and move on with the conversation.

Recognizing that organizational discourses provide predefined understandings that bring forth contestable meanings, the naturalized organizational meaning of organization as a place for education provides a predefined understanding of experience and a vocabulary for action. Thus, proposals for change that relate to this understanding appeals to the tacit logics embedded in the meaning of organization as a place for education, and participants' proposals make sense to others because they align with these shared logics. Thus, when discussing proposed options for using building space, each proposal calls forth shared understandings of the organization and self and the logics embedded in these discourses. As such, justifications for why these proposals are important were not discussed as they are already taken for granted as such among the participants.

Another proposal that emerged during discussion in the breakout session was the desire to create a shared, common space to interact informally with others. Consider the brief excerpt from the conversation in the second breakout session:

Arthur: The Common, the Green, the Quad. It's not really a Quad, but if it was a Quad—anyway the long and the short, where the grass is. That area looks so beautiful is pretty much going to stay the way it is.

Sam: Put a building there? Is that what you're thinking?

Arthur: There was a time when we were talking—part of the interest in . . .

Shane: Volleyball court.

Amy: A lot of broken windows.

Sally: [Arthur] would like that.

[multiple conversations]

Leslie: We have five minutes.

Arthur: Part of the interest in having the student store there is because it's centrally located. I remember talking to [Matt] about this a way, way long time ago, that it would be really interesting to have the Chair and Administrative Offices centrally located for that same purpose, that we'd be sort of the inner circle, and then the outer circle would be the buildings on the outside.

Leslie: And that's what is says here—moving to [AnotherBuilding] would be offices; the [MainBuilding] offices, the book store, and then the Department Chair's lounge to [AnotherBuilding].

Arthur: Yeah. We call it: "The War Room." We'd like it to be a war room because we'd like it to be something, not so much a lounge; but I think what we were talking about is a place where we can get together and post things on the wall and come back to it.

Leslie: Actually collaborate.

Amy: They have approximately five hundred square feet.

Leslie: That's fine.

Arthur: It's better than what we've got! [laughing]

Sam: How much do you have now?

Leslie: It's about five square feet! [laughing]

Sam: What about the lounge, whatever that conference room is on the third floor right now?

Leslie: It's the Admissions Lounge.

Sam: The Admissions Lounge? Yeah.

Amy: That's available square footage, too.

Sam: OK, because that could be—well, maybe not.

Arthur: It's not a classroom, but . . .

Sam: It could be an office. The start of an office space.

Leslie: Yeah, it could be something.

Sam: Well, it's very easy. I'll move up there!

Arthur: I would definitely like to be there!

Leslie: That's a nice space!

Sam: It is a nice space.

Amy: We could do that patio and put some tables and lounge chairs out there.

Bill: We could get the margarita machine going! [laughing]

Leslie: Yeah, that could be great!

Arthur: You know . . . I like your ideas. [laughing]

The participants express a desire for a shared common area in this brief excerpt. In particular, Arthur's call for a "war room" in which the department chairs and administration can have their offices centrally located in an "inner circle" reflects the desire for chairs to be in constant contact with the administration as a way to be a more active part of the decision making on campus. Leslie's interjection of "actually collaborate" added to this appeal by expressing a desire to genuinely engage in ongoing collaborative talk with administration regarding the operations of the college, and she hints that this type of talk is not occurring regularly. Additionally, as the discussion continued, the conversation turned to where and what this space might look like in the future. Amy proposed a patio space with "tables and lounge chairs out there," followed by Bill's suggestion to "get the margarita machine going." This exchange reveals the participants' desire for a space to interact in a casual manner with others. Overall, the proposal for a type of collaborative space suggests that the participants of this session see such a place to interact and work well with others as desirable.

When placing these proposals in relation to the discourses of organization, these appeals align with talk of the organization as a close-knit community. This way of talking creates a way to understand these proposals as those that promote a "friendly feel" or "close community." Yet, similar to the ways in which the participants' proposals for student-oriented ideas relied the tacit logics of a discourse of education, these proposals for a collaborative space to interact reflect a shared assumption that ArtCollege is a community where people work well together and would enjoy a place to interact. Consequently, when proposals arose that aligned with understandings of organization as a close-knit community, they were received as potential desirable options. As such, participants relied upon the commonly shared discourse of community to propose ideas that did not have to be supported with specific logics. Instead, the predefined relational understandings were not articulated as they were already regularly dispersed among the participants of the discussion. Consequently, these examples show how proposals for change are enabled when they rely on shared discourses that call into place predetermined understandings of the organization and the self in relation to the organization.

Discursive Alignment and Closure

The proposals for change already made sense to the participants in the conversation because they aligned with predefined ways of understanding ArtCollege as a place for education or community. As participants of this session initiated ideas for new ways to use building space, they enacted potentially contestable meanings embedded in the language of organizational discourse. When the relational intentions of the organizational discourses were shared across the organization as predominant ways of knowing the organization and self, the proposals that aligned with these meanings made sense. In these cases, the predefined logics within the discourse dominated the conversation of change in the collaborative session. However, while these understandings helped to enable proposals for change to emerge in conversation, other ways of considering the future of the organization were closed from conversation.

Discursive closures are moves in conversation that preclude the emergence of new understandings. When examining the talk during the breakout sessions, a PARC perspective directs attention to meanings that did not emerge or were suppressed. Assessing the talk during the breakout sessions in this way reveals moments in which ideas for discussion emerged, yet were closed from conversation. These discursive closures preclude alternative discourses from being discussed, and when this occurs, some meanings embedded in alternative discourses are blocked from conversation by treating them as unimportant or inadequate for conversation. For instance, in the first breakout session, talk of environmental sustainability in relation to the new building space emerged but was closed from conversation. The following excerpt shows such a moment of closure:

Alan: You know, a big issue I think everybody would like, not just [my department], I would like to see the right recycling. The exact same recycling bins in every classroom.

Renee: We are working on that.

Alan: This is what goes in here and this is what goes in there.

Renee: I am working on that.

Alan: Everyone, everywhere across school.

Renee: We have a committee now that is looking into it. We have to meet with [Mark], but . . .

Jim: Are we talking the same size? Because they are all blue, right?

Matt: The ones that are in the basement are blue and like this big.

Renee: Yeah, they still have those.

Jim: Because I have them available.

Renee: But before we do that, we really need to look at creating a much more comprehensive on-campus recycling program, education, signage. An [outside company] gave me an incredible source for receptacles, for them using recycled pop bottles and such. They are actually making into the map. They're gorgeous, they're cool. So anyway. That is something that's really on our radar screen, and we're starting to work on it.

Matt: In the meantime, I'll give you a bigger one . . .

Renee: But all I'm saying is that that's a band-aid, but it's not a solution. We've got to come up with a solution.

Matt: There's a lot of . . . We need a blue—something that the students can clean up with, so we need to . . .

Jim: Be a little specific, if you want a push broom . . . or a mop . . .

Amanda: I asked [Mark] and he said just write a big note and tape it to the mop handle . . .

Matt: The night guy locks it up. He'll take that mop . . .

Renee: We're getting off the subject. We only have about twenty-five minutes to do everything else we have to do.

Discursive closure renders particular talk unimportant for the conversation. In the excerpt above, Alan proposes a desire for recycling bins in every classroom across the campus. However, this discussion is subsequently closed off from discussion. Renee first explained that such a proposal was already being taken care of and thus recycling bins were not important to discuss in this meeting. When Jim attempted to join the conversation, Renee again asserted in more detail about her efforts to create a comprehensive recycling program that was under development and thus implied that there was no need to discuss recycling in this session. Jim seemed to recognize that this topic was not open for conversation and, with a joke, the conversation quickly lost focus. Renee then ended this exchange, effectively precluding the topic from conversation, by indicating in the last line of the excerpt that this topic was not appropriate to the task at hand and because of limited time suggested that the group get back to more appropriate talk.

The outcome of this closure extends beyond the idea of recycling bins. It closes off the larger discourse of sustainability as well. By closing off discussion of recycling bins, talk of sustainability is also deemed inappropriate. Instead, the discussion focused on ideas aligned with more dominant or preferred discourses such as education and community. Overall, the discourse of sustainability was not incorporated into this discussion of building space during the collaborative session because it did not align with the shared discourses that predefined possible understandings of what the organization is or could be. As a consequence, this closure marginalized the discourse of sustainability. While particular proposals for change were enabled when the talk aligned with the logics of education and community, options that might promote sustainability did not emerge, and dominant meanings of organization and self were not rearticulated during these moments and thus talk of the environmental sustainability was not incorporated as a part of the discussion of ways to use new building space.

TRANSFORMING DISCOURSE

This type of PARC-inspired analysis directs attention to domination of understanding resulting when regularly dispersed meanings align in mutual support. Attending to language use as a political activity and analyzing the interplay among predefined understandings of organization in relation to local practices of talk show how particular options of change emerge in conversation at a particular organization within a particular context of action. In this moment of talk during the collaborative session, participants' proposals that aligned with the logics of education and community emerged as already making sense because these relational understandings were already embedded in the organizational discourse. The politics of this formation of meaning about change remained unquestioned as these proposals aligned with the understanding of the organization as a place for education and community. As such, talk during this session resolidified particular understandings of ArtCollege and served a political function in keeping these meanings unquestioned, uncomplicated, and maintained as the natural and normal way to understand the college. Thus, the meanings embedded in discourses of education and community remained dominant ways to understand and be a part of the organization. In other words, the discourses of education and community generate constellations of meaning that provide vocabularies of action, or scripts, for proposing changes to the college that align with these understandings. In this way, the predefined meanings of the organization provide a way to understand the proposals for change. A PARC perspective calls attention to this relational and political quality of talk.

Additionally, during the session, opportunities to talk about something new arise; however, in this case talk associated with environmental sustainability did not align with predominant ways of knowing the organization and the self. Thus, this talk was precluded from the conversation, as seen through a moment of closure. Examining the local practice of talk, such as the discussion during the collaborative session in relation to particular ways of knowing the organization, provided critical insight into the ways in which understandings of change emerge through alignment of discourses or mechanisms such as discursive closures. Taking a PARC perspective thus attends to the meanings that do not emerge in conversation. Consider in this case that talk during the breakout sessions did not relate to understandings of the organization as a place for art or business.

This brings us to consider the third moment of critical analysis, that of transformation. The moment of transformation aims to fulfill the activist agenda of critical work. When considered in terms of discourse, the objective of transformation is to encourage new ways of talking that are based on different ways of understanding the organization or the self in relation to the organization. Specifically, transformation occurs when the conflicts inherent in the formation of meanings are engaged in active conversation and results in new relational understandings emerging through discourse. For instance, consider what the discourse might have looked like if talk of the organization as a place for art dominated the conversation about the use of new building space. In this case, participants might have seen themselves as artists and given more consideration to the aesthetics of the buildings or for finding ways in which the changes to building space might better promote creativity and other artistic endeavors. Similarly, consider if the conversation relied more on understanding the organization as a business, with participants seeing themselves as analysts or managers. Talk might have attended to ways for generating profits by more efficiently using building space or by reducing costs of building operations. And with regard to environmental sustainability, consider if this talk was not discursively closed and if what emerged from the conversation involved a new relational understanding in which the organization was seen as necessarily environmentally friendly and participants developed subject positions of environmental stewards. This type of relational understanding may have generated alternative possibilities for the use of building space across the campus and may have potentially included talking of ways to promote recycling and a myriad of other possibilities for promoting more environmentally friendly changes to campus.

Engaging in transformative redefinitions is a challenging task that involves inviting alternative ways of talking among organizational participants. Any invitation to complicate the discourse of the organization is challenging and potentially risky. While transformation may take a form similar to participatory action research, fidelity to the critical agenda demands an ongoing sensitivity to the politics of talk and encourages new meanings to emerge among organizational participants rather than from the researcher. While the means for encouraging the transformation of meaning might vary, if following a PARC approach, methods are aimed at attempting to facilitate conversation among organizational participants that might enable alternative concepts or understandings to emerge that promote new discourses constituting alternative ways of understanding the organization and the self in relation to it. For instance, promoting creative euphemisms (Bourdieu 1991) or inspiring rearticulations (Laclau and Mouffe 2001) of meanings might be useful methods. Such attempts are intended to invite participants to talk in new ways and invent alternative discourses that may generate the possibility of discovering alternative ways of relating with others, the organization, and the self.

Motivated by a desire to reveal conflicts inherent, yet suppressed, during the production of meanings, the aim of transformation is to reclaim the indeterminacy of meaning during conversation and allow for alternative ways of talking to guide understandings of the organization and ways to know the self in relation to the organization. Often, this critical task involves finding ways for participants to engage in free and open forms of interaction with the potential to generate new meanings that might guide change initiatives in alternative and potentially more useful ways. Regarding the talk at ArtCollege, future sessions might be organized around talking about change based on various prominent organizing discourses while attending to the alignments and tensions among the different ways of talking about the organization. For instance, if proposals for change guided by an understanding of the college as a place for education run counter to understandings of the college as a business, and if discourse regarding these ways of knowing the organization are able to take place in productive ways, then alternative ways of talking about the college might emerge that could guide change initiatives in alternative ways. However, a PARC-inspired transformation demands that organizational participants recognize that any new ways of understanding the organization that emerge should remain open for renegotiation during ongoing collaborative conversations.

CONCLUSION

This politically attentive relational constructionist perspective reveals the complexities of organizational discourse by directing attention to the interrelatedness of meanings and the overall politics of talk. In this case at ArtCollege, the various ways of knowing the organization enabled some possibilities for change while potentially constraining others. The implication of this talk for ArtCollege is that proposals for future use of building space might help promote educational activities and community, yet these ways of using space might not consider the development of quality art or be financially feasible. Additionally, while environmental sustainability is the overarching aim of the change initiatives at ArtCollege, during the collaborative session it was not considered as a way to understand how new building space might be used. As such, the PARC approach helped expose the politics inherent in language use by demonstrating how talking in particular ways enables some proposals for change while simultaneously precluding other understandings from emerging.

This critical approach to the study of discourse directs attention to the local level of talk and the relational constitution of meaning associated with organization and the self. Rather than engaging in critical approaches, such as critical discourse analysis, that typically attend to broader social processes or cultural practices that reinforce ideological meaning formations, a PARC approach attends to the conversations among stakeholders that simultaneously enable and constrain the understandings that guide organized life. The aim of such an approach focuses not on critique of ideology but on revealing moments of meaning suppression in talk with the hope of finding opportunities for engaging in discursive transformations through moments of free and open conversation that questions the political formations of meaning and engenders new vocabularies of action motivated by alternative ways of knowing the organization and the self.

Our aim in this chapter was to focus critical attention on discourse at the local, emergent level of talk in action while directing attention to the relational and political quality of this talk. The PARC perspective guiding this study helped to expose why some proposals for change emerged in conversation while others were devalued or left undiscussed. Engaging in this type of critical analysis during other moments of conversation among organizational participants can provide useful insight into the challenges members of an increasingly interconnected business and social community face when working collaboratively to reach mutually beneficial decisions. Engaging in a PARC-inspired critical analysis might help reveal the politics of meaning formation and subsequently engender alternative ways to engage discourse to enable new communicative solutions to the complex business and community problems such as those found in organizational change programs and environmental sustainability initiatives.

REFERENCES

Alvesson, Mats, and Stanley Deetz. 2000. *Doing Critical Management Research*. London: Sage.

Alvesson, Mats, and Dan Kärreman. 2000. Varieties of Discourse: On the Study of Organizations through Discourse Analysis. *Human Relations* 53: 1125–49.

Angus, I. 1992. The Politics of Common Sense: Articulation Theory and Critical Communication Studies. In *Communication Yearbook 15,* ed. Stanley Deetz, 535–70. Newbury Park, CA: Sage.

Berger, P. L., and T. Luckmann. 1966. *The Social Construction of Reality: A Treatise in the Sociology of Knowledge*. New York: Random House.

Boden, D. 1994. *The Business of Talk: Organizations in Action*. Cambridge: Polity.

Broadfoot, K., Stanley Deetz, and Donald Anderson. 2004. Multi-levelled, Multimethod Approaches in Organizational Discourse. In *The SAGE Handbook of Organizational Discourse*, eds. David Grant, Cynthia Hardy, Clifford Oswick, and Linda Putnam, 193–212. Thousand Oaks: Sage.

Bourdieu, P. 1991. *Language and Symbolic Power*. Cambridge: Harvard University Press.

Deetz, Stanley. 2003. Reclaiming the Legacy of the Linguistic Turn. *Organization: The Interdisciplinary Journal of Organization, Theory, and Society* 10: 421–29.

Deetz, Stanley, J. MacDonald, and R. Heath. 2006. On Talking to Not Make Decisions: Models of Bridge and Fish Markets. In *Interacting and Organizing: Analysis of a Board Meeting,* ed. F. Cooren, 225–44. Mahwah, NJ: Lawrence Erlbaum.

Deetz, Stanley, and John G. McClellan. 2009. Critical Studies. In *Handbook of Business Discourse,* ed. Francesca Bargiela-Chiappini. Edinburgh: University of Edinburgh Press.

Derrida, Jacques. 1976. *Speech and Phenomenon*. Evanston, IL: Northwestern University Press.

Fairclough, Norman. 1995. *Critical Discourse Analysis: The Critical Study of Language*. London: Longman.

Fairhurst, Gail T., and Linda Putnam. 2004. Organizations as Discursive Constructions. *Communication Theory* 14: 5–26.

Foucault, Michel. 1972. *The Archaeology of Knowledge*. A. S. Smith, trans. New York: Pantheon.

Foucault, Michel. 1980. *Power/Knowledge*. New York: Pantheon.

Gadamer, H. G. 2004. *Truth and Method*, 2nd ed. J. Weinsheimer and D. G. Marshall, trans. London: Continuum (Original work published 1960).

Gergen, K. J., M. M. Gergen, and F. J. Barrett. 2004. Dialogue: Life and Death of the Organization. In *The SAGE Handbook of Organizational Discourse*, eds. David Grant, Cynthia Hardy, Clifford Oswick, and Linda Putnam, 39–59. Thousand Oaks: Sage.

Habermas, J. 1984. *The Theory of Communicative Action: Vol. 1. Reason and the Rationalization of Society*. T. McCarthy, trans. Boston: Beacon.

Habermas, J. 1987. *The Theory of Communicative Action: Vol. 2. Lifeworld and System of Society*. T. McCarthy, trans. Boston: Beacon.

Heidegger, Martin. 2000. *Introduction to Metaphysics*. G. Fried and R. Polt, trans. London: Yale University Press. (Original work published 1953.)

Horkheimer, M., and Theodor Adorno. 1972. *Dialectic of Enlightenment.* J. Cumming, trans. New York: Herder and Herder. (Original work published 1947.)

Laclau, E., and C. Mouffe. 2001. *Hegemony and Socialist Strategy: Towards a Radical Democratic Politics*, 2nd ed. London: Verso.

Lindlof, T. R., and B. C. Taylor. 2002. *Qualitative Communication Research Methods*, 2nd ed. London: Sage.

Murphy, A. G. 1998. Hidden Transcripts of Flight Attendant Resistance. *Management Communication Quarterly* 11: 499–535.

Van Dijk, T. 1993. Principles of Critical Discourse Analysis. *Discourse and Society* 4: 249–83.

Wodak, R. 1997. Critical Discourse Analysis and the Study of Doctor-Patient Interaction. In *The Construction of Professional Discourse*, eds. B. Gunnarsson, P. Linell, and B. Nordberg, 173–200. London: Longman.

3

Asian Business Discourse(s)

Francesca Bargiela-Chiappini

This chapter offers a European perspective on a relatively recent phenomenon in business discourse research, which is the development of a distinct body of scholarship in East and Southeast Asia. In its current manifestation, Asian Business Discourse(s) concentrates on the analysis of pragmalinguistic aspects of (oral and written) communication in the workplace and their socioideological underpinnings. Similar research first appeared in Europe in the 1980s and consolidated in the 1990s to form the eclectic field of business discourse. It was not until the early 2000s that articles and the occasional book-length monograph authored by Asian scholars and published in English began to be noticed internationally. An edited collection and a special journal issue helped to position Asian scholarship uniquely within business discourse. This chapter discusses select issues raised by this development, particularly against the European origins of business discourse and the field's subsequent dialogue with other Western disciplines. In so doing, it engages the field with critical perspectives from anthropology, cultural studies, and critical linguistics, among others.

In the context of a critical appraisal of specific epistemological and ontological positions within business discourse, the choice of the parenthetic plural form "Asian Business Discourse(s)" (or ABDs for short) is significant: it encapsulates the tension between "business discourse" as a European social epistemology (with methodological consequences) and the plurality of "discourses" that are emerging from the distinct sociohistoric business environments that compose the vast geopolitical expanse known as "Asia." In this chapter, I will argue that ABDs is an enterprise with Western antecedents but with increasingly localized expressions, which reflect the concerns and expectations of specific geopolitical and socioeconomic *locales*.

The chapter opens with a selective historiography of business discourse and concludes with reflections on essentialist discourses and the dangers of using homogenizing labels, such as *Asian*. In between these two bookends, and within the limits of a short essay, I will sketch out some of the issues raised by the recent contribution of ABDs to the wider field of business discourse scholarship.

The examples of research work by Eastern Asian scholars discussed below are indicative of a growing interest in the application of ethnographic and discourse analytic approaches to the interpretation of verbal and written communication in the workplace. Some authors (e.g., Tanaka 2006; Nair-Venugopal 2006) also interrogate the ideological import of corporate language policy and question the continuing gap between work practices and business communication pedagogy (Cheng and Warren 2005).

WHENCE BUSINESS DISCOURSE?

The introduction has already characterized business discourse as a European, multidisciplinary enterprise, which in recent years has looked across the Atlantic for dialogue with business communication and organizational communication. The recent opening to Asian perspectives further encourages a critical appraisal of some of the early, Eurocentric assumptions in the light of diverse sociocultural realities. A brief historical outline of business discourse will help situate these developments both geographically and diachronically.

Tracing the origins of the field of research, which has come to be known as "business discourse," is a relatively short journey into the past. In Britain at least, the 1970s and 1980s are often associated with research on language needs analysis. The literature on needs analysis in the 1980s certainly shows that company surveys and questionnaires were widely used in order to assess which and when languages were needed, for what and by whom (Coleman 1984, 1988).

In the same period, business negotiations attracted little attention in contemporary applied linguistics and sociolinguistics circles; the word *negotiation* was almost entirely associated with sales interactions. Scandinavian scholars represent a notable exception for their study of the discourse and pragmatics of business negotiations, especially intercultural negotiations.

In the early 1990s, finally negotiation as a key communicative event became a significant topic of study in relation to business as a site of language contact (Ehlich and Wagner 1995; Trosborg 1995; Bargiela-Chiappini and Harris 1997a).

An equally significant development in the 1990s was the marked shift from written to spoken discourse and the increased use of data from authentic workplace interaction (Firth 1995). This coincided with some linguists venturing into companies, not only to interview business practitioners but also to record negotiations, meetings, and other types of spoken interaction (e.g., Bargiela-Chiappini and Harris 1997b; Yeung 1998). A number of these studies involved multinationals and multilingual settings. Ethnographic work in companies also inspired the first debates on methodological issues (Bargiela-Chiappini 1991, 1993) based on an overdue dialogue between the social sciences: management and organizational studies finally met pragmatics and discourse analysis.

One of the earliest definitions of "business discourse" reflects the importance of knowledge of the context of language production, which can only be appreciated through a multidisciplinary research perspective: "It is language-in-use . . . that 'business discourse' is concerned with. Not, therefore, through isolated, contrived linguistic forms, but rather through historically and socially embedded written and spoken interactions involving individuals and groups in and across corporate organizations" (Bargiela-Chiappini and Nickerson 2002, 272).

To summarize, during the 1990s, research on business discourse witnessed three important changes: (1) the shift from almost total absorption with language needs analysis and the study of language of intercultural negotiations to tentative engagement with management and organizations studies and their newest offshoot, organizational discourse; (2) conversation analysis and discourse analysis, mainly medical and legal (e.g., Drew and Heritage 1992) expanded to include "professional discourse" (Gunnarsson et al. 1997; Geluykens and Pelsmaekers 1999); and finally, (3) a variety of analytical perspectives on workplace interaction became available through increased involvement in the field of sociologists, psychologists, ethnographers, anthropologists, and communication scholars.

In Europe and Australia, discourse analysis and organizational analysis were deployed in the multimodal analysis of work practices (cf. Iedema and Wodak 1999); probably the most notable outcome of this fusion was the birth of organizational discourse (OD) analysis. The understanding of discourse as constitutive of organizations characterizes many, if not most, contributions to the first *Handbook of Organizational Discourse* (Grant et al. 2004). The ontological status afforded to discourse separates OD from sociolinguistic studies of organizations, where organizations are treated as objects rather than processes (Putman and Fairhurst 2001), and conversational data are seen as "illustrative of social processes and effects, rather than actually constitutive of social order" (Coupland 2001, 13).

Arguably the interpretative potential of a discourse approach to the analysis of "organizing" is fully realized when discourse is granted ontological primacy; for example, when reality is seen as constituted by discourse and transformation of social practices can be achieved through discursive interventions. Other discourse analytical approaches stop short of a political interventionist agenda that proposes transformation of existing practices or generation of new ones, for example in sociolinguistics and pragmatics.

The critical and political nature of discourse-based approaches to business and organizations can be plotted onto an "engagement continuum" (see figure 3.1). For example, the evolution of business discourse research in the 1990s and 2000s, especially under the influence of social constructionism and critical approaches, can be tentatively located between the interpretative and the constitutive points. Organizational discourse analysis in its critical and reflexive manifestations probably oscillates between constitutive and transformative (e.g., Iedema and Scheeres 2009), while the proposed reappraisal of the Western agenda of business discourse, which informs the second part of this chapter, is suggestive of discourses that are transformative in the short term and generative in the long term.

DISCOURSE as . . .

Descriptive   Interpretative   Constitutive   Transformative   Generative

__________*__________*__________*__________*__________

Figure 3.1. The engagement continuum. (From Bargiela-Chiappini 2004, 8.)

NAMING, CLAIMING, AND TRESPASSING: IDEOLOGIES OF TERRITORIALITY

As the engagement continuum suggests, naming accompanies a field from inception and through its evolution; business discourse is no exception. In fact, its emergence in a period of great productivity in discourse studies and discourse analytical approaches meant that choice of a label was not only an exercise in identification but also an implicit statement about theoretical and methodological allegiances and differentiation, and "distanciation."

For example, when we first thought of "business discourse" as a possible label to describe our research (Bargiela-Chiappini and Nickerson 1999), we tried to distance ourselves from contemporary debates, at times quite pointed, between the discourse camp and the communication camp, exemplified in the United States by debates on disciplinary identity (e.g., Reinsch 1996). Such debates have continued unabated and are captured over a decade later by Jian et al. (2009) in a review article that has prompted a good deal of critical reflection (Kärreman and Alvesson 2008; Barker 2008; Putman 2008; Taylor 2008; Bargiela-Chiappini 2008).

It seems almost inevitable that disciplinary divisions should exist, and persist, often motivated by national educational politics more than academic parochialism. Collegial exchange around ontological and epistemological issues is an antidote against intellectual protectionism and ethnocentrism. Labels such as "business discourse" and "Asian Business Discourse(s)" are exposed as political in a number of ways. To begin with, business discourse uses two contentious lexemes. The first, business, indexes a field of human activity that is often target of criticism by media and scholars alike. The second, discourse, is host to a variety of analytical approaches and methodologies that belie ontological incommensurability. Overall, business discourse retains a strong European flavor, even though in the last decade it has become more eastward-looking.

Moreover, right from its inception, business discourse has claimed a wide territory; it was and it continues to be a broad church, and it could not be otherwise if it is to be concerned with analyzing the "talk and writing between individuals whose main work activities and interests are in the domain of business and who come together for the purpose of doing business" (Bargiela-Chiappini and Nickerson 1999, 2). The latest development, the dialogue with East and Southeast Asian scholars (Bargiela-Chiappini and Gotti 2005; *Journal of Asian Pacific Communication* 2005 and 2006) has added a further dimension of complexity of the original European character of the field, raising an array of issues relating to a nonethnocentric understanding of the new research.

It is in the spirit of this enlarged community that this chapter argues that business discourse can only develop if it is prepared to trespass its current disciplinary and geographic boundaries in an ongoing process of redefinition through sharing. The use of "discourse" can be both evocative and provocative. What seems without dispute is that in order "to understand the language of discourse . . . we need to understand the world in which it resides; and to understand the world in which language resides, we need to go outside linguistics" (Schiffrin 1994, 419). How far outside linguistics, and Europe, business discourse has been venturing is nowhere more apparent than in the Asian Business Discourse(s) project (Bargiela-Chiappini and Gotti 2005, *Journal of Asian Pacific Communication* 2005, 2, and 2006, 1).

One possible characterization of Asian Business Discourse(s) is in terms of the development of two existing areas of indigenous scholarship: (1) the contrastive studies of Japanese and American/Australian English of the

1990s, arguably promoted by the intensification of trade between Japan and the West but also by the spread of Japanese management ideas and the growth of research in business communication in Hong Kong and in Malaysia; and (2) growing interest in the discourse analysis of business in a number of other East Asian languages, including Chinese (Zhu and Li 2009), Korean (Jung 2009), and Vietnamese (Chew 2009).

Awareness of the historical roots of ABDs heightens the necessity for debate around how we Western discourse analysts represent the work of our Asian colleagues, how we seek to understand them and the practices they analyze, and how the use of English contributes to powerful positioning within business discourse research worldwide by determining who can speak and through which media. The next three sections take up each of these aspects in turn.

CULTUR-ING THE OTHER

The generic yet politically laden "Asian" label requires that we reflect on the consequences of referring to a multitude of distinct sociohistorical areas and communities as a convenient "whole." Labeling is constructing, usually in one's own image and for one's own purposes. History reminds us that the West encountered non-Western cultures in the fifteenth century not to learn from them but to convey truth: "This meant that there was no dialogue between Europeans and non-Westerners, but merely an imparting of 'truth' from the former group to the latter" (McCumber 2005, 206).

The enlargement of the original Anglophone basis of business discourse further calls for interrogation of Western, essentialist concepts of "culture" in the form of an active engagement with indigenous psychologies and philosophies (Bargiela-Chiappini and Nickerson 2003; Bargiela-Chiappini and Harris 2006; Bargiela-Chiappini 2009b).

Whether "culture" is something tangible and observable or whether it is a discursive construction continues to be debated across disciplines. The fact that a whole volume could be devoted to analyzing definitions of culture harvested exclusively from the literature published in English (Baldwin et al. 2006) is a sign that there is no impending agreement on the essence of the "thing." Clearly, different ontologies of "culture" will offer different perspectives on the phenomenon, which in turn will demand different methodological approaches to the analysis of the "data."

For the purpose of our reflections on representations of the "cultural other" rendered necessary by business discourse looking East, we may wish to recall that the rise and fall of the fortunes of "culture" in anthropology is often associated with anticolonialist and "nativist" discourses. In the 1980s and 1990s, for example, on the wave of poststructuralism and postmodernism, culture became a contested concept for at least four reasons: (1) the liberal and radical guilt about anthropology's association with Euro-American colonialism, (2) the disappearance of the supposedly "untouched" or "primitive" peoples who were the favored subjects for classical ethnographies, (3) the rise of "native" ethnographers who contest the right of European and American scholars to tell the truth about their people, and (4) the general loss of confidence in the possibility of objectivity (Sewell 1999, 37).

The contestation of the idea/ideology of culture(s) is ongoing (see Hutnyk 2006); some anthropologists have even dropped culture as the subject matter of their discipline (Street 1993; Yeongoyan 1986). Instead, they observe and write about the unfolding processes of *social practices*, a shift in emphasis from the earlier ontology of culture as an object, which seems to point to a new and more attractive notion of "culture as a verb" (Street 1993, 38). If we have uncovered an alternative to "culture" within a new processual and dynamic context of practice, does "culture" in the plural become irrelevant? Should we abandon the cultural paradigm within ABDs and concentrate instead on localized practices (Nair-Venugopal 2009) in combination with an appreciation of indigenous theories of communication?

KNOWING THE OTHER—FROM WITHIN

Understanding the "cultural other" from within their own sociohistorical condition is a first step toward avoiding rushed and crude generalizations about an idealized and generic "other" that fits all comparative purposes. One possible point of departure, at a theoretical level, is an approach through ontologies of communication. Arguably, Western theories of communication[1] tend to posit systemic differences among cultures and therefore lead to division (Chen and Starosta 2003, 7). Looking for a possible "Asian" ontology underpinning human communication, Chen (Chen and Starosta 2003, 5) turns to the great religious and philosophical traditions that have shaped the region:

> Asian cultures tend to assume a holistic view of the universe, especially in those areas influenced by Buddhism, Confucianism, Taoism and Shintoism. In other words, Asians tend to believe that the universe is a great whole in which all is but a transitional process, with no fixed substance of its substratum. Human communication is then a holistically interconnected network and even in a state of change and transformation.

This assumption is the background of an ontology that considers all things as relationally connected; communication is a relations process that requires adaptation and relocation of the participants in the universal system of interdependence. Harmony sustains the connectedness of the whole and is treated as *the aim* of human communication. The nonlinear cyclical approach to reasoning that emerges in communication and distinguishes Asian interactants from their Western counterparts reflects the endless, nonlinear cycle of the transforming process of the universe (Chen and Starosta 2003, 5–6).

Common features of Asian communication include intuition, for example, "feeling" rather than "analysis"; empathy, manifested in deep concern for others' feelings and affective self-detachment; silence, "as a form of speech"; attentiveness to the internal workings of the mind rather than external verbalization; indirectness where subtlety is required to avoid confrontation and embarrassment (Chen and Starosta 2003, 10). Strong rapport breeds mutuality between interactants who find themselves involved in a relationship of complementary obligation. In organizational and institutional settings workers rely not only on each other but also on their leaders, who find themselves giving more advice than their Western counterparts and giving "face" to their workers in order for their own "face" to be enhanced (Chen and Starosta 2003, 12).

These observations are subject to considerable variation across cultural and work contexts; their value resides not in their generalizability but in their intimations of "difference," which should spur the reflexive researcher to look beyond fixed categories. Japanese anthropology, for example, proposes the view that local "cultures" are constituted through historical processes of continuous dialectics between internal and external factors. To this effect, the multiple historical encounters of Japan, first with the "East" (China) and later with the "West" (Europe), document how the origins of a distinctive Japanese self-identity are to be found within a complex process of appropriation of a foreign food (rice) and the creation of a powerful mythology based on the transformation of the land from wilderness to abundant rice crops (Ohnuki-Tierny 2006). Similarly, centuries later, the Japanese imperial governance and constitution were modeled on the Prussian system, and attempts were made by the Japanese government to raise Shintoism to the level of a state religion (Ohnuki-Tierny 2006).

These instances of cross-globe, long-term, deep influences show up the East–West dichotomy as not only "useless and false" (Ohnuki-Tierny 2006, 13) but also positively dangerous, especially when appeals to its ontological authority are made to justify differences that lock peoples and communities into essentialist categorizations. The in-between status of Japan, historically oscillating between two dichotomies, "the West plus Japan vis-à-vis Asia-Pacific, and the West vis-à-vis Japan plus Asia Pacific" (Shimizu 2006, 19) is a reminder of the ethnocentric bias and political motives behind the attribution of a substantive and holistic character to entities caught up in historical flux. At best, we could continue to deploy the East–West as a heuristic tool (Shimizu 2006) while remaining aware that both East and West—and Asian and European—incorporate dichotomies emerging from crossovers that date back centuries.

Resistance to reification and ontological essentialism are prerequisites for a dialogue with the Other, in this case the "Asian-s." (Echoes of Orientalist interpretative practices and their critique will be explored later.) Here, my concern is to argue for a "hermeneutic reconstruction of discursive preassumptions" that shape "pre-understanding, and are capable of going unchallenged" (Kögler 2005, 252). Such preassumptions, I would further argue, become accessible through self-reflexive practices by indigenous scholars. We stay with Japan for an illustration of the hermeneutic process of self-interpretation, not least because Japan in the past has often prided itself of having developed a unique worldview; "Japaneseness" being the conceptual core of "the studies of the Japanese" (*nihonjin-ron*) (Tanaka 2009).

How can the Japanese understand themselves "from within," and is there something we in the West can learn from this process? The Japanese philosopher and thinker Ōhashi Ryōsuke (2002) proposes a hermeneutic of "Japaneseness," which is based on a "dialogue of 'Japaneseness'" with itself. Ōhashi intriguingly remarks that "a hermeneutic of 'Japaneseness' requires first the perception of Europeanness as the 'other in itself' for the Japanese self" (Ōhashi 2002, 25). Thus far, "Japaneseness" appears to be contrasted with a West (allegedly) outside it; what is now required is a dialogue of Japaneseness with itself, which will allow a hermeneutic to develop of Japanese modernity and "the West" as "the other in itself" (Ōhashi 2002, 27). This would recognize the character of Japanese history as renewed and reborn from the implication and appropriation of the "other-world," be it China or the West. But a further step back is required. While acknowledging the incorporation and adaptation of the external "other," a hermeneutic of Japanese modernity needs to go back to the religious and philosophical roots of its worldview, the influence of which one can appreciate in a range of well-known artistic forms as well as in the Japanese language itself.

This hermeneutic approach represents a reversal of the dominant attitude that contrasts "'Japaneseness' with the Western culture outside it" (Ōhashi 2002, 27). It is a move that depends on the engagement of Japanese scholars with the "other in themselves," to paraphrase Ōhashi. Such a hermeneutic appreciation of the Other as an "interpretative agent who draws on implicit background assumptions" and is therefore "projected as a potentially reflexive and critical agent" could help us engage with the "cultural others" without essentializing their "otherness" and reifying them. Unfortunately, there is still limited work published in English that documents hermeneutic studies in the Asian region (see Marra 2002 for a collection on Japanese hermeneutics), but the potential of this alternative approach to cultural analysis makes it very attractive to the analyst wishing to move beyond classic comparative analyses.

ENGLISH AND ENGLISHES

The danger of ready-made, fixed categorization is heightened in business discourse research by the dominance of English as its international language of dissemination, whether through publications, conferences, or networks. This seems to be the case also within ABDs, and while such "choice" makes communication possible among colleagues who may not share any other language, it also poses the question of what kind of "knowledge" is being traded in and around ABDs. As already amply documented, business discourse is inherently European, with offshoots in Australia, New Zealand, and Canada (cf. *The Handbook of Business Discourse*). Much research on business discourse has become available in English, although there are important exceptions such as Francophone research, which is usually published in French (see Feuillettaz and De Saint-Georges 2009).

Linguistic inequality is almost inevitable when a single language, namely English, is referred to as the "world language" and the "language of international trade." It is disturbing to learn that access to English as a passport to a successful life can in fact lead to social and linguistic inequality in a country with a very high literacy rate such as Taiwan (Chang 2004). Minority language and identity continue to be "terrains of struggle, of contradiction and ambiguity" (Chang 2004). Asian scholars have recently addressed some of the cultural differences and preferences that underline this struggle (e.g., Nair-Venugopal 2006) while seeking to engage critically with its ideological import.

The widespread notion of English as *the* language of corporate communication worldwide affects also multilingual workplaces where the issues are quite different from those of other multilingual situations and need consideration within the contexts of local linguistic "ecologies." Verbal communication in a multilingual environment requires attention to the specific needs and competencies that are best fulfilled by the various languages: for example, certain tasks could be accomplished more effectively if workers were allowed to use their native language(s), or a local variety of English. On the other hand, cross-division meetings or companywide training sessions may require the adoption of a *lingua franca*, unless the speakers are able (and willing) to code-switch and accommodate to speakers of other languages who are present (cf. Nair-Venugopal 2006).

Calls to resistance to linguistic imperialism (e.g., Phillipson 1992) attract academic approval in the West but in other contexts "may incur dramatically real consequences, particularly in politically repressive regimes of both the left and the right" (Bolton 2005, 77). In place of a militancy often originating from inner-circle countries and disseminated worldwide, the WE ethos proposes support for linguistic and racial diversity, engendered cultures, and languages but also for the international spread of English (Bolton 2005, 78).

The non-native educated speakers of English who seek to operate on equal terms with native speakers within a disciplinary field dominated by inner-circle varieties are confronted with the imposition of a standard language model that seriously disadvantages them. This is particularly noticeable in academic circles in which non-native language performance in English leads to an overall negative evaluation by native reviewers in spite of sound contents (Ammon 2003).

An ethical approach to English as *the* "language of international business" that accepts the challenge of "difference" and linguistic variety requires a pedagogy that raises awareness of the ideological baggage that language, any language, carries: "If we do not make our students aware of the ideologies inherent in Inner, Outer and Expanding Circle Englishes, we are indeed not fully educating them to the best of our abilities, certainly an ethical lapse on our part as teachers" (Baumgardner and Brown 2003, 248).

Arguably, the role of English in Asian business contexts is either very prominent; for example, in multilingual Hong Kong or Malaysia, or is becoming increasingly so, even in largely monolingual communities; for example, Japan and Thailand. This situation raises questions about the role of local languages, especially in multilingual interactions. The strategic significance of code-switching in multilingual workplaces (cf. Nair-Venugopal 2000; Haugh and Watanabe 2009) is an indication of the need to analyze the use of English in conjunction with that of other (Asian) languages. To this effect, a new network (currently consisting of representatives from Malaysia, China, Japan, Korea, Thailand and India) of East and Southeast Asian scholars has been set up under the ELAB banner (English as a Language of Asian Business), with the explicit remit of investigating multilingual business interaction where English is one of the languages, and not necessarily the most important. Placing English *among* the Asian languages in operation in the workplace rather than giving it place of honor frees indigenous research from the constraints of preexisting paradigms; for example, outer-circle Englishes. From this new outlook of coexisting languages, the dynamics of which are intimately connected with everyday work practices and identification processes, Asian Business Discourse scholars can hope to develop a research agenda and pedagogic materials that are responsive to local needs. The next section samples ABD research in its variety and originality.

ASIAN BUSINESS DISCOURSES: RECENT STUDIES

The focus on "language as action" (Bargiela-Chiappini and Nickerson 1999a) that characterizes much (Asian) business discourses, whether spoken or written, reflects the concern with analyzing authentic data and feeding the findings into professional and pedagogic practice (Candlin 2002; Candlin 2003; Cheng 2009). Issues of relevance of academic research on business and professional practice have traditionally been at the top of the business communication agenda on both sides of the Atlantic (e.g., Charles 2009; Dulek and Graham 2009) and in Hong Kong (Cheng 2009).

When linguistic preferences imposed by management clash with the employees' needs, expectations, and effective practices, the financial and political consequences of corporate language policy become all too apparent. For example, Tanaka (2006) and Nair-Venugopal (2006) discuss the adoption of English in work interactions in two very different socioeconomic contexts, namely Japan and Malaysia, respectively. Far from being a neutral *lingua franca*, English is shown to be enmeshed with the politics and policies of multilingual communication. The picture that emerges from the Japanese study is that of a company that "endures" English as the language imposed by the new owners who, in turn, demonstrate little cultural sensitivity to their Japanese employees. The losses caused by a blanket use of English and poor intercultural communication skills are measured not only in terms of personal "face" and interpersonal relations but also in terms of financial losses derived from the inability to interpret, for example, nonverbal expressions of disagreement or dissent; worse, when the difficulties are tentatively aired by the Japanese, they tend to be dismissed as nonrelevant in the new corporate culture (Tanaka 2006).

Based on the findings of her study of two large Malaysian firms, Nair-Venugopal (2006) critiques the "standard English for all" paradigm pedaled by many business communication textbooks. Excerpts from in-work training sessions illustrate how the speakers ably accommodate to their audiences within the stylistic range afforded by Malaysian English, and even code-switch to, and code-mix with, Malay in response to the trainees' varying linguistic competence levels. Although the availability of such skills cannot always be taken for granted in multilingual work settings, Nair-Venugopal's examples are a graphic condemnation of the insistence on imposing "standard" English(es) for communication in the workplace where other Englishes are available and indigenous languages are equally, if not more, suited to the tasks in hand.

Research on written business discourse is no less revealing. Two studies based on companies in China (Hong Kong) and Thailand will serve as illustrations. Kenneth Kong (2006) examines internal e-mails written in English in Hong Kong firms and looks at the effects of hierarchical status on language use. In particular, the author concentrates on the expression of directives among three categories of employee dyads: peer to peer, subordinate to superior, and superior to subordinate. A counterintuitive finding of this study is the presence of a significant number of accounts in directives from superiors to subordinate (with respect to the peer-to-peer category), when the rank differential would not normally call for such a degree of mitigation. Kong explains the discrepancy in terms of the superiors' awareness of the wide power differential with their addressees, which increases the potential for severe face loss and resistance. In symmetrical relationships these concerns appear to be far less prominent.

These observations need to be placed in the context of a complex and varied cultural background (Hong Kong), where respect for power and hierarchy has traditionally been considered a strong determinant of employees' compliance. Kong surmises that the trend toward a more consultative style of management in Hong Kong firms may explain the managers' choices of increased mitigation in their written directives. This attitude also reflects the concern that superiors are expected to demonstrate toward employees in order to maintain harmony in the workplace. To conclude, Kong's findings point to a possible convergence between traditional Confucian principles (see Chen and Starosta 2003) and models of consultative management already operational in some Western corporate contexts.

An Asian context in which possible Western influences on textual strategies appear to be less salient is Thailand. In spite of the relatively standardized nature of the business-letter genre across languages, Ora-Ong Chakorn (2006) identifies noteworthy differences in letters of requests written in English by Thai speakers and by native English speakers. The difference are structural (positioning of the request), rhetorical (type of appeal used), and pragmatic (use of politeness strategies). In the Thai letters, the request is usually introduced in the middle or second half of the letter and is preceded by another structural element. Confirming the findings of earlier research on other Eastern Asian languages, the rhetoric of Thai letters relies on a combination of logos, ethos, and pathos; interestingly, pathos (emotional or affective appeal to the reader) alone is only found in the Thai dataset. This leads Chakorn to conclude that through the use of collective references Thai letter writers seem to appeal more openly to relationship building and collaboration than do native English writers.

SOME LESSONS FOR PRACTICE

The studies just reviewed confirm the discrepancy between textbook prescriptions and language use in the workplace: the "scripted discourse" of many business communication textbooks published in English stands in sharp contrast to the complex ways in which corporate workers effectively switch between registers and codes (Nair-Venugopal 2006; see also Cheng 2009). Similarly, business communication textbooks tend to ignore delicate yet meaningful variations in the performance of potentially face-threatening acts such as, for example, disagreements. Research based on the Hong Kong Corpus of Spoken English demonstrates the range of possible pragmalinguistic realizations of disagreement that the prescriptive literature ignores, as well as the importance of intonation in moderating the negative impact of disagreement (Cheng and Warren 2005). The damage inflicted by wrong prescriptions has potentially serious consequences on the successful management of real-life professional interactions. Cheng and Warren (2005) note that the fact that Hong Kong students are taught to be more "direct" in their verbal behavior, thus clashing with real-life expectations, is doubly problematic because such attitude runs counter to the preference among Hong Kong Chinese for indirect and other-oriented communication.

The call for "partnership research" (Bargiela-Chiappini and Nickerson 2001) is being heeded. Researchers are discovering the benefits of collaborating with practitioners and professionals toward developing joint modes of interpretation and analysis of issues of practice that are often constructed discursively (Iedema and Sheeres 2009; Cheng 2009). In the Asian region, the Hong Kong Polytechnic University is host to a research team based in the Research Centre for Professional Communication in English (RCPCE), which is seeking to contrast the effects of prescriptivism in business education by working with professionals in key industries in Hong Kong on the construction of taxonomies of communicative competencies (Cheng 2009).

The question of collaborative research between academics and their corporate counterparts is central to (Asian) business discourse research in at least three ways.

(1) Without spoken and written data there would be no business discourse. As the first comprehensive overview of the field shows (Bargiela-Chiappini et al. 2007), researchers in and outside academia depend entirely on access to businesses for their work, be it for written documentation and correspondence or for recordings of meetings and interviews. Personal contacts appear to be the most effective way of gaining access. (2) Business discourse relies on collaborative understanding between researchers and their corporate partners, which entails mutually agreed terms and sharing of findings. As we know, what a scholar deems "useful" and "sufficient" may be different from what a business organization expects its academic partners to concentrate on. Moreover, there are issues of timing and delivery that need to be agreed upon: businesses will require "answers" within a shorter time frame than afforded by a comprehensive study of, say, meeting behavior conducted according to

qualitative research guidelines. Finally, (3) issues of confidentiality are likely to affect the sharing of certain data and findings within and beyond corporate boundaries: for example, on-site recordings may be forbidden altogether and researchers are then forced to resort to alternative ways of presenting their findings (e.g., Tanaka 2006). Building and maintaining trust between the researcher and her corporate collaborators means that treatment of data may have to be negotiated and agreed upon. This was the case when I was given access to the field on the understanding that I would report to the CEO the anonymized findings from employee interviews in exchange for retaining exclusive access to the recordings.

Objective difficulties encountered in gaining access to the field and negotiating and maintaining long-term relationships are partly based on a lack of understanding of the contribution that qualitative research can make toward improving communication within and across business organizations (Ora-Ong Chakorn, personal communication). Negotiating a shared perspective with corporate partners on the nature of the issues that affect business performance, especially in intercultural contacts, is essential to establishing the premises of a successful partnership (Tanaka, personal communication). Collaboration with corporate partners is facilitated when academic researchers already work as consultants to businesses: the benefit of a double identity removes the need for an often laborious process of establishing professional credentials and mutual trust.

This brief discussion of select recent research originating from East and Southeast Asia has illustrated the contribution to scholarship, pedagogy, and professional practice that ABDs are making toward an indigenous understanding of workplace communication, based on irreplaceable "insider knowledge." Partnership with scholars from the region presents Western business discourse researchers with the challenge of rethinking deeply rooted epistemological assumptions and Eurocentric understandings honed by fieldwork in familiar cultural *locales* and fed by disciplinary knowledge emerging from Judeo-Christian thought and the Enlightenment. Therefore, rather than concluding this chapter in a traditional manner, for example, with directions for future research (which I think should come from the pen of Asian scholars), I would like to offer some food for thought to scholars in the West, which I hope will inspire a deeper dialogue with the East for the benefit of business discourse research worldwide.

CONCLUSION: AN EPISTEMOLOGICAL NOTE

Given its eclectic constitution and its openness to influences from other fields, disciplines, and "cultural" traditions, business discourse is set to remain a fluid research domain with a marked experimental vocation. In some respects, and against the projected evolution in similar scholarly fields, for example, business communication (Baker Graham and Thralls 1998), the "disturbing" and unsettling nature of much business discourse research is likely to slow down concerted efforts toward disciplinary consolidation and a unifying identity. Influenced by critical studies (Deetz and McClellan 2009), (Asian) business discourse is beginning to develop an increasingly self-reflexive and self-questioning orientation with regard to its objectives, modes of operation, research outcomes, and applications (Bargiela-Chiappini 2009b).

Rather than seeking paradigmatic conformity, (Asian) business discourse should be active where boundaries are breaking down and accepted ordering principles are contested; (self)reflexivity should become its *modus operandi*. In this vein, we should be alerted to the fact that the "Asian" in ABDs is potentially reminiscent of the first and perhaps most notorious ethnocentric discourse emanating from the West: I am thinking here of "orientalism," the totalizing famously deconstructed by Edward Said. Briefly, orientalism is an interpretative practice that denies "the other's humanity" through "vague, reductive, preposterous generalizations and pre-fabricated judgments, insulated from any real hermeneutic context" (Kögler 2005, 252).

The second ethnocentric discourse is a permutation of orientalism and "a telling trope of the global reality": it is the mythical West-and-the-Rest dichotomy, dissected by Sakai Naoki (2005). In its cartographic form, this discourse belies the political significance of a chronotope sustained by a putative internal unity. In other words, "the West is a name whose indexing function is evoked in order to represent spatially the events of the past, the present and possibly the future in chronological order" (Sakai 2005, 183). In developmental terms, the West inscribes itself as ahead of the Rest, as advanced and, through a totalizing label, as internally coherent. Thus, the West-Rest taxonomy "naturalizes and essentializes what is given as a temporary social distinction between subject positions" (Sakai 2005, 184).

A third and perhaps more subtle "orientalist-type" discourse is that of the West as a metaphysical project (McCumber 2005). If metaphysics is understood as a set of beliefs and doctrines with practical consequences, then its impact is felt beyond the realm of theory. Arguably, the most basic concept of metaphysics is "Being," and Aristotle's conception of being has been influential enough to be identified as constitutive of the West (McCumber 2005, 199). However, the word *being* poses a serious semantic challenge: as the Japanese philosopher Ōhashi Ryōsuke (2002) reminds us, there are two translations for this word in Japanese while Chinese has no copula. To this philological conundrum, one must add the Western understanding of speech "as the imparting of information, and of language as a medium for conveyance of truth"

(McCumber 2005, 203), which dominated thought and scholarship until the controversial phenomenologist philosopher Martin Heidegger published his much quoted *Being and Time.*

From this critique, the West that emerges is more than a geographic location: it is "an immense collection of diverse historical phenomena, ideas, and approaches to life, many of which contradict one another" (McCumber 2005, 198). But deconstructing the unity of the "West" is only the first and the easiest step in our self-reflexive journey: the economic and political program of colonialism, which has made the West synonymous with "the enterprise of global domination" (McCumber 2005, 197) continues to this day, albeit in different and often more subtle forms.

In this context, we need to be aware of the implications of carving out "Asia" as another fictitious unity for the convenience of scholarship and in opposition to the West, whence business discourse research arguably originates.

At the time of writing this chapter, some East and Southeast Asian scholarship is still emerging (see Jung 2009; Chew 2009), while others have reached a more advanced stage of development (e.g., Nair-Venugopal 2009; Cheng 2009; Zhu and Li 2009; Tanaka 2009). What Asian scholars and their Western counterparts must be aware of and continue to discuss is the sociopolitical and historical antecedents of ABDs so that collaborative research conducted under this hospitable banner becomes a socially transformative enterprise.

ACKNOWLEDGMENTS

I would like to thank Sandra Harris and Hiromasa Tanaka for their helpful comments on an earlier version of this chapter. I am also very grateful to the two anonymous reviewers for their constructive comments and ask for forbearance where their advice has not been heeded.

REFERENCES

Ammon, U. 2003. Global English and the Non-native Speaker. In *Language in the Twenty-first Century*, eds. H. Tonkin and T. Reagan, 23–34. Amsterdam: Benjamins.

Baldwin, J., S. Faulkner, M. Hecht, and S. Lindsley. 2006. *Redefining Culture: Perspective across Disciplines*. London: Routledge.

Bargiela-Chiappini, Francesca. 1991. Language and Management Studies: Towards an Integrated Approach to Business Discourse Analysis. Third ENCoDe International Conference, Paris.

Bargiela-Chiappini, Francesca. 1993. Issues in International Business Communication: An Anglo-Italian Case Study. Fifth ENCoDe International Conference, Preston, UK.

Bargiela-Chiappini, Francesca. 2004. Introduction: Reflections on a New Research Paradigm. Special Issue on Organisational Discourse. *International Journal of the Sociology of Language* 166: 1–18.

Bargiela-Chiappini, Francesca. 2008. Discourse and/or Communication: Living with Ambiguity. *Discourse and Communication* 2, 3: 327–32.

Bargiela-Chiappini, Francesca, ed. 2009a. *The Handbook of Business Discourse*. Edinburgh: Edinburgh University Press.

Bargiela-Chiappini, Francesca. 2009b. Introduction: Business Discourse. In *The Handbook of Business Discourse*, ed. F. Bargiela-Chiappini, 1–15. Edinburgh: Edinburgh University Press.

Bargiela-Chiappini, Francesca, Ora-Ong Chakorn, C. L. G. Chew, Y. Jung, K. C. C. Kong, S. Nair-Venugopal, and Hiro Tanaka. 2007. Eastern Voices: Enriching Research on Communication in Business: A Forum. *Discourse and Communication* 1: 131–52.

Bargiela-Chiappini, Francesca, and M. Gotti, eds. 2005. *Asian Business Discourse(s)*. Bern: Peter Lang.

Bargiela-Chiappini, Francesca, and S. Harris, eds. 1997a. *The Languages of Business: An International Perspective*. Edinburgh: Edinburgh University Press.

Bargiela-Chiappini, Francesca, and S. Harris. 1997b. *Managing Language: The Discourse of Corporate Meetings*. Amsterdam: Benjamins.

Bargiela-Chiappini, Francesca, and Catherine Nickerson. 1999. In *Writing Business: Genres, Media and Discourses*, eds. Francesca Bargiela-Chiappini and Catherine Nickerson, 1–32. Saddle River, NJ: Pearson.

Bargiela-Chiappini, Francesca, and Catherine Nickerson. 2001. Partnership Research: A Response to Priscilla Rogers. *Journal of Business Communication* 38: 240–41.

Bargiela-Chiappini, Francesca, and Catherine Nickerson. 2002. Business Discourse: Old Concepts, New Horizons. *International Review of Applied Linguistics* 40: 273–86.

Barker, J. R. 2008. Directions for Thought Leadership in Discourse and Communication: A Commentary on Jain et al., *Discourse and Communication* 2, 3: 333–38.

Baumgardner, R. J., and K. Brown. 2003. World Englishes: Ethics and Pedagogy. *World Englishes* 22: 245–53.

Candlin, C. N., ed. 2002. *Research and Practice in Professional Discourse*. Hong Kong: City University of Hong Kong Press.

Candlin, S. 2003. Issues Arising When the Professional Workplace is the Site of Applied Linguistic Research. *Applied Linguistics* 24: 386–94.

Chakorn, Ora-Ong. 2006. Persuasive and Politeness Strategies in Cross-Cultural Letters of Request in the Thai Business Context. *Journal of Asian Pacific Communication* 16: 103–46.

Charles, Miriliisa. 2009. Future Horizons: Europe. In *The Handbook of Business Discourse*, ed. Francesca Bargiela-Chiappini. Edinburgh: Edinburgh University Press.

Chen, G-M., and W. J. Starosta. 2003. Asian Approaches to Human Communication: A Dialogue. *Intercultural Communication Studies* XII, 4, 1–16.

Cheng, W. 2009. Future Horizons: Asia. In *The Handbook of Business Discourse,* ed. Francesca Bargiela-Chiappini, 481–96. Edinburgh: Edinburgh University Press.

Cheng, W., and M. Warren. 2005. // → well I have a DIFferent // THINking you know //: A Corpus-Driven Study of Disagreement in Hong Kong Business Discourse. In *Asian Business Discourse(s),* eds. Francesca Bargiela-Chiappini and M. Gotti, 241–70. Berne: Peter Lang.

Chew, C. L. G. 2009. Vietnam. In *The Handbook of Business Discourse*, ed. Francesca Bargiela-Chiappini, 372–86. Edinburgh: Edinburgh University Press.

Coleman, H. 1984. Perceptions of Language Use in a Bilingual Industrial Community. *International Journal of the Sociology of Language* 49: 51–72.

Coleman, H. 1988. Analyzing Language Needs in Large Organizations. *English for Specific Purposes* 7: 155–69.

Coupland, N. 2001. Introduction: Sociolinguistic Theory and Social Theory. In *Sociolinguistics and Social Theory*, eds. Nicholas Coupland, Srikant Sarangi, and Christopher N. Candlin, 1–26. Harlow, Essex (UK): Pearson Education.

Deetz, Stanley, and John G. McClellan. 2009. Critical Studies. In *The Handbook of Business Discourse,* ed. Francesca Bargiela-Chiappini. Edinburgh: Edinburgh University Press.

Drew, P., and J. Heritage, eds. 1992. *Talk at Work: Interaction in Institutional Settings*. Cambridge: Cambridge University Press.

Dulek, R., and Margaret Baker Graham. 2009. Future Horizons: North America. In *The Handbook of Business Discourse*, ed. Francesca Bargiela-Chiappini, 465–80. Edinburgh: Edinburgh University Press.

Ehlich, K., and J. Wagner, eds. 1995. *The Discourse of International Negotiations*. Berlin: Mouton de Gruyter.

Firth, A., ed. 1995. *Negotiations in the Workplace: Discourse and Interactional Perspectives*. Berlin: Mouton de Gruyter.

Geluykens, R., and K. Pelsmaekers, eds. 1999. *Discourse in Professional Contexts*, 3–22. Munich and Newcastle: LINCOM EUROPA.

Grant, David, Cynthia Hardy, Clifford Oswick, and Linda Putman, eds. 2004. *The SAGE Handbook of Organizational Discourse*. Sage Publications.

Gunnarsson, B.-L., P. Linell, and B. Nordberg, eds. 1997. *The Construction of Professional Discourse*. London and New York: Longman.

Gupta, A., and J. Ferguson. 1997. Culture, Power, Place: Ethnography at the End of an Era. Explorations in Critical Anthropology. In *Culture, Power, Place,* eds. A. Gupta and J. Ferguson, 1–32. Durham and London: Duke University Press.

Haugh, M., and Y. Watanabe. 2009. Analysing Japanese "Face-in-interaction": Insights from Intercultural Business Meetings. In *Face, Language and Social Interaction*, eds. Francesca Bargiela-Chiappini and M. Haugh, 78–91. London, Equinox.

Hutnyk, J. 2006. Culture. *Theory, Culture and Society* 23: 351–38.

Iedema, R., and H. Sheeres. 2009. Organisational Discourse. In *The Handbook of Business Discourse*, ed. Francesca Bargiela-Chiappini, 80–91. Edinburgh: Edinburgh University Press.

Iedema, R. A., and R. Wodak. 1999. Introduction: Organizational Discourses and Practices. *Discourse and Society* 10: 5–20.

Jian, G., A. Schmisseur, and Gail T. Fairhurst. 2009. Organisational Communication. In *The Handbook of Business Discourse,* ed. Francesca Bargiela-Chiappini. Edinburgh: Edinburgh University Press.

Journal of Asian Pacific Communication. Special double issue on Asian business discourse(s) 15 (2005): 207–320; 16 (2006): 1–158.

Jung, Y. 2009. Korea. In *The Handbook of Business Discourse*, ed. Francesca Bargiela-Chiappini. Edinburgh: Edinburgh University Press.

Kärreman, D., and Mats Alvesson. 2008. The Communicative Constitution of What? A Response to Jian et al. Relationship. *Discourse and Communication* 2: 321–26.

Kögler, H.-H. 2005. Recognition and Difference: The Power of Perspectives in Interpretative Dialogue. *Social Identities* 11: 247–69.

Marra, M. F., ed. 2002. *Japanese Hermeneutics: Current Debates on Aesthetics and Interpretation*. Honolulu, HI: University of Hawaii Press.

McCumber, J. 2005. Dialogue as Resistance to Western Metaphysics. *Social Identities* 11: 197–208.

Nair-Venugopal, S. 2000. *Language Choice and Communication in Malaysian Business.* Bangi, MY: Penerbit University Kebangsaan Malaysia.

Nair-Venugopal, S. 2006. An Interactional Model of English in Malaysia: A Contextualised Response to Commodification. *Journal of Asian Pacific Communication* 16: 51–75.

Nair-Venugopal, S. 2009. Malaysia. In *The Handbook of Business Discourse*, ed. Francesca Bargiela-Chiappini. Edinburgh: Edinburgh University Press.

Ōhashi, R. 2002. The Hermeneutic Approach to Japanese Modernity: "Art-Way," "Iki," and "Cut-Continuance." In *Japanese Hermeneutics: Current Debates on Aesthetics and Interpretation*, ed. M. F. Marra, 25–35. Honolulu, HI: University of Hawaii Press.

Ohnuki-Tierney, E. 2006. Against "Hybridity": Culture as Historical Processes. In *Dismantling the East-West Dichotomy. Essays in Honour of Jan van Bremen*, eds. J. Hendry and H. W. Wong, 11–16. London: Routledge.

Phillipson, R. 1992. *Linguistic Imperialism*. Oxford: Oxford University Press.

Putman, Linda L. 2008. Images of the Communication-Discourse Relationship. *Discourse and Communication* 2: 339–46.

Putman, Linda L., and Gail T. Fairhurst. 2001. Discourse Analysis in Organizations: Issues and Concerns. In *The New Handbook of Organizational Communication: Advances in Theory, Research and Methods*, eds. F. M. Jablin and L. L. Putman, 78–160. Thousand Oaks, CA: Sage.

Reinsch, N. L. J. 1996. Business Communication: Present, Past and Future. *Management Communication Quarterly* 10: 27–49.

Sakai, N. 2005. The West—A Dialogic Prescription or Proscription? *Social Identities* 11: 177–95.

Sarangi, S., and C. Roberts, eds. *Talk, Work and Institutional Order*. Berlin: Mouton de Gruyter.

Schiffrin, D. 1994. *Approaches to Discourse: Language as Social Interaction*. New York: Wiley-Blackwell.

Sewell, W. H. Jr. 1990. The Concept(s) of Culture. In *Beyond the Cultural Turn: New Directions in the Study of Society and Culture*, eds. V. Bonnell and L. Hunt, 35–61. Berkeley: University of California Press.

Shelby, A. 1996. A Discipline Orientation: Analysis and Critique. *Management Communication Quarterly* 10: 98–105.

Shimizu, A. 2006. West-Japan Dichotomy in the Context of Multiple Dichotomies. In *Dismantling the East-West Dichotomy: Essays in Honour of Jan van Bremen*, eds. J. Hendry and H. W. Wong, 17–21. London: Routledge.

Street, B. V. 1993. Culture is a Verb: Anthropological Aspects of Language and Cultural Process. In *Language and Culture*, eds. D. Graddol, L. Thompson, and M. Bryman, 23–43. Clevedon: BAAL and Multilingual Matters.

Tanaka, Hiro. 2006. Emerging English-speaking Business Discourses in Japan. *Journal of Asian Pacific Communication* 16: 25–50.

Tanaka, Hiro. 2009. Japan. In *The Handbook of Business Discourse*, ed. Francesca Bargiella-Chiappini, 332–44. Edinburgh: Edinburgh University Press.

Taylor, J. R. 2008. Communication and Discourse: Is the Bridge Language? Response to Jian et al. *Discourse and Communication* 2: 347–52.

Trosborg, A., ed. 1995. *Hermes: Special Issue on Intercultural Negotiation*. Aarhus, Denmark: Aarhus Business School.

Westwood, R. 2001. Appropriating the Other in the Discourses of Comparative Management. In *The Language of Organization*, eds. R. Westwood and S. Linstead, 241–82. London: Sage.

Yengoyan, A. A. 1986. Theory in Anthropology: On the Demise of the Concept of Culture. *Comparative Studies in Society and History* 28: 368–74.

Yeung, L. 1998. Linguistic Forms of Consultative Management Discourse. *Discourse and Society* 9: 81–101.

Zhu, Y., and L. Li. 2009. China. In *The Handbook of Business Discourse*, ed. Francesca Bargiela-Chiappini, 345–59. Edinburgh: Edinburgh University Press.

4

"Harmonious Disagreement" in Japanese Business Discourse

Misa Fujio and Hiromasa Tanaka

Increased intercultural contact as a result of the globalization of business has highlighted the need to investigate not only intercultural business interaction, in which English is often used as a *lingua franca*, but also intracultural business contact, where local discursive practices can be scrutinized as essential material for comparative analyses. As discussed in an earlier chapter (Bargiela-Chiappini, this volume), Asian Business Discourses (ABDs) have become an integral field of business discourse research, which in its plurality encompasses a multitude of localized discourses and therefore practices. Much business communication research has been dominated thus far by Western epistemologies; yet analysis of localized discourses, for example in the Asian business context, would benefit from the application of non-Western interpretive frameworks (Bargiela-Chiappini 2009).

In this chapter, we present a Japanese perspective on business discourse based on the discussion of extracts from a forty-minute meeting recorded in Yokohama between employees of a small company and an independent management consultant. In the analysis, we attempt to apply an epistemological framework based on concepts developed by Japanese scholars. We also seek to bridge the gap between business discourse analysis and the study of organizations in Japan by setting the analysis of the meeting data against current business practices as shaped by native management theories.

Given the empirical nature of this chapter's contribution to the volume, we have chosen to concentrate on selected excerpts of meeting talk, in which we show how disagreement is tactically managed to preserve an impression of interactional "harmony." Before we introduce the analytical framework, a brief outline of Japanese business discourse research is offered as a way of contextualizing the analysis.

In spite of the difficulty of obtaining authentic business data in Japan, the number of empirical studies by Japanese scholars has steadily increased since the 1990s. Yamada's (1997a 1997b) extensive discussion of differences in back-channeling, topic management, and interaction style in Japanese and American business meetings is based on both intercultural and intracultural data. Sumihara (1993) and Marriott (1995) report miscommunication triggered by different management styles between Japanese and Americans and Japanese and Australians, respectively. Following studies such as these, Japanese communication has been labeled as collectivist, authoritarian, and high context. In contrast, there are other empirical studies that have identified additional features of Japanese business interaction. For example, Miller (1994, 1995) and Fujio (2004) have sought to deconstruct Japanese stereotypes by examining meeting data of Japanese and U.S. employees, from which it emerges that Japanese participants do not necessarily follow the indirect communication style that had been attributed to them in earlier research but are in fact capable of being quite direct. Such findings point to the fact that communication is not influenced by "cultural factors" alone; instead, power relations, the purpose of the meeting, affect, the personality of the individuals, the tension between individual and corporate goals, and linguistic constraints all come into play (Tanaka 2006).

A SOCIOHISTORICAL CONTEXTUALIZATION

Besides discursive approaches to Japanese business, a complementary line of inquiry that has thus far been neglected in Japanese business discourse research is represented by management and organizations studies. Research in these fields has traditionally characterized Japanese business as a set of systems, the effectiveness of which is said to account both for Japan's rapid economic development and for the allegedly unique and inscrutable behavior of Japanese business organizations and their employees. Abegglen (1958), who pioneered this line of research, has credited Japanese Human Resource Management philosophy with the country's fast economic recovery after WWII. He notes that lifetime employment, seniority-based compensation, and in-company labor unions were the three systems that enabled Japan's phenomenal economic growth. William Ouchi (1981) developed Abegglen's arguments into what became known as Theory Z, according to which Japanese management inculcates strong organizational loyalty and team working in the workforce, which ultimately enhance productivity. Based on a tacit understanding of the importance of teamwork supported by unwavering loyalty and "harmony" in interpersonal relations, decision making in Japanese organizations seeks to reach total agreement (Cordeiro 1999). A consequence of this broadly participatory process is that no one is individually credited with success or held responsible for failure.

It is widely recognized that throughout its economic development, from the premodern era to the present, Japan has created a strong work ethic and elaborated distinct models of management praxis, reflections of which are traceable in everyday organizational discourses. Among the foundational concepts of current participatory management are conflicting Japanese ideologies, such as "traditional morality" (MacVeigh 2000), where hierarchy, loyalty, obedience, and diligence sustain interpersonal "harmony" against a mimetic appropriation of Western management (Bargiela-Chiappini and Tanaka, forthcoming).

Past research traces some foundational elements of Japanese management discourse back to indigenous East Asian and Japanese philosophies. Confucianism (Wakabayashi 2001) and *Bushidō* (Jackson and Tomioka 2003) are two ideologies that have had considerable influence on Japanese management discourse. The influence of these two ideologies, especially Confucianism, has been discussed by some indigenous studies. For example, Moriya (2005) claims that the Japanese company is a family-like community that emphasizes organizational "harmony" and wholeness. Wakabayashi (2001) links the family norm of Japanese companies with the paternalistic aspect of Confucianism: "Namely, the company provided jobs, incentives, training, wage increases, promotion, and job security, while workers demonstrated loyalty by committing to the firm's production goals and staying with the firm, disregarding alternative employment opportunities elsewhere." (5)

This brief attempt to contextualize organizational discourse in Japan alerts us to the complex interplay of influences and values that shape situated contexts of practice. In the next section, we introduce a conceptual framework based on constructs indigenous to Japan, which we see realized in the meeting discourse analyzed later in the chapter.

CONCEPTUAL FRAMEWORK

Management theories have traditionally been considered culture free; therefore, several attempts were made to transplant Japanese management ideas outside Japan, with mixed results. This would seem to point to the "situatedness" of management practice and to the interdependence of management ideologies and local discourses (Saka 2003). We therefore argue for a study of business communication within the context of management ideologies and practices; findings from discursive analyses of workplace interaction can be illuminated by insights from organizational behavior research. In this section, we propose an analytical framework that builds on concepts developed by Japanese scholars as a first step toward a progressive "decolonization" of business discourse research epistemology and toward a local control of socially situated inquiry.

Japan's historical and environmental context has made Japanese business processes, business-government relations, work ethic, and management somewhat distinctive from those of many Western countries, especially the United States (Johnson 1982; Vogel 1979); this means that Japanese scholars often sound essentialist in their discussion of Japanese "culture." The specificity of certain situational factors lends itself to ready exploitation in *Nihonjin-ron* ("the studies of the Japanese"), which tends to describe the Japanese as a monolithic nation with unique characteristics. We, however, need to be aware of the danger of using the term *culture* as an explanatory concept (Piller 2009), which is why this chapter concentrates on Japanese discourses and uses concepts that have emerged from Japanese language interaction research. Thus, we look at Japanese language users as the locus of our cultural framings, where national culture is not a given but "a discursive construction that social actors draw upon in selective ways" (Piller 2009, 325). Moreover, we need to interpret such constructions against the ideological background discussed earlier.

In his seminars held at the International Research Center of Japanese Studies (1996, 1998), Eshun Hamaguchi argued that the underlying value in Japanese society is "contextualism," in which relations among individuals are seen as more important than the individuals involved in them. The two dimensions of human relations, horizontality and verticality, map the (apparently conflictual) harmony and hierarchy value combination that is quite influential in shaping interpersonal relations in Japan. The often discussed indirectness of the Japanese may be attributed to the sensitivity required in gauging relational processes and positionings among interlocutors.

In her monograph *Wakimae no goyoron [Pragmatics of Wakimae]* (2006), Sachiko Ide discusses the modality of Japanese language use by employing the notion of *wakimae* or discernment. Ide points to multiple contextual elements that interlocutors need to consider in order to "fit in" a Japanese speech community. Such elements include consideration of the other interlocutors' positions, status, responsibilities, and degree of closeness (*uchi-soto* relations). Particularly important to the assessment of the social relationship are the vertical dimension corresponding to the hierarchical order and the horizontal dimension corresponding to interpersonal closeness, or *uchi-soto* (insider-outsider) (Mikami 1953; Takiura 2005). Tanaka (2011) explores the dynamic nature of hierarchy and *uchi-soto* relations in his study of a Japanese corporate meeting. Tanaka shows how managers' choice of honorifics depends on the topic under discussion. In the data, the participants change their positionality along the vertical and horizontal axes. When managers talk as representatives of the company's management, they will distance themselves from other participants by using honorific forms. In the same meeting, when a manager complains about senior management, thus siding with his subordinates in the meeting, he emphasizes solidarity with them by using plain-form speech.

The competence of speakers to assess and to adjust to the social coordinates defining their position in the situation, or *wakimae*, relies on another well-know dualism besides *uchi-soto*. The sociologist Yoshio Sugimoto, among many other scholars, argues that the *honne/tatemae* [real intention/explanation to outsiders] distinction is key to interpreting interpersonal relations in Japan: "Thus an employee who expresses dedication to his company boss in accordance with the corporate *tatemae* of loyalty and harmony, may do so because of his *honne* ambition for promotion and other personal gains" (2003, 28). Sugimoto is also critical of the "in-group harmony" value promoted by what he calls "Nihonjinron-style stereotyping" (17), which he lists as one of the "values" framing contemporary analyses of Japanese society to this day.

In line with the emic approach adopted in this chapter, we define *harmony* as a "conflict-free situation," a concept that involves certain cultural practices arguably specific to Japan. This choice acknowledges both the dangers of "culturalism" and the difficulties surrounding a discursive yet situated approach to the analysis of Japanese business interaction, of which the dynamics of "harmony maintenance" are integral if not exclusive.

Wakimae dynamics are especially visible in the case of confrontational or conflictual positionings in interaction. Kondo's (2007) large-scale study of Japanese intracultural business interaction found that the speakers' concern for potential conflict results in the recycling of topics. Another study (Tanaka and Bargiela-Chiappini 2011) echoes Kondo's findings and shows that topic digression is used in order to avoid creating a confrontational stance. Situational constraints also affect topic development. Kameda (2001, quoting Motokawa 1988) surmises that "if other people come to the same conclusion as the one I have in mind, then we can share the conclusion and we are happy in harmony." Kameda claims that in order to minimize conflict, Japanese speakers tend to share the contextual information first and express their opinion or judgment at the very end of the interaction. This behavior is based on the assumption that sharing contextual information will lead to a shared opinion, thus ensuring interactional "harmony."

A very good example of this is the construction of disagreement in Japanese discourse. According to Ide and Uchida (2001), turn exchanges in Japanese and English interaction are noticeably different. Agreement usually accompanies speakers' change in Japanese; whereas in English conversation, disagreement is often a turn-taking marker. Ide and Uchida argue that Japanese speakers develop solidarity by creating harmony through continuous expression of agreement. Nakai (2002) found that Japanese language learners in the United States have difficulties in showing topic involvement because of their limited capability to express agreement and empathy. In Japanese discourse, when disagreement is expressed it tends to appear much later in the interaction (Ide and Uchida 2001; Ide 2006). An interactant may not feel qualified to show disagreement without first acquiring all contextual information and weighing its implications. Thus, Japanese interactants often wait until the end of a conversation before showing disagreement.

In summary, in order to achieve self-discernment, a Japanese listener is required to make an extensive effort to capture the subtle influences that shape the social context of discourse. Because of the different access to contextual knowledge among the interlocutors and their vertical and horizontal positionings, meeting participants are forced to concentrate on listening. Yamada (1997b) explains differences in verbal exchange between U.S. and Japan meeting participants in terms of two modes of participation: speaker talk versus listener talk, respectively. In a speaker talk context such as in the United States, it is a speaker who is responsible for communicating, and therefore the speaker is expected to articulate her message. On the other hand, in a listener talk context, such as in Japan, it is the listener who is responsible for and expected to understand the speaker, using *sasshi*, or guesswork. Therefore, the role of the listener in Japanese discourse is "not only key, but the main mode of communication" (Yamada 1997b, 38). Also, guesswork is one of the reasons why silence is tolerated in Japanese interaction. Silence is necessary for guesswork, as well as being sociolinguistically accepted as "the ultimate form of unspoken interdependence" (Yamada 1997b, 77).

DATA AND ANALYSIS

Data

The data collected for this study is a meeting among six staff members of Toyoko Network, a Japanese consulting company, and an independent consultant, Mr. Tabata. Toyoko Network's core business is knowledge creation through elaboration of clients' ideas and customization of their training programs. Mr. Tabata is a prominent corporate trainer in Japan, and Toyoko has a long-established business relationship with him; the data discussed here refer to an informal meeting that took place on company premises. Mr. Tabata called the meeting with the purpose of gathering the opinions of Toyoko staff on some training materials that he developed. Tabata is especially interested to obtain information on how long it will take to apply the materials, how they can be sold, and what kind of price range will be appropriate; on the other hand, Toyoko Network, as a consulting company, is looking for a business opportunity in the form of a joint project. However, no apparent negotiation is observed in the meeting; instead, the participants just continue to exchange opinions and sound out each other's intentions to the very end of the meeting.

As for the analytical procedure, the two authors first analyzed the conversation independently and then exchanged findings before agreeing on a shared interpretation. This method worked effectively in terms of contextualizing discursive practices since one of the authors is familiar with the staff at Toyoko Network and its business. In line with a semiethnographic approach, background and contextual information available to one of the authors was incorporated in the analysis and used to inform the interpretation, while the other author, without detailed knowledge of the company, focused on analyzing the discourse. In addition, the meeting purpose and the business outcomes following this meeting were clarified with one of the participants, and based on this additional information the analysis and interpretation were updated.

Below is the list of the seven male meeting participants and their age; real names have been replaced by pseudonyms:

An independent consultant: Tabata, 68
Company President: Hanawa, 65
Senior Vice President, Research: Nojima, 59
Senior Vice President, Sales: Kasai, 54
Sales Director: Umemoto, 48
Sales Representative: Ochiai, 26
Intern from Local Board of Education: Tsuda, 50

Kasai was approached by one of the authors to record the meeting after obtaining the consent of the participants. Due to space constraints, only select excerpts are discussed in this section; first, to show the basic listening attitude that typically precedes agreement or a disagreement in meetings, and second to illustrate the dynamics of what we have called "harmonious disagreement," a phenomenon that is typical of Japanese discourse.

Preparing the Ground for "Harmonious Disagreement"

Excerpt 1 refers to the beginning of the interaction, where Mr. Tabata explains the purpose of the meeting by introducing his newly developed teaching materials and encouraging Toyoko members to use them and give him feedback on their experience. His explanation, however, is not structured in a way that includes all the necessary information; for example, how he is going to sell the materials, how they are structured, and what kind of price range he is thinking of. Instead, all these items are clarified by a series of questions from the other participants and, thus, information is acquired as the meeting unfolds. The words in parentheses were inserted by the authors for ease of understanding. See the transcription key at the end of the chapter for information about symbols and numbers in the excerpts.

Excerpt 1

1.1 Tabata: *Kyou ne, onegai shi, shitakatta koto wa [hai] kami ni tsukutte kita n dakedo, jigyou no are jya nai n dakedo ne, chotto ni san pun, ni san pun desu ga hanashi te, ato wa XXX manējimento, uh, kabushikigaisha ni kyonen shite, kyouzai hanbai gaisha wo tsukuru n desu yo kenshū kyouzai no hanbai gaisha wo, sore ga 80% no ueito. (1.13) To yū fūni, dakedo, sono shuppan toka kangaeteru n dakedo, soryā mā, jigyou no, ikutsuka yatterutte koto ni shiyou to omotte, shuryoku wa kyouzai uritaitte [Hum].* "Today what I want to ask you is [Yes] I have written (it) on the paper. Not work-related. Just a little, two or three minutes, two or three minutes (I'm going to) talk, and the rest is XXX (sound of paper distribution) management. Oh, and last year I established a corporation. The company sells materials, training materials. It accounts for 80 percent of my business. (1.13) This way, I'm thinking of publishing (materials), well yeah, of course, (I'm) trying to do some other business (.) but the main business is to sell materials [Hmm]."

Mr. Tabata's first utterance is complete neither in form nor in function. His attempt to verbalize the purpose of the meeting seems to shift to background information about his company. It is only in the last sentence that he mentions its core business—the sale of training materials. It is unclear what Mr. Tabata is trying to accomplish in his first turn except perhaps sharing background and contextual information with Toyoko staff. The unexpressed contents are gradually revealed through a series of questions from the floor.

1.2 Tabata: *(1.05) De, sono kyouzai tte nowa kihonteki na kyouzai de, shi, shinnyūshain kenshū, chūken shain, kakarichou, kachou tte yonkaisou no kaku kaigou ga nanatsu gurai aruno kana (.) dakara, [un] sono kaisou iso tēma betsu kenshū, mokkan tokane [un] souyū no wo zenbu tsukutte, yaku rokujyū aitemu rokujyū (.) kaigou uruwake (.) jissai ne, shinnyūshain nara jyūgo gurai kana.* "(1.05) and the materials are basic materials for the courses of four levels of training sessions, such as new employees, middle career, *kakaricho* (junior managers), *kacho* (middle managers). (There are) about seven kinds (for each level). (.) So [Hmm] training by levels or by themes such as management by objectives. [Yes] I will create all of those, about sixty items sixty (.) meetings [Hmm] We will sell (.) Actually, new employees' training, one material covers fifteen meetings."

(1.16)

1.3 Umemoto: *Sou suru to aitemu no kumiawase?* "Then, (are they) going to combine these items?"

1.4 Tabata: (.) *un, dakara kou kumiawasete, katte, echiketto nara echiketto kautoka sa.* "(.) Yeah, (they purchase the material) and combine like this. (If they want etiquette in their training), buy an etiquette program."

1.5 Tabata: *Kouyū monodesu (.) kouyū no (4.07) kouyū no.* "It's like this (.) like this (4.07) like this."

(1.68)

1.6 Hanawa: *Mojyūru ka [sareteite].* "Modularized [they are]"

1.7 Umemoto: *[Etto, kore ga sono, wan aitemu tte kanji ne].* "[Well, is this one item, so to say?]"

1.8 Tabata: *[Sou sou sou, dakara kore ga manyuaru to shite, sore wa ne, kougi dake dakara, amari ryou ga nai wake de].* "[Yes, yes, yes, this is a manual, so it is only for lecture, that's why it's not thick.]"

1.9 Hanawa: *Kore ga manyuaru ga haitte iru wake desu ne.* "[So this manual is enclosed.]"

1.10 Tabata: *Kore ensyūyou no ga haitte iru kara goukei yon yonjyū mai gurai ni naruwake, yonjyū pēji gurai ni naruwake ne.* "This contains exercise materials so it contains four, forty papers. Forty pages altogether."

1.11 Hanawa: *[Ah Ah Ah pēji sū ni shite ne].* "[Ah, Ah, Ah, the number of pages.]"

. . .

1.12 Hanawa: *Kore wa manyuaru desu ne.* "This is the manual, isn't it?"

1.13 Tabata: *Iya ryouhou.* "No. Both."

1.14 Hanawa: *Ryouhou desu ka?* "Both?"

1.15 Tabata: *Ryouhou. Shīto tsuiten da. Ushironi.* "Both. A sheet is attached in the back."

1.16 Hanawa: *Ah, ushiro ni tsuiteru. Ah kore desu ne. Ah.* "Ah, in the back. Ah, this is it. Ah."

(2.07)

1.17 Tabata: *Kore wo ne, intānetto de hanbai suru.* "This, I will market through the Internet."

1.18 Kasai: *Hum. (1.98) Ato wa minna kobetsu ni purinto auto surun desu ka?*

"Hum. (1.98) The customers will print out all the rest?"

1.19 Tabata: *=Purinto auto suru.* "=Will print out."

1.20 Kasai: [*Shīto to ka.*] "[and the sheets.]"

As seen in Excerpt 1, what an item is, what a manual is like, and how to sell on the Internet are all issues clarified by questions from Umemoto lines (1.3, 1.7), Hanawa (1.9), and Kasai (1.18). In each question, the speaker is confirming his understanding by eliciting an affirmative answer from Mr. Tabata, while Mr. Tabata complements the questioners' understanding by adding some examples. As a speaker, Mr. Tabata appears not too concerned about organizing his talk or getting his messages across effectively. Instead, it falls on the listeners to try to understand Mr. Tabata by asking questions; in other words, by supplying missing information as if putting together pieces of a jigsaw puzzle. In this meeting then, the listeners play a major role in co-constructing discourse as pointed out by Yamada (1997b). The same pattern continues until six minutes and twenty-six seconds into the meeting, when Mr. Tabata finally completes his very first utterance ("Today what I wanted to ask you is") by adding, "I'm hoping that you can try them. I don't know how long it will take or what it will be like." The interactional style that emerges from this meeting is one in which the listeners collaborate and reach shared understanding first and hold back their opinions until later (Ide and Uchida 2001; Ide 2006).

Harmonious Disagreement

The important role of the listeners is also observed when business interests seem to be conflicting. The listeners are very tactful in adjusting their replies to the speaker's utterance and at the same time in showing their disagreement indirectly. In excerpts 2 and 3, the business objectives of Mr. Tabata and of Toyoko Network turn out to be incompatible. E-mail exchange with one of the participants revealed that Mr. Tabata expected Toyoko Network to try the materials and give him feedback while Toyoko was more interested in exploiting the business opportunities afforded by marketing the materials. Therefore, setting the price too low would not secure Toyoko enough profit if it decided to be involved in a project with Mr. Tabata. Company members show their disagreement indirectly in several ways:

Excerpt 2

2.1 Tabata: *Dakara nedan teki ni wa dou (.) douyū fūni sureba iika kangaete nain dakedo.* "So costwise (.) I haven't much thought about how to price."

(2.11)

2.2 Umemoto: *Aitemu goto ni nedan settei sarerun deshou ne (.) Tabun ne sore wa (.) kakujitsu desu yo ne?* "You will price each item separately, won't you? That must be the case."

2.3 Kasai: *Hum*. "Hum"

(2.04)

2.4 Tabata: *Dakara sore kumiawasete ne (.) Mikka kan kouza dattara futatsuzutsu (.) yarutoka (.) maa futsukakan dattara . . .* "So (users) will combine them. (.) For three-day program (.) two per day or (.) er for two days . . ."

2.5 Umemoto: *=Sono kumiawase no (.) sono moderu mitaina monomo . . .* "=For the combination (.) Some kind of examples of the combination . . ."

2.6 Tabata: *=Sore wa nai ne.* "=There is no example."

2.7 Umemoto: *=Nai. Sore wa. (2.30) Sore wa soudan?* "No example. (2.30) (If anybody needs it) it will be [based on] negotiation?"

2.8 Hanawa: *[Mukou ni] erabaseru wake desu ka? Kau gawa ni?* "(Do you) [make them] choose, the consumers?"

(6.01)

2.9 Tabata: *Dakara kachou kenshū nanatsu toka sa (.) kakarichou yattsu toka no mondai dake ne.* "So it is a matter of choice (.) seven items for *Kacho* training or eight items for *Kakaricho* training."

2.10 Hanawa: *Ah hai hai hai.* "Ah, yes, yes, yes."

In Excerpt 2, two noticeable interactional features are observed: long and frequent pauses and incomplete utterances. In line 2.2, Umemoto produces his first utterance as an emphatic assumption—"That must be the case"—but in his next turn (line 2.5) his tone is more subdued: his incomplete sentence creates lingering ambiguity. Following line 2.6, which reveals that Mr. Tabata has not thought about the price for combined programs, Umemoto in his third turn (line 2.7) pauses for 2.30 seconds, waiting for Mr. Tabata's further explanation. Failing to receive a reply, Umemoto asks a question, using another incomplete utterance.

This could be interpreted as a device to avoid exposing Mr. Tabata's unpreparedness, which could make him lose face; in other words, Umemoto shows discernment of his own positionality. At the same time, Umemoto indirectly conveys concern about the price issue by an oblique reference to it; the pauses appear to be signaling hesitation, so the turns could be interpreted as implicit disagreement.

It is during the discussion on pricing that the only instance of open disagreement in the whole meeting is traceable (see excerpt 3). However, instead of being resolved through negotiation, the disagreement settles down into yet another indirect utterance, thus preserving the impression of interactional "harmony."

Excerpt 3

3.1 Hanawa: *Dakara 20 nara 20 setto. De, touzen sono bun dake okane itadaku wake desu yone.* "So if twenty sets are sent (to a customer), you receive that much."

3.2 Tabata: *Iya 20 setto jya nai yo*. "No, not for 20."

3.3 Hanawa: *Morawanai n desu ka?* "Not going to receive (for twenty)?"

3.4 Tabata: *Morawanai yo. Wan setto uttara.* "No, once I sold one set."

3.5 Umemoto: *Wan setto desuyo. [Dakara genbutsu wa wan setto dakara.]* "(The price is) just for one set. [Cause what is actually sold is one.]"

3.6 Tabata: *[Jibun de kopī sureba iinda.] [Hā] Dakara wākushīto toka souyū no wa sa . . .* "[So the customers can make copies by themselves.] So, worksheets or something like that . . ."

3.7 Hanawa: *Mā tatoeba gosen en toka ichiman en toka kaitearu n desu keredomo (.) kouyū nedan nan desu ka?* "This says, for example, five thousand or ten thousand yen. (.) Is this the actual price?"

(2.53)

3.8 Hanawa: *Yasui.* "Cheap."

3.9 Kasai: *Yasūi.* "CHEAP."

3.10 Tabata: *Dakara jibun de kopī shite tsukaeba ii jyan.* "So, they will make copies themselves."

3.11 Hanawa: *Sore ni shitemo yasui jya nai desuka. Gosen en, ichiman en jya. Datte nou hau ryou toka nan toka.* "Even so, still cheap, isn't it? Just five thousand or ten thousand yen. Considering (it includes) know-how or anything."

(1.16)

3.12 Umemoto: *Mā furoppī tte wake niwa ima ikanai kara (.) zenbu saitei CD ka DVD ka.* "Now that we don't use a floppy, (we should include) either a CD or DVD."

3.13 Hanawa: *=Mā nedan no mondai wa korekara mata okangae ni narareru deshou kara ne*. "=Well, (Mr. Tabata) will have a further thought on the price."

3.14 Tabata: *Iyā soko ga mondai nanda yo.* "Well, that is the thing."

3.15 Hanawa: *Sore wa wakari masu yo.* "I understand."

3.16 Tabata: *Hito ni iwaseru to ne (.) sonna ne (.) yasui n jya dame datte (.) tema bakkari kakatte*. "Some people say the price, cheap one, does not make sense. Just too laboring for the price."

3.17 Hanawa: *Iya ippanteki ni kangaerya (.) dou kangaete mo gosen en, ichiman en jya yasui yo ne.* "Well, generally speaking, five thousand or ten thousand yen is too cheap, isn't it?"

3.18 Kasai: *Yasui desu ne*. "It is."

3.19 Tabata: *Datte wan aitemu da mon. Wan kaigou da mon.* "But it's just for one item, one meeting."

3.20 Hanawa: *Mā kore de sho (.) Sore ni shitemo ne.* "Well, this is it. Even so."

The first several turns in excerpt 3 (lines 3.1 to 3.7) reveal that the expectations about pricing differ between Mr. Tabata and Mr. Hanawa. Mr. Hanawa, who has thus far always supported Mr. Tabata's ideas, for the first time shows surprise at the consultant's suggestion, in lines 3.3, 3.7, 3.8, and 3.11. In lines 3.1, 3.3, and 3.7, Hanawa uses a yes/no question to confirm the price, and in lines 3.8 and 3.11, he mentions that Mr. Tabata's price is set too low. In line 3.11 Hanawa insists on his opinion by using a tag question. Compared to his previous turns, Hanawa's utterance here assumes a more critical tone, partly because he is the president of Toyoko and is in the position to decide whether or not to be involved in this project with Tabata. However, after Umemoto's utterance in line 3.12, Hanawa in line 3.13 tries to change the topic and avoid further negotiation. In line 3.15 he even shows agreement with Tabata in pursuit of a "harmonious" conclusion. Further, Tabata (line 3.16) quotes a third party in his attempt to avert potential conflict.

In excerpt 3, nobody explicitly claims that Mr. Tabata should reconsider his price; besides, no further price negotiation takes places in the remaining section of the meeting. In other words, even if disagreement is implied, it never develops into a negotiation around differing positions; instead, the topic is changed and the threat of disagreement is "naturally" averted by a change of topic. This phenomenon is consistent with findings by Kondo (1997), which point to disagreements being resolved in an indirect, "harmony"-preserving fashion.

The meeting ends without a clear agreement regarding whether Toyoko will collaborate with Mr. Tabata either in selling his materials or in a pilot study in which Toyoko staff will use the materials and give him feedback on their experience. By postmeeting e-mail exchange, it eventually turns out that Toyoko will undertake a pilot study and will collaborate in selling the materials, and this without a formal written contract being signed but based instead on a mutual tacit agreement. Contextualization is essential for understanding this meeting outcome. First, Toyoko has a very long-established relationship with Mr. Tabata, who also holds an advisory role in Toyoko; second, there is no financial disadvantage for Toyoko (though no tangible advantage either) in doing business with Mr. Tabata in that the company has not agreed to any specific sales objectives: Tabata's materials will be just one of their product lines. In other words, although many of the staff members who participated in the meeting were concerned with the business potential of a deal with the consultant—because of possible low market demand and a low set price—these were not compelling enough reasons for declining Mr. Tabata's project at the cost of endangering their long-standing relationship.

DISCUSSION

The analysis in the above section shows the importance of the listening function in Japanese discourse. In excerpt 1 the listeners complement the speaker, co-construct the discourse, and share contextual information until they reach mutual understanding. It is only when all relevant information is acquired and shared by the interactants that agreement or disagreement can be expressed, though not necessarily verbalized in conflictual terms. Excerpts 2 and 3 illustrate how participants holding a potentially negative opinion choose to convey it through discursive indirectness in order to preserve interactional "harmony," and to this effect they use significant pauses and subtle topic shifts. These discursive features reflect an important characteristic in the structure of Japanese meetings. Japanese participants tend to wait until the end of the meeting before showing disagreement, while listening to the speakers very carefully regardless of whether they agree with them or not. This interactional style contrasts with a certain "Western" meeting style, where disagreement is often a turn-taking marker (Ide 2006). On their part, discourse scholars working on English interactions have long argued that direct disagreement is a token of high conflict (Handford and Koester 2010; Kotthoff 1993), while the tendency to avoid disagreement has been identified by a number of other Western business discourse studies, such as Boden (1994), Holmes and Stubbe (2003), and Koester (2006). The interactional patterns revealed by this study contrast also with behaviors observed in intercultural meetings involving Japanese business people who have been shown to be quite outspoken in negotiating meaning and expressing disagreement of other non-Japanese participants (Fujio 2004).

The different way in which disagreement is managed between Japanese and non-Japanese speakers could arguably be a major cause for misunderstanding or incomprehension in intercultural communication. In this sense, investigation into intracultural communication can make a significant contribution toward understanding local business practices, while research into intercultural communication may reveal whether and how local practices are maintained or adapted in response to contextual and situational influences. Given the centrality of verbal communication to business practice, ethnographically framed discursive and interpretive approaches are especially suited to capture the detail of situated workplace interaction within the specificity of localized practice. For instance, according to Kondo's survey (2007), one of the four issues in Japanese business that non-Japanese business practitioners claim is inefficiency in the workplace. The present analysis of careful grounding of disagreement may explain why Japanese business practices look inefficient to non-Japanese business people who may be less concerned about preserving interactional and interpersonal "harmony" and more interested in immediate business outcomes. Our findings show the complexity of the process of disagreement constructed in a particular Japanese organizational discourse, and add to the current research on disagreement (e.g., Boden 1994; Holmes and Stubbe 2003; Koester 2006) by showing how Japanese relation-building processes deal with disagreement in somewhat different ways.

The chapter has also attempted to link management systems with verbal communication in the workplace. The authors argue that the observed co-constructed nature of grounding and exercise of "harmonious disagreement" is a manifestation of shared Japanese business ideology embedded in management systems. Past research on Japanese management systems characterizes Japanese organizations in terms of group orientation and team spirit (Ouchi 1981). As we discussed earlier, management systems are potentially situated and contextualized and not easily transferable. The premise of much management theory and practice in Japan is often claimed to be the fundamental native value of "harmony." The in-company labor union system, for example, requires organizational discourse where total agreement can be reached among those who have divergent interests. This is only possible through a cumbersome process of decision making based on shared management philosophy, values, and beliefs (Ouchi 1981). In this chapter, we showed how business participants effectively co-construct a localized discourse that reflects a continuous concern for the preservation of interactional "harmony," not as a value exclusive to Japan, but perhaps rather more as a response to ideological and social conditioning that promote hierarchy, status, and authority among the organizing principles of corporate life.

CONCLUSION

This study's primary contribution to the business discourse research lies in the close examination of intracultural business communication focusing on select interactional features of Japanese discourse. As discussed in the previous section, discourse observed in localized interaction reflects the typical and ordinary business practices of the region, which are free from the linguistic and cultural "adjustments" observed in intercultural communication.

The findings of this study point to the interdependence of local interactional patterns and organizational discourse and challenge the solidity and homogeneity of management systems that are often taken for granted. The dynamics of "harmonious disagreement" is a window on how a local discourse constructs companywide, team-oriented organizational systems and norms in Japanese companies. In other words, (Japanese) management systems do not preexist observable local business discourses; rather, we would argue that such systems are being crafted by practitioners and analysts as instances of social reality, such as in the case of the concrete, existential episode of human interaction analyzed in this chapter (see Chia 2003, 112). The potential interaction of local and organizational discourse found in this study suggests that management should enact careful consideration when implementing certain systems and policies across different organizational cultures.

This discursive approach to the study of business interaction in Japan as situated cultural praxis extends the scope of the traditional, prescriptive scholarship that has relied on quantitative methodologies and predictive models; as such, it opens up a new avenue for cross-disciplinary research. In terms of cross-cultural management scholarship, intracultural research based on indigenous conceptual frameworks warns against the blanket and uncritical application of essentialist and ethnocentric categories, usually formulated in Western contexts of practice.

The "mystery" (Cleary 1999) that Japan continues to represent in a certain (romantic) Western tapestry of Eastern mythology could be represented as a consequence of the persistence of a certain "idea of the West" that decentralizes and isolates the Other. The thesis of the mutuality of the "gaze" between the West and Japan—proposed by Bargiela-Chiappini and Tanaka (forthcoming)—posits a two-way direction of influence in the areas of business management and training, in which Japan is seen as the importer (and adapter), as well as the exporter, of ideas and practices.

As discussed in the introduction, Asian Business Discourse(s) are becoming an integral part of business discourse research. More empirical studies are urgently needed, not only in Japan but also in other countries in the region. Such research should extend the range of analyzed contexts and settings and thus begin to construct a map of the similarities and differences, which will in turn provide material for much-needed comparative studies and deeper insight into intercultural encounters. Future business discourse research will benefit from an iterative pattern of zooming into the detail of intra- and intercultural business practices and then zooming out to identify patterns emerging from comparative and contrastive studies.

TRANSCRIPTION KEY

[ ]	interruption or overlap
(1.0)	one-second pause
(.)	micro pause
=	immediate latching on
XXX	indecipherable syllables

ACKNOWLEDGEMENTS

We are grateful to Francesca Bargiela-Chiappini for her dedicated support and to Michael Handford and Bertha Du-Babcock for their perceptive and constructive comments on an earlier version of the chapter.

REFERENCES

Abegglen, J. C. 1958. *Japanese Factory: The Origins of National Diversity in American Industry.* Cambridge, MA: MIT.

Bargiela-Chiappini, Francesca. 2009. Introduction: Business Discourse. In *The Handbook of Business Discourse,* ed. F. Bargiela-Chiappini, 17. Edinburgh: Edinburgh University Press.

Bargiela-Chiappini, F., and Hiro Tanaka, forthcoming. The Mutual Gaze: Japan, Business Management and the West. In *The Gaze of the West: Framings of the East*, eds. S. Nair-Venugopal et al.

Boden, D. 1994. *The Business of Talk: Organizations in Action.* Cambridge, UK: Polity Press.

Chia, R. 2003. Ontology: Organization as "World-Making." In *Debating Organization: Point-Counterpoint in Organization Studies*, eds. R. Westwood and S. Clegg, 98–113. Oxford: Blackwell.

Cleary, T. F. 1999. *Code of the Samurai: A Contemporary Translation of the Bushido Shoshinshu of Taira Shigesuke.* North Clarendon, VT: Tuttle Press.

Cordeiro, W. P. 1999. Can We Learn Management Technique from the Japanese Ringi Process? *Business Forum*, www.allbusiness.com/human-resources/employee-development-problem-solving/393248-1.html (accessed on April 4, 2010).

Fujio, M. 2004. Silence during Intercultural Communication: A Case Study. *Corporate Communications* 94: 331–39.

Hamaguchi, E., ed. 1996. *Nippon bunka to wa ishitsuka.* Tokyo: Nippon Hoosoo Kyookai.

Hamaguchi, E., ed. 1998. *Nippon bunka to wa nani ka: <fukuzatukei> no kanten kara.* Tokyo: Nippon Hoosoo Kyookai.

Handford, M., and A. Koester. 2010. It's Not Rocket Science: Metaphors and Idioms in Conflictual Business Meetings. *Text and Talk* 301: 27–51.

Holmes, J., and M. Stubbe. 2003. *Power and Politeness in the Workplace.* Auckland: Pearson Longman.

Ide, S. 2006. *Wakimae no goyoron [Pragmatics of Wakimae]*. Tokyo: Taishukan Publishing Company.

Ide, S., and R. Uchida. 2001. Hanashite no baton tacchi: eigo de wa teisei no tokini nihongo de wa doui no tokini. *STEP Eigo Joohoo* 5/6: 60–63. Tokyo: Nippon Eigo Kentei Kyookai.

Jackson, K., and M. Tomioka. 2003. *The Changing Face of Japanese Management*. London: Routledge.

Johnson, C. 1982. *MITI and the Japanese Miracle*. Stanford, CA: Stanford University Press.

Kameda, N. 2001. The Implication of Language Style in Business Communication: Focus on English versus Japanese. *Corporate Communications* 63: 144–49.

Koester, A. 2006. *Investigating Workplace Discourse*. Abingdon: Routledge.

Kondo, A. 2007. *Nihonjin to gaikokujin no bijinesu komyunikeishon ni kansuru kenkyuu [Research on Business Communication between Japanese and Foreigners]*. Tokyo: Hitsuji Shobo.

Kotthoff, H. 1993. Disagreement and Concession in Disputes: On the Context Sensitivity of Preference Structures. *Language in Society* 22: 193–216.

MacVeigh, B. 2000. Education Reform in Japan: Fixing Education or Fostering Economic Nation-Statism. In *Globalization and Social Change in Contemporary Japan*, eds. J. S. Eades, T. Gill, and H. Befu, 76–92. Melbourne: Transpacific Press.

Marriott, H. 1995. Deviations in an Intercultural Business Negotiation. In *The Discourse of Negotiation*, ed. A. Firth, 247–68. UK: Pergamon Press.

Mikami, A. 1953. *Keigo hou no a sen Gendai go hou josetsu*. Kuroshio Shuppa.

Miller, L. 1994. Japanese and American Indirectness. *Journal of Asian Pacific Communication* 5: 37–55.

Miller, L. 1995. Two Aspects of Japanese and American Co-worker Interaction: Giving Instructions and Creating Rapport. *Journal of Applied Behavioral Science* 312: 141–61.

Moriya, T. 2005. *Nippon kigyou eno seikashugi dounyu: kigyounai kyoudoutai no henyou [Implementation of Performance-based Personnel Appraisal: Transformation of Corporate Communities]*. Tokyo: Moriyama shoten.

Motokawa, T. 1988. "Sushi Science vs. Hamburger Science": Science, Technology and Human Values. Handout at a public lecture, Duke University Program, April 20, 1988, 6–7.

Nakai, K. Y. 2002. Topic Shifting Devices Used by Supporting Participants in Native/Native and Native/Non-native Japanese Conversations. *Japanese Language and Literature* 361: 1–25.

Ouchi, W. G. 1981. *Theory Z*. Reading, MA: Addison-Wesley.

Piller, I. 2009. Intercultural Communication. In *The Handbook of Business Discourse*, ed. F. Bargiela-Chiappini, 317–29. Edinburgh: Edinburgh University Press.

Saka, A. 2003. *Cross-national Appropriation of Work Systems: Japanese Firms in the UK*. Cheltenham: Edward Elgar.

Sugimoto, Y. 2003. *An Introduction to Japanese Society, Second Edition*. Cambridge, New York, and Melbourne: Cambridge University Press.

Sumihara, N. 1993. A Case Study of Cross-cultural Interaction in a Japanese Multinational Corporation Operating in the United States: Decision-making Processes and Practices. In *Diversity and Differences in Organization: An Agenda for Answers and Questions*, eds. R. R. Sims and R. F. Dennehy, 135–38. Westport, CT: Quarum Books.

Takiura, M. 2005. *Nippon no keigo ron: Poraitonesu riron karano saikentou.* Tokyo: Daishukan shoten.

Tanaka, Hiro. 2006. Corporate Language Policy Change: The Trajectory of Management Discourse in Japan, the Oppressed or the Oppressor? *Quaderns de Filologia. Estudis Lingüístics* 11: 279–88.

Tanaka, Hiro. 2011. Politeness in a Japanese Intra-organizational Meeting: Honorifics and Socio-dialectal Code Switching. *Journal of Pacific Asian Communication* 202, forthcoming.

Tanaka, Hiro, and Francesca Bargiela-Chiappini. 2011. Asian Business Discourses. In *The Routledge Handbook of Discourse Analysis*, eds. J. P. Gee and M. Handford. Abingdon: Routledge.

Vogel, E. F. 1979. *Japan as Number One: Lessons for America.* Cambridge, MA: Harvard University Press.

Wakabayashi, M. 2001. Transforming Employee-Organization Linkages in Japanese Companies: Integrating Process of Employees' Career Making with Organizational Dynamics. In *2001 AJBS Conference Best Papers Proceedings*, eds. V. Mäkeläinen, H. Kitinoja, and T. Peltola, 4–14. Seinäjoki, Finland: Seinäjoki Polytechnic.

Yamada, H. 1997a. Organization in American and Japanese Meetings: Talk versus Relationship. In *The Languages of Business*, eds. F. Bargiela-Chiappini and S. Harris, 117–35. Edinburgh: Edinburgh University Press.

Yamada, H. 1997b. *Different Games, Different Rules.* Oxford: Oxford University Press.

5

Analyzing Political Space through Discourse

The Case of the U.S. Coast Guard and the Live Fire Zones on the Great Lakes

Gail Fann Thomas and Kimberlie Stephens

During the early twentieth century, governmental agencies were often seen as formalized political institutions meant to handle problems in the best interest of the public (Hajer 1995). Public problems were often considered technical problems to be solved, policy studies reflected an operations research perspective focusing on efficiency, and government administrators promulgated public policy in a top-down, command-and-control fashion (Hitch 1958). Professional administrators assumed the role of experts in making rational, value-free decisions and who managed a centralized, standardized system (Osborne and Gaebler 1992) and primarily used a legalistic "decide-announce-defend" communication strategy (Forester 2008). Citizens assumed the role of clients, who were expected to respect and defer to the bureaucrats' expertise (Wilson 1941). This technocratic approach, often referred to as the "old public administration," engendered a hubris among many public administrators that has since become unsustainable (Denhardt and Denhardt 2000).

As public problems have grown increasingly complex and citizens have become less trusting of government decisions, individuals more often demand a stronger voice in public policy decisions that affect them. With electronic communication tools such as e-mail, Facebook, YouTube, and Twitter, citizens have new opportunities to build strong coalitions that influence decisions about environmental issues, public health, and numerous other social problems. In response to this new landscape, federal, state, and local government agencies are increasingly experimenting with public participatory arrangements that allow a network of actors' voices to be included in the policy-making process (Castells 1996; Hajer 1995). This shift to a more inclusive process is sometimes referred to as "the new public service," with a goal of creating a political system that is more networked, decentralized, dialogic, and responsive to the public's needs (Denhardt and Denhardt 2000; Fung and Wright 2001; Goodin, Rein, and Moran 2006).

Paralleling this more decentralized, citizen-centric movement, numerous public administration theorists have suggested a turn to interpretive theory, especially discourse theory, to develop a better understanding of the more complicated and contested space in which public policy making is occurring (Denhardt and Denhardt 2000; Fischer and Forester 1993; Hajer and Laws 2006; van den Brink and Metze 2006). Discursive analysis is gaining prominence in the scholarship of policy making because it offers a reflective position for understanding how multiple actors use discourse to establish and resist power in this space (Hajer and Laws 2006).

Following Fischer (2006), we use the term *space* in this chapter (and discuss it in more detail in the next section) to refer to the discursive space where actors' voices reside. In this way, the notion of space provides an opportunity to examine who is/not participating, who is/not permitted to participate, and what is/not being said (Hajer and Laws 2006), or in other words, how different actors' discourse shape a space. Thus, examining this space allows us to investigate the relationships among discourse, power, and policy making.

While the term *discourse* is widely used and has many definitions, we use Hajer's (2006) definition for this study: "An ensemble of ideas, concepts and categorizations through which meaning is allocated to social and physical phenomena and which is produced and reproduces in an identifiable set of practices" (447). The connection between language and action reflects the long-range variety of discourse articulated by Alvesson and Kärreman (2000), such that discourse represents the ways that individuals talk about issues that in turn works to frame the way individuals understand and act in regard to those issues. In this way, discourse analysis in this study aims to capture the primary ideas and concepts asserted through language and draw connections between that language and the broader frames that they seem to represent. Unlike traditional policy-making analysis that emphasizes structure and processes, discursive approaches allow researchers to look into the "black box" to examine the intersubjective understandings and normative politics that take place within the space (Fischer 2006). In particular, we use a critical perspective in our analysis. This type of analysis allows researchers to describe, interpret, and reflect on text to reveal discursive sources of power. It also shows how these sources of power are initiated, reproduced, resisted, and transformed within specific social, economic, political, and historical contexts (van Dijk 1988).

Few researchers have taken a systematic, empirical look at how different actors' discourse shape a social space and the effect that discourse has on regulatory processes and outcomes (Fischer 1998). Additionally, little is known about how shifts within the political space actually occur (Suddaby and Greenwood 2005). This study explores the notion of contested space through discursive analysis in a case study in which the U.S. Coast Guard's Ninth District (USCG) attempted to create a new government safety zone ruling that was associated with a new live fire training policy for the Great Lakes. In this context, rule making refers to an agency's authority, given to it by Congress, to create and enforce a rule. In many cases proposed rules receive little or no public comment, and after the specified time frame, the rule is put into place and enforced. In some cases, however, these comment periods serve as political spaces in which discursive interaction takes place. The USCG case represents one such occasion. Our study, therefore, sets out to answer these research questions:

1. How did the agency's initial proposal of the rule frame the discursive space?
2. How did the various actors interact to shift the framing of the political space?
3. What was the effect of the discursive deliberation on the agency and policy outcomes?

The remainder of this chapter offers our theoretical perspectives, research methods, the USCG case, a discursive analysis, a discussion of the analysis, and concluding remarks.

THEORETICAL PERSPECTIVES

According to Fischer (2006), space "is not just filled with competing interests but rather is understood as something that is created, opened, and shaped by social understandings" (25). Discursive meanings become the focus of attention, where identities of the actors, institutions, and practices are brought into sharp contrast (Jordon and Weedon 1995). A discursive analysis allows researchers to reveal what is important and what is not. It shows how some participants are included and others excluded. Social space, as explained by Fischer (2006), "can be understood as woven together by a set of discursive relationships that determine the meanings and understandings of the identities within them. Through these discursive practices, the power relations of the surrounding societal context are brought into the social space" (26). To this end, Fischer suggests several questions that can inform an analysis of a social space: Who determines the form of participation that takes place in a given space? Who initiates, chooses the methods, and takes part? What do the people who enter these spaces bring with them? In other words, what are their thoughts and beliefs about what is really going on in the space, and how do they strategically orient themselves to this understanding? What do people want to gain? What are their expectations? How do they perceive the costs and benefits of the activity?

Fischer's questions offer a valuable approach for understanding discourse. However, another aspect that provides an understanding of the different subjectivities represented within the discursive space is to abstract from the ideas and concepts being expressed to the frames that lend action and power in the space. Goffman (1974) initially asserted the concept of frames as "schemata of interpretation." In other words, frames provide a lens through which issues are viewed. Frames can be constructed and developed over time, as demonstrated in the social movement literature (Davis, McAdam, Scott, and Zald 2005; Steinberg 1998). Frames can also act to legitimate certain activities and attribute power to specific individuals or entities (Benford and Snow 2000).

The notion of frames has been applied in the policy context, as well. Policy frames are a means for "selecting, interpreting, and organizing information to construct a policy argument" (Schon and Rein 1994). Meaning of these frames within a political space are not inherent but are constructed through language and human interaction (Houston 2001). Jewell and Bero (2006) claim that individuals from distinct interest group affiliations construct policy frames in the process of participating in policy discourse. They identify two specific types of frames: abstract-technical frames that use technical language from scientific journals, financial data, and/or case law; and concretized-moral frames that use personal or organizational anecdotes.

In addition to understanding the role that frames play in shaping a political space, power is also an essential aspect of the discourse. Fischer (2006) says that space is not neutral and that space is essential to exercise power. Power relations constituted in these spaces enable what is said and how it is understood. Power and knowledge are used by a network of actors to shape the political space (Bourdieu 1977; Foucault 1986). By examining the ways in which specific types of frames are used within the discursive space, and the ways in which competing frames are constructed and reconstructed over the course of time, it is possible to see how discourse can question the sources of power and ultimately influence action and impact change.

Method

The documents used to conduct this study included the USCG's proposed ruling announcement in the *U.S. Federal Register*, over nine hundred individual public comments that were logged in the public docket in response to the proposal, interviews with the USCG's Ninth District management team, transcripts from the public meetings that were conducted in conjunction with the proposal, and the *U.S. Federal Register* announcement of the withdrawal of the proposal. The event transpired over a six-month period beginning in August 2006 and ending in January 2007.

Public comments were captured from the *Federal Register* website in the fall of 2007. The *Federal Register* website also included transcripts of the nine public hearings that were held in October and November 2006. Six unstructured interviews were conducted with the USCG Ninth District management team over a two-day period in September 2007. The interviews were tape recorded and later transcribed for analysis. The purpose of the interviews was to understand the chain of events from the USCG's perspective.

We conducted the analysis in two phases. In the first phase, two coders reviewed 929 public documents from the docket to determine the overall tone or attitude of the public comment. Tone, as defined by Locker (2004), is the attitude, feeling, or emotion that is conveyed by the author. Key words and phrases from the documents were used to make a qualitative assessment of overall tone. For example, comments might include straightforward phrases such as "I fully support the live fire proposal" or "I am against shooting on the Great Lakes." Other written statements were more subtle, using words such as *deception* or *protection* to communicate support or a lack of support for the proposal. Documents in support of the proposal or that demonstrated positive attitudes toward the USCG were designated as positive. Those demonstrating disapproval of the proposal, often relying on negative words or phrases to describe the proposal, were assigned a negative rating. Those expressing indifferent attitudes or equal positive and negative feelings were assigned a neutral rating. The coders also identified the stakeholder group that the individual commenter represented, such as government representative, a private business owner, a nonprofit organization representative, or an individual member of the general public. The comments were then categorized into attitude rating and stakeholder groups to provide a picture of how each group relied on positive, neutral, or negative language in the discursive process.

The second phase of the analysis included a more critical discursive analysis to map the political space over the six-month period. The discursive analysis was used to identify the latent content and deep structure (Alvesson and Kärreman 2000), with an aim to discover the themes, types of argument, sources of power, and the overarching frames communicated by each group of stakeholders (Boyatzis 1998; Stillar 1998). As suggested by Alvesson and Kärreman (2000), when conducting a long-range discursive analysis, it is valuable to triangulate the themes and ideas extracted from the discourse with other sources. In this case, the interview transcripts were used to verify connections between the USCG's talk in the proposal, withdrawal, and public meetings and their actions and thinking.

The discursive analysis was used to create a picture of the changing political space over the course of this issue. For the sake of clarity, we treated the USCG announcement, the public response through the comments, the USCG's discourse at the public meetings, and finally the USCG's withdrawal announcement as punctuated time points. Tracking this space over time allowed us to assess the themes and types of argument, determine how these themes and arguments translated into overarching frames, and then to identify the implications of the frames on the political space at each point in time. Figure 5.1 below depicts our discourse analysis process.

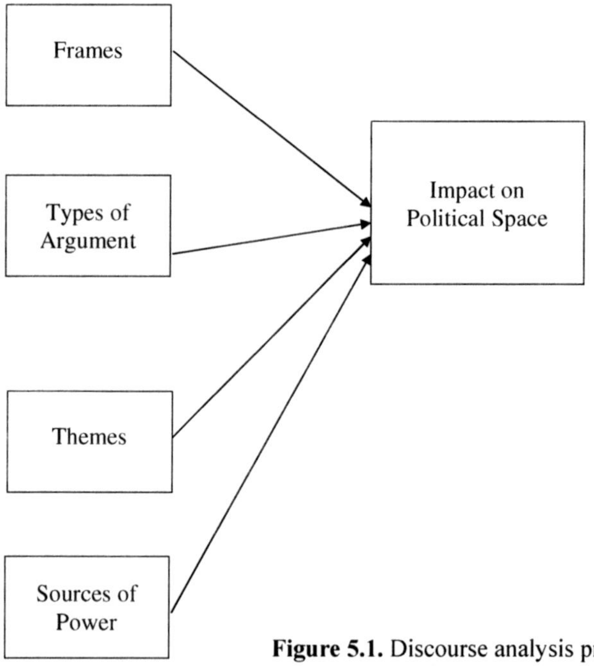

Figure 5.1. Discourse analysis process.

THE U.S. COAST GUARD AND THE GREAT LAKES

The U.S. Coast Guard is a military, multimission, maritime service that, in 2002, became part of the Department of Homeland Security. It is one of the nation's five armed services. Its core roles are to protect the public, the environment, and U.S. economic and security interests in any maritime region in which those interests may be at risk, including international waters and

America's coasts, ports, and inland waterways. In the Great Lakes area more than 5,500 active duty, reserve, civilian, and auxiliary men and women are responsible for the Saint Lawrence Seaway and parts of the surrounding states, including 6,700 miles of shoreline and 1,500 miles of the international border with Canada. As "Guardians of the Great Lakes," the USCG conducts search and rescue, maritime safety and security, environmental protection, maritime law enforcement, aids to navigation, and icebreaking (USCG History).

Also, an important consideration in this case is the recent history of the Great Lakes. These lakes have long been a source of food, drinking water, recreation, and industry for the citizens of the region. However, due to the Lakes' size and the slow inflow and outflow of water, pollution has also been a persistent problem. In 1969 the Cuyahoga River, which feeds into Lake Erie, caught fire because of the oil on its surface. Breeding of the bald eagle was also down because of the contamination of the fish and other wildlife on which the eagles depended for food. In the 1970s the United States and Canada signed the Great Lakes Water Quality Agreement. This agreement represented an international recognition of the importance of restoring the health of the Great Lakes and precipitated a series of actions aimed to clean up the lakes and surrounding waterways. In the decades since the agreement, both the United States and Canada have worked together to reduce pollutants of all varieties, including phosphorous load, airborne pollutants, lead, and mercury. The efforts expended by residents of the states bordering the Great Lakes have resulted in a view of the lake as a national treasure. It is this context into which the USCG's Safety Zone proposal was submitted.

THE U.S. COAST GUARD RESPONDS TO A 9/11 INITIATIVE

In 2006, the USCG added new automatic weapons to the lighter arms already included on many of their cutters and small craft responsible for patrolling the Great Lakes. The new weapons were installed in response to the added antiterrorist mission assigned to the USCG as part of the increased Homeland Security Initiative since 9/11. Along with the new equipment came a need to train members of the USCG on proper use of these weapons. As a result, in early 2006, live fire exercises commenced on the Great Lakes. Training consisted of shooting live ammunition at floating targets in the lake. Temporary training zones were established for training sessions that usually lasted less than four to six hours and took place in remote sections of the Great Lakes. Each time the USCG conducted a live fire training, time-intensive, case-by-case administrative steps were required to notify the public. After conducting twenty-four exercises on the Great Lakes, the commander of the Ninth District of the USCG, based in Cleveland, Ohio, decided to formalize the live fire safety zones, thus eliminating the ad hoc approval process. In an effort to minimize the resources and time that training would take away from other search-and-rescue functions that the USCG serves in the Great Lakes, the zones were created in several areas close to existing USCG stations, approximately five miles offshore. The proposed rule included a total of thirty-four zones.

In keeping with federal regulations, the USCG hired two different companies to do an environmental assessment to evaluate whether or not a full environmental impact study would need to be conducted. In addition, the USCG Ninth District commander and his staff wrote an announcement that detailed the coordinates of all thirty-four of the zones and published it in the *U.S. Federal Register*. The announcement was published on August 1, 2006, and per federal regulatory minimum requirements was opened for a thirty-day public comment period. Members of the USCG Ninth District expected that the comment period would receive a few comments and the comment period would close, as expected on August 31, and the rule would become permanent.

One week before the close of the comment period, an article was published in the *Bay City Times* that described the USCG's proposed rule. This article was the first published public announcement of the USCG's plans outside the *Federal Register* and it, along with acknowledgement of the rule by multiple state representatives, initiated an influx of public participation in the form of new newspaper articles and an avalanche of public comments. As a result of many requests received after publication of the article in the *Bay City Times*, the USCG agreed to extend the public comment period another sixty days, as well as to conduct nine public meetings explaining the rule-making process and providing citizens an opportunity to voice their concerns. This ninety-day period yielded a total of more than nine hundred public comments that were sent to the USCG Ninth District and posted in the Federal Docket. In addition to the public comments, more than 250 newspaper articles were published in local newspapers. In the end, the USCG decided to withdraw the proposal for the live fire safety zones. Table 5.1 shows a time line of the events.

The *Federal Register* proposal announcement and withdrawal, the written public comments posted to the *U.S. Federal Register* docket, transcripts from the public meetings, and transcripts from the six USCG management team interviews constitute the data that were analyzed for this study.

Analysis

We analyzed the political space in this case using four punctuated time points, mentioned above. Analyzing this space over time, we show how the USCG initially used a legal, regulatory frame, assuming that they were simply promulgating requirements from USCG headquarters. By the time the USCG

TABLE 5.1. USCG Live Fire Exercise: Time Line of Events

Date	Event
8/01/06	Filing of the rule making in *Federal Register*
8/24/06	Article published in the *Bay City Times*
8/31/06	Original close of public comments
9/12/06	Comment period is extended sixty days
9/19/06	Four public meetings are announced in the *Federal Register*
10/12/06	Three additional public meetings are announced in the *Federal Register*
10/16/06	First public hearing in Duluth, MN
10/18/06	Public meeting in Grand Haven, MI
10/19/06	Public meeting in Port Huron, MI
10/23/06	Two more public meetings are announced in the *Federal Register*
10/23/06	Public meeting in Cleveland, OH
10/30/06	Public meeting in Rochester, NY
11/01/06	Public meeting in Milwaukee, WI
11/03/06	Public meeting in Charlevoix, MI
11/06/06	Public meeting in Erie, PA
11/08/06	Public meeting in Sturgeon Bay, WI
11/13/06	Public comment period closes
1/05/07	USCG withdraws rule making

withdrew their proposal in January 2007, the political space had changed significantly. This section provides an analysis of the overarching frames, themes, types of argument, and power that shaped the political space.

The USCG Ninth District's Initial Announcement of the Live Fire Safety Zones

On August 6, 2006, the USCG announced its proposal for the live fire rule. The appendix shows an excerpt of the five-page announcement. Analysis of the announcement in the *U.S. Federal Register* revealed that the USCG used a legal, regulatory discursive frame to guide their actions in the live fire case. If we consider the questions proposed by Fischer (2006), "who initiates the discourse, chooses the methods for interaction, and who takes part?" we begin to understand the legal, regulatory discursive framework and the interweaving of discourse, power, and space in the policy-making process.

Rather than starting with more informal discussions with key stakeholders that might have helped gauge possible resistance, the USCG chose to announce the new permanent live fire safety zones in the official government *U.S. Federal Register*. Analysis of the USCG management team transcripts showed at least three reasons for this decision. First, the management team had already conducted twenty-four live fire training exercises using temporary rules and had not received any public complaints. Second, the USCG's Ninth District believed they were simply complying with higher USCG headquarters and federal government orders to be able to respond to possible maritime threats on the Great Lakes. Last, the USCG's Ninth District believed they were complying with the law, although the minimum legal requirement, by posting the announcement in the *U.S. Federal Register* for thirty days. These reasons illustrate the legal, regulatory approach the USCG took to framing the approach to their decisions.

The choice to use the *Federal Register* for the initial announcement represents a legal, authoritative approach. As a genre, the *Federal Register* carries legal, government authority. *Genre* is defined as "socially recognized types of communicative action habitually enacted by members of a community to realize particular communication and collaborative purposes" (Yates and Orlikowski 1992, 299). The *Federal Register* is an official gazette of the U.S. government designed to provide legal notice of administrative rules and notices in a comprehensive and uniform manner (*Federal Register*'s Main Page). It also creates a space for persons or organizations to comment on a notice.

By complying with the *Federal Register*'s legal minimum, thirty-day open comment period, the USCG created a political space for the public to voice their support or resistance. Even so, many people saw the act as contradictory and constrained. On one hand the announcement stated, "We encourage you to submit comments and related materials." On the other hand, individuals were required to follow specific rules for submitting comments. Commenting parties had to "indicate the specific section of this document to which each comment applies, and give the reason for each comment," or that those who feel this rule would have a negative economic impact on their business should explain "why you think it qualifies and how and to what degree this rule would economically affect it." These justifications were in addition to the particular requirements for submission that included mailing comments "in an unbound format, no larger than 8½ by 11 inches, suitable for copying and electronic filing." The announcement further stated:

> By issuing this notice of proposed rulemaking and accepting public comments, the Coast Guard does not waive its use of military-function exception to notice and comment rulemaking under 5 U.S.C. 553(b).

So while the USCG agreed to accept public comments, they also said that they were not waiving their rights to the rule-making exceptions that say that military and foreign affairs functions of the United States are exempt from the rule-making comment procedure. Last, the USCG's Ninth District stated, "We do not now plan to hold a public meeting." The choice of official government publication medium, the lack of communication with the public through other means, as well as the technical nature of the announcement framed this action as an issue of compliance with the law, a necessity to accomplish the mission required by the government. In this way, the USCG technically opened a discursive space but did so under very narrow terms and initiated the discussion as one of a legal, regulatory nature, where facts and legal authority dictated who had the power to take action. The USCG viewed themselves through their discursive frame that thus shaped their expectations for who should participate in the discursive space created through the announcement. Since, to them, it seemed like a cut-and-dry proposal that was necessary for them to fulfill their mission, they anticipated little to no participation in the discursive space.

In addition to disciplining the discursive space, the USCG eventually created public resistance in the way that they chose to announce the proposal. Even though the document was labeled a "proposal," the announcement was presented as if a final decision had been made. First, the announcement frequently mentioned the authority of specific United States Code (U.S.C.) and Executive Orders to support their rights to implement the live fire zones on the Great Lakes. Then, almost one-half of the five-page announcement listed the coordinates of the thirty-four safety zones (see the appendix). Later in the announcement, the USCG explained how their assessments would exempt them from a number of federal requirements. For instance, they stated:

> We expect that the economic impact of the proposed rule to be so minimal that a full Regulatory Evaluation is unnecessary.

Regarding children and environmental risks, they stated:

> We have analyzed this proposed rule under Executive Order 13045, Protection of Children from Environmental Health Risks and Safety Risks. This rule is

not an economically significant rule and would not create an environmental risk to health or risk safety that might disproportionately affect children.

In summary, the USCG use of technical language, reliance on legal requirements, and placing the burden of justification for the need to participate in the discursive space on those who seek to comment initiated a discourse in which the USCG possessed the power and right to act. In retrospect, it is clear that the USCG failed to consider the historical lens through which the public viewed the Great Lakes and the extent to which the public would see their role and their rights to be involved in the rule-making process as more central. A summary of the themes, frames, and political space immediately following the release of the USCG announcement is included in table 5.2 below.

The Public Responds

The public's reaction to news of this announcement offered a contrast to the USCG's legal, regulatory discursive frame. The public docket, which included 929 written comments from government representatives, nonprofits, local associations, private businesses, and individual citizens represents the second of our four punctuated time points. This section presents the findings of the tone, frame, power, and space analysis.

An analysis of the written public comments revealed a highly negative tone. Although there were slight differences in the degree of negativity across stakeholder groups, there is no question that overall the public did not support the USCG's Safety Zone proposal. Table 5.2 below shows the number of comments received from the major stakeholders, as well as the percentage of those comments that were negative, neutral, or positive in tone.

TABLE 5.2. Content Analysis Results of Public Comments Documents

	# of Comments	% Positive	% Neutral	% Negative
Government representatives	30	20%	30%	50%
Nonprofit and local associations	60	2%	16%	82%
Private business	14	7%	36%	57%
Individuals	825	17%	12%	71%

The largest percentage of negative comments came from the nonprofit and local associations (82 percent) followed by individual citizens (71 percent). The lowest percentage of negative comments came from the government representatives (50 percent) and private businesses (57 percent).

The overarching frame from the public comments was "participatory, democratic." Three major themes revealed the public's expectations about the live fire initiative: a direct request for more public participation, transparency, and a demand that all stakeholders' concerns be taken into consideration.

The first theme among the public comments was a demand that the Coast Guard create more space for citizens' voices. Some people requested public meetings.

> I ask that the USCG hold a public meeting at which the reasons for this action and potential hazards to the lake and the safety of its users may be explained and citizens allowed to express their viewpoints. (government official)

Others also wanted the public comment period extended.

> We request that hearings be held in all of the Great Lakes states that would be affected by these live fire zones. We also request an extension of the comment period so that Native American tribes with international fishery treaties may be notified and that local governments throughout the Great Lakes may also receive notification in a timely manner and give input. (nonprofit association representative)

In addition to the direct requests for expanded space for the citizens' voices, some of the people demanded a more transparent decision-making process. These comments asked the USCG to provide justification for their actions, also requesting further information about the hazards and safety. For example, one public comment stated:

> We believe these questions deserve public discourse far more transparent than has taken place to date, and that should begin with a series of public hearings on the proposed safety zones referenced in the Aug 1 *Federal Register*. (nonprofit association representative)

The use of the word *transparent* implies that the public had expectations that the USCG would make their decisions more public, including a justification for their actions. Some people questioned the need for the exercises and requested a rationale for the decision.

> The burden of proof is on the Coast Guard to demonstrate that live fire exercises on the Great Lakes are both necessary and safe. Until this has been done to the public's satisfaction, we ask that you postpone implementation of the plan as described. (nonprofit association)

Other people questioned the specifics of the proposal. For example, some wondered how the decision had been made to create thirty-four live fire zones, instead of twenty-five or thirty.

> While we support measures to ensure our nation's security, we have been provided with no justification for the need to have 34 sites designated for weapons training within the Great Lakes. (nonprofit association)

The requests for justification challenged the legal authority asserted by the USCG to unilaterally decide to conduct trainings on the Great Lakes. Inherent in the comments was an expectation that the USCG must answer to the public, much like an elected official must be sensitive to his/her constituents.

The third theme that arose through review of the public comments was an expectation that the USCG would take into account the varying concerns of individuals, associations, and businesses. This expectation was likely influenced by discourse in the initial *U.S. Federal Register* announcement, which made statements such as "this proposed rule would not have a significant economic impact on a substantial number of small entities." The public likely felt the need to communicate the extent to which the USCG had failed to consider the full impact of its actions. Comments below express an expectation that the USCG take into consideration all its stakeholders concerns. For example, this business person spoke about the USCG's "narrow vision" and an apparent lack of respect for the public.

> We expect solid and well-reasoned efforts to consider not only the needs and mission of the Coast Guard, but consideration for the public, for the mariner, and for "partners" in maritime commerce. Lastly, as shown in the narrow vision for Live Fire Zones, this latter respectful approach seems to be lacking. (private business)

Business owners often made their case using economic arguments, detailing the extent to which the live fire zones might disrupt their business.

> If the Coast Guard used this area 1–3 times per year, depending on the time of year it could potentially affect as many as 24 trips depending on the month and day of the week and increase our fuel consumption by 6,000 gallons. At $3/gallon this would amount to $18,000.

Some people expressed concerns about boating and fishing:

> I am opposed to the Great Lakes being used for target practice and request that the United States Coast Guard reconsider their request. . . . By setting up the live fire zones in recreational areas, they will be discouraging the use of the Great Lakes for both boating and fishing. (government official)

Individuals, nonprofits, and local associations provided scientific reports and argued the merits of the environmental assessments that the USCG had conducted. Some individuals were particularly concerned with the use of lead bullets.

> We have worked long and hard to prevent further lead contamination of the lakes through forbidding use of lead sinkers and lead shotgun shells. For the health of our fish and waterfowl, please forbid the use of lead shot in U.S. Coast Guard tests. (individual citizen)

Others expressed concerns about the larger ecosystem.

> The Great Lakes presently are exhibiting symptoms of extreme stress from a combination of sources that include toxic contaminants, invasive species, nutrient loading, shoreline and upland land use changes, and hydrologic modifications. In large areas of the lakes, historical sources of stress have combined with new ones to reach a tipping point at which ecosystem-level changes occur rapidly and unexpectedly, confounding the traditional relationships between sources of stress and the expected ecosystem response. (nonprofit association representative)

Individual citizens often used strong moral arguments to express their concerns. Rather than using scientific, economic, or legal arguments, they would draw on personal anecdotes to lodge an emotional argument against the live fire proposal.

> I was born literally a stones throw from Lake Michigan and live here in West Michigan all my long life, working about 12 years on the Great Lakes.

Finally, some respondents relied on legal arguments to undermine the discourse used by the USCG. The following quotation shows one comment that drew on another set of legal regulations that seemed to reject the unilateral assertion put forth by the USCG.

> I also met with other members of the Great Lakes delegation in Congress. We are in full agreement that the Coast Guard is not acting lawfully in deciding to conduct live fire exercises without full environmental review, and we are prepared to organize throughout the region against target practice in the Great Lakes.

What does a participatory, democratic frame do in this political space? How does the discursive frame work to influence the policy discourse? In order to answer these questions it will be fruitful to look at the expectations implied in the discursive frames used by both the USCG and the public and how these expectations drew from identity and caused power within the space to shift.

As with any communication, different positions or subjectivities are inherent in discourse. In this particular case, the announcement by the USCG viewed itself as holding the position of an organization that had been assigned a mission: to protect the waterways from terrorism. The reader in such a discourse becomes those who will be protected. These positions come out of the identity of the USCG as Guardians of the Great Lakes, where guardian is viewed as synonymous with protector, one who would keep the lakes safe, whether through search-and-rescue missions or through antiterrorism missions. This identity resulted in the expectation that the public would, in general, appreciate the efforts of the USCG to offer protection from terrorism and thus would have little or no problem with the proposed live fire zones required for training. The legal frame communicated in the USCG discourse reflected the expectation of minimal resistance through its use of minimal public engagement. The USCG only fulfilled the legal obligations for engagement and went no further.

The general public, in contrast, had a different view of its identity in relationship to the USCG that was reflected in the frame used through public comment discourse. Citizens, business owners, and nonprofit representatives viewed the USCG as an agency that exists to provide protection and, by extension, freedom to citizens of the United States, and specifically in this case those who live, work, and recreate on and around the Great Lakes. This identity created an expectation for a more active role by citizens in the Great Lakes area and produced a discursive frame that not only communicated the expectation to be included but also precipitated action from citizens. The participatory, democratic frame met the legal, regulatory frame to create conflict within the political space. The participatory, democratic frame challenged the authority of the legal underpinnings of the announcement by reminding the USCG that the authority of the government is granted by its citizens. In this way, the discursive space was reshaped in this case by redefining the subjective position of the USCG. The public's claims for participation and consideration challenged the USCG's position as the organization with the power to determine what actions were required and subjugated them to a position of having to defend their claims for authority. For instance, the call for organization of political representatives made by the government official referenced above drew on the democratic frame to reorient the power relations in the political space. By referencing the legal, regulatory frame within the context of the democratic frame, the government official was able to challenge the claims to power of the USCG and simultaneously shift the power in the discursive space to all those individuals, business owners, and public officials who were participating. In this way, regardless of whether it was an organization or an individual, the public used a discourse of democracy that placed responsibility on the USCG to ensure the concerns of its citizens as well as their rights to health and safety and security.

To summarize, the discourse used in these public comments relies on the participatory, democratic frame that challenges the legal, regulatory frame used by the USCG and creates space for citizens to express their opinions. Citizens complicate and politicize the space by offering legitimate concerns such as economic, recreational, environmental, and legal arguments. The public confronts the USCG's unilateral assertion of power by calling into question the source of that power. In terms of the impact on the political space, the extent of public participation by such a large and diverse group of stakeholders, in essence, expanded the discursive space, creating space for a myriad of voices. The discourse also influenced the power dynamics within the space. The democratic discourse claims power for citizens shifting the burden to justify action from the public to the USCG. Attempts by the public to shape this political space were evidenced in the USCG's changing discourse in response to the democratic framing used in the public comments.

U.S. Coast Guard and the Public Meet

Due to the magnitude of the public's response to the USCG live fire announcement, the USCG decided to conduct nine public hearings at different locations around the Great Lakes. The public hearings were recorded and transcribed, resulting in over one thousand additional pages that were entered into the public docket. This section provides an analysis of the November 3, 2006, public hearing that was conducted in Charlevoix, Michigan. Our analysis focused primarily on the USCG's participation and revealed that they began to shift from a strictly rational, legal discursive frame to include a more empathetic participatory, democratic frame. The following analysis shows how the public's resistance to the USCG's initial announcement in the *Federal Register* caused the USCG to reframe their arguments, expand the political space enabling the new action, and at the same time constrain the space by maintaining control over the interaction among the actors.

The transcript of the interview with the Ninth District commander showed that he had two purposes for conducting the public hearings. First, and foremost, he wanted to let the public know that the Ninth District was listening. Second, he wanted to provide information about the threat and explain the decisions behind the live fire safety zones. Evidence of USCG's shift to a listening posture came when the commander provided his initial remarks at the public meeting:

> I want to tell you that we are here tonight because we care so much about your comments, and they are important to me, in consideration of the 34 proposal zones for training. I want you to know that no decision has been made on this matter; that your comments, each and every one will be taken into consideration before a decision is made.

Here the commander appeared to signal an inclusion of stakeholder perspectives in the political space. These statements were in stark contrast to the initial nonresponsive, legalistic approach the USCG took when they first announced the proposal in the *U.S. Federal Register*. The commander went even further in his next statement:

> You know, outside my office in Cleveland there's a mural, and the mural is one depicting the Great Lakes, and there's a caption under it entitled, "Guardian of the Great Lakes," and the word "guardian" existed long before the current movie by a similar name. The Great Lakes depiction is one of treasure, and the U.S. Coast Guard and the Ninth Coast Guard District, in partnership with our colleagues in the Canadian Coast Guard, in Transport Canada, and RCMP, are honored to be the guardians of that treasure. We take our mission seriously, in protection of the environment; in protection of lives; in protection of commerce; and in protection of the communities.

Again, the contrast from the initial announcement is sharp. The commander offered a dramatic visual and strong metaphor to depict the long history and philosophy of the USCG. The Lakes were cast as a treasure, and the commander provided an opening in the political space by mentioning the environment, commerce, and the communities, thus legitimating many of the public's concerns. Rules, regulations, and laws were noticeably absent during this part of his talk.

Then the Commander talked about the history of the Great Lakes—in 1977, when they first carried side arms to conduct routine boardings, in 1990 when they increased their oil pollution exercises, and after 9/11 when they began instituting security regulations. After this, the commander talked about the latest change—installing a mounted automatic weapon aboard the boats. At this point, he offered an apology:

> I'm here to tell you that we have not effectively communicated with you, the communities around the Great Lakes, about this change. I hope you leave . . . with a better sense that your Coast Guard has managed the change well.

The political space is opened up and being shaped. The commander expressed regret for the way the proposal was announced to the public. The power dynamic began to shift. The comments about guardians of the lakes and apologizing for not better explaining the change showed that the USCG was ready to listen. The commander also shifted from a unilateral, top-down approach in the initial announcement and repositioned himself in the political space by asking the public to evaluate the USCG's ability to manage the implementation of the new live fire training policy.

While the USCG stated that their first objective was to listen to the concerns of the public that served to open the political space, the genre of the public hearing served to constrain the space. During all nine of the public hearings, a moderator began with a prepared statement:

> The purpose of the meeting is to gather information. Your comments should provide specific information and facts related to the impact of the zone on the commenter. . . . Please note, you will have three minutes to supply your comment. This time is imposed to allow as many people as possible, the opportunity to be heard. . . . I will use the countdown clock, which is here to my right, so that you can see the time you have remaining. At the conclusion of three minutes, you will be asked to be seated, to allow others to make their comment.

The public hearings, like the *Federal Register*, were conducted using standardized, formal procedures. Citizens were allowed to comment within the specified time period, but they we not permitted to ask questions of the USCG members. Only one-way communication was allowed.

The second theme of the meetings was the USCG's rationale for creating the live fire zones. This portion of the meeting consisted of four experts: the chief of the Response Division, the Weapons Training program manager, and two private environmental consultants who had conducted environmental studies for the USCG. The consultants provided an in-depth scientific evaluation of the environmental risks. Using scientific and technical arguments, the subject-matter experts described and provided graphical displays of the results of their laboratory and field experiments. At one point in their testimony, one of the environmental consultants said:

> It's not just a waving of hands, and we not only looked at the potential for risk, but we quantified that risk, as you'll see in the slides.

Additionally, they talked in much detail about the risk of the bullets in three pathways: the sediment, the water, and the food web. They concluded that there was no elevated risk.

After the environmental consultants completed their presentation, the weapons training officer gave a technical description of the two weapons, the three-step USCG training process, the procedures they would use to manage the safety zones, and the rationale for the length of the live fire exercises. Last, the chief of the Response Division provided an explanation for the decision to create thirty-four safety zones. Decision criteria, he argued, were resource availability and legal requirements. He also provided an explanation of the notification system the USCG decided to use.

Each of the USCG speakers provided technical and scientific arguments for the proposed safety zones and the risks associated with the ruling. Each discussed a well-studied process, providing precise definitions, measurements, and procedures. The meeting ended with an assurance from the commander:

> Again, I want to assure you that no decision in this matter has been made, that all of your comments will be taken into careful consideration, and the Coast Guard will aggressively work in notification and communications with you and the communities around the Great Lakes.

In summary, the result of the USCG's participation in the face-to-face public hearings transformed the political space. In sharp contrast to the initial announcement that was predominately framed as legalistic and regulatory, the public hearings were framed as an opportunity for the USCG to understand the concerns of the public and to help the public understand the rationale for their live fire proposal.

The U.S. Coast Guard Withdraws Their Proposal

On January 6, 2007, the USCG announced the withdrawal of the live fire safety zone proposal in the *Federal Register*. Analysis of the two-page *Federal Register* announcement showed that the USCG shifted away from a legal, regulatory frame to a participatory, democratic frame. At this point, the political space was considerably more open as compared to the initial announcement. The voices of the various constituents were legitimized, and the USCG offered a promise to collaborate with the public in any future decisions regarding the live fire training policy. The power within the space was significantly more decentralized.

The themes in the January 2007 withdrawal notice included the reason for the withdrawal, a detailed description of the public's concerns, and a promise to collaborate with the public in the future. The reason for withdrawing the proposal is demonstrated in this quote:

> The [Notice of Public Rulemaking] NPRM is being withdrawn, however, because of comments received from the public regarding the number and location of the proposed safety zones, the frequency of use, notifications procedures as well as other concerns raised by the public.

The USCG not only legitimated the publics' concerns but also the concerns had the effect of abolishing the proposal. The USCG chose to use a more empathetic voice of concern rather than use a hierarchical, authoritarian voice. Rather than restrict the political space, they expanded the space and enabled other frames to define the problem and offer alternative solutions.

Forty percent of the *Federal Register* withdrawal notice provided a detailed summary of the concerns that were expressed by members of Congress, state and local government representatives, recreational boaters, commercial users, Native American tribes, local businesses, and members of the general public in the Great Lakes region. The notice explained:

> The Coast Guard will reevaluate the proposal in light of the issues raised in the comments the Coast Guard received during the course of the rulemaking. Whatever option the Coast Guard pursues, it intends to address the concerns of the Great Lakes community and to work with the region's stakeholders to develop an acceptable solution that meets the readiness needs of the Coast Guard Forces and addresses the public's concerns.

This promise frames the future political space as one that will be more collaborative. Communication will be two-way, and the public will be included much earlier in the process. To show the shift over the four time periods—announcement of the ruling, public responses to the announcement, the public hearings, and the proposal withdrawal—table 5.3 provides a summary of the frames, themes, types of argument, and sources of power.

TABLE 5.3. Analysis of Changing Political Space over Proposal Period

	U.S. Coast Guard's Announcement	Public Comments—Response to USCG Announcement	USCG at Public Hearings	USCG Proposal Withdrawal
PRIMARY FRAME	• Legal, regulatory	• Participatory, democratic	• Participatory, democratic • Legal, regulatory	• Participatory, democratic
Themes	• Accomplishment of USCG mission • Requirement to conduct training • Authority under law	• Public has a right to formally participate in the process • Expectations for transparency in policy-making process • Public has a right to have concerns taken into consideration	• Desire to listen to publics' concerns • Desire to explain proposal and risks • USCG as Guardians of the Great Lakes • Mission to accomplish	• Desire to listen to participants • Desire to take concerns into account • Desire to accomplish mission while considering citizen concerns
Types of Arguments	• Legal arguments • Scientific arguments	• Moral arguments • Economic arguments • Legal arguments • Scientific arguments	• Moral arguments • Economic arguments • Legal arguments • Regulatory arguments • Scientific arguments	• Moral arguments
Political Space	• Created under obligation of law • Limited • Constraints on entering • One-way communication	• Expanded, hundreds entered space through public comment • Constrained to written participation • One-way communication • Contested	• Further expansion, hundreds more enter space • Opened to face-to-face communication • Constrained to one-way communication	Discourse Promises • Open space in future • Two-way communication • Early participation by stakeholders
Source of Power	• *U.S. Federal Register* process • Authority from Congress and USCG Headquarters	• Power from democratic ideals • People grant authority to government	• Public concerns are legitimized by the USCG • USCG shifts from top-down approach to citizens' authority to evaluate USCG's ability to implement this policy	• Power in open, discursive participation

DISCUSSION

This case has presented a practical example that demonstrates the way in which political policy space can be opened, created, and shaped by a variety of actors. The initial public policy space of the thirty-day comment period was created by the USCG out of legal obligation associated with filing a proposed rulemaking in the *Federal Register*. In this way, the USCG held a governmental and legal authority in dictating the terms in which the space could be used. They failed, however, to see the significance of having created this space until after the negative reactions erupted. Also, given the fact that the comment period was not publicized by the USCG, perceptions that they were trying to maintain power over that space by avoiding input were reinforced. Interviews with members of the USCG about this case suggest that they were not trying to be deceptive, but they did indicate that the USCG failed to consider the context in which the public might view this proposal, and thus failed to see how the policy space might be reshaped by a variety of stakeholders.

Using Fischer's (2006) questions, motivations for the public to use a democratic frame to shape the policy space can be seen more clearly. Fischer asks about the context or perspective from which the constituents come, as well as their expectations and what they hope to gain. A major source of contention in this case came as a result of the historical context of the Great Lakes. Since many of the stakeholders had been involved in the clean up and maintenance of the Great Lakes, any act that appeared to compromise the health of the lakes was seen as a threat. This was amplified by the fact that the lakes are the source of drinking water for millions of people in the surrounding states, and therefore, threatening the health of the lakes by extension threatens the health of individuals who rely on them for drinking water. An additional aspect of the context that influenced this situation was the self-defined role of the USCG as "Guardians of the Great Lakes." This claim, considered in conjunction with the live fire proposal, created a contradiction for the public between what the USCG professed to be and how their actions aligned with that image.

In this way the democratic frame was powerful because it placed an emphasis on listening to the voices of interested parties. By using this frame, supported by concretized moral, economic, scientific, and legal arguments, the stakeholders who participated in the public discourse were able to expand the political space and decentralize the power within the space. The earliest signs of the power shift were seen when the public requested an extended public comment period and the USCG granted the public hearings. The content of the public hearings was evidence that the voices that had entered the discourse were defining the issues that were important, as the meetings featured a segment that responded to the major objections made by public participants, including an explanation of the environmental assessment conducted, justification for locations of the zones, as well as language that was intended to reiterate the "Guardian" role of the USCG.

Despite the efforts made by the USCG to communicate a commitment to the public's concerns while still moving forward with plans to establish the live fire zones, the public discourse maintained a predominantly negative tone, voicing concern for the same issues and claiming the same rights to safety, security, and health over the course of the public meetings. In this way, the discursive frame used by the public did not change, and thus the incremental reshaping of the discursive space was due primarily to the USCG's shifting frame away from the legal, regulatory frame toward a more democratic, participatory frame. Over time, the discourse evolved from one that was hierarchical and top-down to one that was more participatory and democratic.

Ultimately, the legalistic, regulatory frame did not have the power the USCG's Ninth District had expected. Instead of persisting with a decide-announce-defend strategy, the USCG's Ninth District decided to take a listening stance that legitimated the public's concerns. Over time, the discourse moved from inform to consult, and ultimately the USCG made a promise to the citizens of the Great Lakes to involve and even collaborate with them before establishing a safety zone requirement (Arnstein 1969).

CONCLUSION

Traditional policy-making analysis has focused on structure and practices where researchers examine material and procedure factors that impact policy decisions (Fung 2006). The purpose of this study was to develop insights into the sociocultural practices of policy making through language. Using the live fire case, we showed how the USCG used a legal, regulatory frame to constrain actors from participating in a policy dialogue. The USCG's initial approach was technocratic and hierarchical, stressing the execution of a policy that had been handed down from headquarters in the name of antiterrorism and national security. This approach mirrors the "old public administration" model (Denhardt and Denhardt 2000).

In the months immediately following 9/11, the USCG may have gained stronger public support for this policy change. But, as time passed, U.S. citizens grew less tolerant of increased government restrictions. As a result, the USCG faced considerable resistance from local politicians, business people, and citizens. Their resistance created an opening in the political space that was subsequently shaped through interactions among the USCG and various constituents. Through these interactions via public comment, public hearings, and the media, the actors problematized the meaning of the USCG as Guardian of the Great Lakes. While the commander believed that the terrorist training fell within his purview as Guardian of the Great Lakes, the public demonstrated the contradictions inherent in the execution of the live fire exercise. Using moral, economic, and scientific arguments, the public wove a democratic participatory frame that eventually overcame the USCG's legal regulatory frame. This network of actors' voices as part of the political process is more akin to the "new public service" model, where agencies are more responsive to the public's needs (Denhardt and Denhardt 2000).

The study also demonstrates the possibilities of examining the "black box" of policy making using systematic discourse analysis. Examining the political space allowed us to track the discourse that shaped the political space and the resulting consequences of the discourse (Boden 1995; Barrett, Thomas, and Hocevar 1995; Livesey 2001, Titscher, Meyer, Wodak, and Vetter 2000).

Managerial Implications

Using a discursive approach, in addition to the traditional procedural approach to policy making, allows public managers to reimagine avenues for policy development. Managers can become attuned to the sociocultural aspects of policy development by observing the impact that language has on shaping policy. As mentioned by Fischer (1998), managers can envision themselves as facilitators of public learning and public empowerment. Instead of deliberating behind the scenes and then announcing a policy, managers can build purposeful strategies to include multiple voices in the policy formulation stages. This approach imports local knowledge into decisions and considers the context of the major stakeholders (Fischer 2006). Public managers get a deeper understanding of the historical forces that shape public opinion and can devise frames and strategies that empower local citizens and increase accountability.

APPENDIX: PROPOSAL EXCERPTS

DEPARTMENT OF HOMELAND SECURITY
Coast Guard
33 CFR Part 165
[CGD09-06-123]
RIN 1625-AA00
Safety Zones; U.S. Coast Guard Water Training Areas, Great Lakes

AGENCY: Coast Guard, DHS

ACTION: Notice of proposed rulemaking

SUMMARY: The Coast Guard proposes to establish safety zones throughout the Great Lakes. These zones are intended to restrict vessels from portions of the Great Lakes during live fire gun exercises that will be conducted by Coast Guard cutters and small boats. These safety zones are necessary to protect the public from the hazards associated with the firing of weapons.

DATES: Comments and related materials must reach the Coast Guard on or before August 31, 2006.

ADDRESSES: You may mail comments and related material to Commander (dre) Ninth Coast Guard District, 1240 E. 9th Street, Room 2069, Cleveland, OH 44199. The Ninth Coast Guard District Planning and Development Section (dpw-1) maintains the public docket for this rulemaking. Comments and material received from the public, as well as documents indicated in this preamble as being available in the docket, will become part of this docket and will be available for inspection or copying between 8 a.m. (local) and 4 p.m. (local), Monday through Friday, except Federal holidays.

FOR FURTHER INFORMATION CONTACT: Commander Gustav Wulfkuhle, Enforcement Branch, Response Division, Ninth Coast Guard District, Cleveland, OH at (216) 902-6091.

SUPPLEMENTARY INFORMATION:

Request for Comments
We encourage you to submit comments and related materials. If you submit a comment, please include your name and address, identify the docket number for this rulemaking [CGD09-06-123], indicate the specific section of this document to which each comment applies, and give the reason for each comment. You may submit your comments and material by mail (see ADDRESSES). If you submit them by mail or delivery, submit them in an unbound format, no larger than 8½ by 11 inches, suitable for copying and electronic filing. If you submit them by mail and would like to know that they reached the facility, please enclose a stamped, self-addressed postcard or envelope. We will consider all comments and material received during the comment period, which may result in a modification to the rule.

Public Meeting
We do not now plan to hold a public meeting. But you may submit a request for a public meeting (see **ADDRESSES**) explaining why one would be beneficial. If we determine that one would aid this rulemaking, we will hold one at a time and place announced by a later notice in the **Federal Register**.

Regulatory Information
The Coast Guard is proposing to establish these safety zones to conduct training essential to carrying out Coast Guard missions relating to military operations and national security. Accordingly, these proposed safety zones fall within the military function exception to the Administrative Procedure Act (APA), 5 U.S.C. 553(a)(1). Notice and comment rulemaking under 5 U.S.C. 553(b) and an effective date of 30 days after publication under 5 U.S.C. 553(d) are not required for this rulemaking.

Lake Ontario:

Ontario Zone 1 (Eastern): Beginning at 43°44′18″ N, 076°30′22″ W; then south to 43°36′05″ N, 076°30′22″ W; then east to 43°36′05″ N, 076°22′58″ W; then north to 43°44′18″ N, 076°22′58″ W; then west to the point of origin.Show citation box

Ontario Zone 2 (Middle): Beginning at 43°27′59″ N, 077°34′32″ W; then south to 43°24′19″ N, 077°34′36″ W; then east to 43°24′20″ N, 077°22′55″ W; then north to 43°28′06″ N, 077°23′04″ W; then west to the point of origin.Show citation box

Ontario Zone 3 (Western): Beginning at 43°24′19″ N, 079°02′25″ W; then south to 43°21′50″ N, 079°00′47″ W; then east to 43°23′48″ N, 078°50′29″ W; then north to 43°26′29″ N, 078°52′05″ W; then west to the point of origin.Show citation box

Lake Erie:

Erie Zone 1 (Eastern): Beginning at 42°12′01″ N, 080°45′11″ W; then south to 42°05′22″ N, 080°38′23″ W; then east to 42°12′35″ N, 080°18′01″ W; then north to 42°15′18″ N, 080°23′52″ W; then west to the point of origin.Show citation box

Erie Zone 2 (Eastern Middle): Beginning at 41°59′51″ N, 081°16′23″ W; then south to 41°56′15″ N, 081°16′02″ W; then east to 41°58′39″ N, 081°00′12″ W; then north to 42°02′20″ N, 081°01′00″ W; then west to the point of origin.Show citation box

Erie Zone 3 (Western Middle): Beginning at 41°47′40″ N, 081°47′44″ W; then south to 41°41′50″ N, 081°46′22″ W; then east to 41°41′24″ N, 081°40′26″ W; then north to 41°47′26″ N, 081°37′49″ W then west to the point of origin.Show citation box

Erie Zone 4 (Western): Beginning at 41°35′30″ N, 082°30′04″ W; then south to 41°30′07″ N, 082°31′02″ W; then east to 41°30′22″ N, 082°25′07″ W; then north to 41°35′30″ N, 082°25′07″ W; then west to the point of origin.Show citation box

Lake Huron:

Huron Zone 1 (Southern): Beginning at 43°43′07″ N, 082°24′23″ W; then south to 43°27′45″ N, 082°24′34″ W; then east to 43°27′45″ N, 082°20′16″ W; then north to 43°42′51″ N, 082°17′14″ W; then west to the point of origin.Show citation box

Huron Zone 2 (Harbor Beach): Beginning at 44°12′00″ N, 082°40′30″ W; then south to 44°04′02″ N, 082°37′41″ W; then east to 44°04′44″ N, 082°29′24″ W; then north to 44°12′00″ N, 082°33′08″ W; then west to the point of origin.Show citation box

Huron Zone 3 (Saginaw Bay): Beginning at 44°19′24″ N, 083°10′40″ W; then south to 44°09′48″ N, 083°15′55″ W; then east to 44°12′08″ N, 082°50′35″ W; then north to 44°19′30″ N, 082°55′15″ W; the west to the point of origin.Show citation box

Huron Zone 4 (Thunder Bay South): Beginning at 44°45′45″ N, 083°07′19″ W; then south to 44°38′00″ N, 083°03′18″ W; then east to 44°38′00″ N, 082°54′11″ W; then north to 44°45′45″ N, 082°57′42″ W; then west to the point of origin.Show citation box

Huron Zone 5 (Thunder Bay North): Beginning at 45°17′02″ N, 082°51′48″ W; then south to 45°05′54″ N, 082°51′22″ W; then southeast to 45°01′10″ N, 082°47′22″ W; then east to 45°01′07″ N, 082°35′48″ W; then north to 45°16′13″ N, 082°39′33″ W; then west to the point of origin.Show citation box

Huron Zone 6 (Northern): Beginning at 45°44′35″ N, 083°58′16″ W; then south to 45°39′48″ N, 083°59′55″ W; then east to 45°38′41″ N, 083°49′26″ W; then north to 45°42′39″ N, 083°50′22″ W; then west to the point of origin.Show citation box

Lake Michigan:

Michigan Zone 1 (Charlevoix): Beginning at 45°30′00″ N, 085°25′18″ W, then southwest to 45°22′41″ N, 085°26′47″ W, then northeast to 45°27′45″ N, 085°13′50″ W, then northwest to 45°32′46″ N, 085°16′25″ W then southwest to the point of origin. Show citation box

Michigan Zone 2 (Frankfort): Beginning at 44°47′23″ N, 086°41′12″ W; then south to 44°34′06″ N, 086°48′54″ W; then east to 44°35′55″ N, 086°33′03″ W; then north to 44°46′41″ N, 086°28′43″ W; then west to the point of origin.Show citation box

Michigan Zone 3 (Manistee): Beginning at 44°22′18″ N, 086°53′41″ W; then southwest to 44°14′34″ N, 087°01′06″ W; then southeast to 44°09′18″ N, 086°51′36″ W; then northeast to 44°21′49″ N, 086°40′14″ W; then northwest to the point of origin.Show citation box

Michigan Zone 4 (Ludington): Beginning at 43°59′40″ N, 086°46′24″ W; then south to 43°51′24″ N, 086°49′50″ W; then east to 43°51′11″ N, 086°42′28″ W; then north to 43°59′21″ N, 086°39′15″ W; then west to the point of origin.Show citation box

Michigan Zone 5 (Grand Haven): Beginning at 43°13′03″ N, 086°46′57″ W; then south to 43°00′27″ N, 086°46′04″ W; then east to 43°00′17″ N, 086°27′13″ W; then north to 43°13′49″ N, 086°32′00″ W; then west to the point of origin.Show citation box

Michigan Zone 6 (St. Joseph): Beginning at 42°12′52″ N, 086°50′10″ W; then south to 42°05′41″ N, 086°53′55″ W; then east to 42°05′24″ N, 086°43′45″ W; then north to 42°12′19″ N, 086°39′42″ W; then west to the point of origin.Show citation box

Michigan Zone 7 (Michigan City): Beginning at 41°58′36″ N, 087°02′53″ W; then south to 41°48′42″ N, 087°02′53″ W; then northeast to 41°52′51″ N, 086°51′40″ W; then north to 41°59′06″ N, 086°48′00″ W; then west to the point of origin.Show citation box

Michigan Zone 8 (Chicago): Beginning at 41°55′18″ N, 087°15′49″ W; then south to 41°48′29″ N, 087°17′46″ W; then east to 41°47′45″ N, 087°08′57″ W; then north to 41°55′18″ N, 087°08′48″ W; then west to the point of origin.Show citation box

Michigan Zone 9 (Waukeegan): Beginning at 42°22′28″ N, 087°39′14″ W; then south to 42°17′49″ N, 087°39′27″ W; then southeast to 42°13′42″ N, 087°37′35″ W; the east to 42°14′02″ N, 087°31′36″ W; then north to 42°22′58″ N, 087°33′02″ W; then west to the point of origin. Show citation box

Michigan Zone 10 (Kenosha): Beginning at 42°39′28″ N, 087°33′19″ W; then south to 42°30′17″ N, 087°31′09″ W; then east to 42°30′21″ N, 087°23′23″ W; then north to 42°38′55″ N, 087°24′30″ W; then west to the point of origin.Show citation box

Michigan Zone 11 (Milwaukee): Beginning at 43°05′13″ N, 087°32′48″ W; then south to 42°54′37″ N, 087°34′27″ W; then east to 42°54′50″ N, 087°26′27″ W; then north to 43°05′13″ N, 087°25′55″ W; then west to the point of origin.Show citation box

Michigan Zone 12 (Two Rivers): Beginning at 44°08′20″ N, 087°24′08″ W; then south to 43°49′06″ N, 087°27′34″ W; then east to 43°48′59″ N, 087°20′19″ W; then north to 44°06′04″ N, 087°16′43″ W; then northwest to the point of origin.Show citation box

Michigan Zone 13 (Sturgeon Bay): Beginning at 44°41′22″ N, 087°08′43″ W; then south to 44°32′49″ N, 087°13′21″ W; then east to 44°32′32″ N, 087°04′10″ W; then north to 44°40′33″ N, 087°01′41″ W; then west to the point of origin.Show citation box

Michigan Zone 14 (Washington Island): Beginning at 45°19′17″ N, 086°35′58″ W; then southwest to 45°12′50″ N, 086°41′39″ W; then southeast to 45°10′50″ N, 086°30′48″ W; then northeast to 45°17′29″ N, 086°25′32″ W; then northwest to the point of origin.Show citation box

Lake Superior:

Superior Zone 1 (Whitefish Bay): Beginning at 46°41′30″ N, 084°54′00″ W; then south to 46°36′00″ N, 084°55′00″ W; continuing south to 46°34′30″ N, 084°54′36″ W; then east to 46°33′18″ N, 084°50′54″ W; continuing east to 46°32′48″ N, 084°46′00″ W; then north to 46°33′12″ N, 084°45′54″ W; then northwest to 46°36′06″ N, 084°49′48″ W; continuing northwest to 46°42′00″ N, 084°52′18″ W; then southwest to the point of origin.Show citation box

Superior Zone 2 (Sault Ste. Marie): Beginning at 46°56′16″ N, 085°39′01″ W; then southeast to 46°51′55″ N, 085°24′04″ W; then northeast to 46°53′07″ N, 085°12′37″ W; then northwest to 46°58′20″ N, 085°29′44″ W; then southwest to the point of origin.

ACKNOWLEDGMENT

The authors acknowledge and thank Daphne A. Jameson for her insightful comments and suggestions. We also thank Sarah Martin and Jovanna Rosen, research assistants at the U.S. Naval Postgraduate School.

REFERENCES

Alvesson, M., and D. Kärreman. 2000. Varieties of Discourse: On the Study of Organizations through Discourse Analysis. *Human Relations* 53: 1125–49.

Arnstein, S. 1969. A Ladder of Citizen Participation. *JAIP* 35: 216–24.

Barrett, F. J., G. F. Thomas, and S. P. Hocevar. 1995. The Central Role of Discourse in Large-scale Change: A Social-Constructionist Perspective. *Journal of Applied Behavioral Science* 31: 352–72.

Benford, R. D., and D. A. Snow. 2000. Framing Processes and Social Movements: An Overview and Assessment. *Annual Review of Sociology* 26: 464–81.

Boden, D. 1995. *The Business of Talk: Organizations in Action*. Cambridge, UK: Polity Press.

Bourdieu, P. 1977. *Outline of a Theory of Practice*. Cambridge, UK: Cambridge University Press.

Boyatzis, R. E. 1998. *Transforming Qualitative Information*. Thousands Oaks, CA: Sage Publications.

Castells, M. 1996. *The Information Age: Economy, Society and Culture. Volume I. The Rise of Network Society*. Malden, MA: Blackwell Publishers.

Davis, G. F., D. McAdam, W. R. Scott, and M. N. Zald. 2005. *Social Movement and Organization Theory*. Cambridge, UK: Cambridge University Press.

Denhardt, R. B., and J. V. Denhardt. 2000. The New Public Service: Serving rather Than Steering. *Public Administration Review* 60: 549–59.

Federal Register Main Page. n.d. Retrieved August 3, 2009, from http://gpoaccess.gov/fr/.

Fischer, F. 1998. Beyond Empiricism: Policy Inquiry in Postpositivist Perspective. *Policy Studies Journal* 26: 129–46.

Fischer, F. 2006. Participatory Governance as Deliberative Empowerment: The Cultural Politics of Discursive Space. *American Review of Public Administration* 36: 19–40.

Fischer, F., and J. Forester, eds. 1993. *The Argumentative Turn in Policy Analysis and Planning*. Durham, NC: Duke University Press.

Forester, J. 2008. Participation as Dialogue, Debate, and Negotiation: Entangled Promises and Practices. In *Governance Reform under Real-world Conditions: Citizens, Stakeholders, and Voice*, eds. S. Odugbemi and T. Jacobson. Washington, DC: The World Bank.

Foucault, M. 1986. Of Other Spaces. *Diacritics—A Review of Contemporary Criticism* 16: 22–27.

Fung, A. 2006. Varieties of Participation in Complex Governance. *Public Administration Review* 66: 66–75.

Fung, A., and E. O. Wright. 2001. Deepening Democracy: Innovations in Empowered Participatory Governance. *Politics and Society* 29: 5–41.

Goffman, E. 1974. *Frame Analysis.* Cambridge, MA: Harvard University Press.
Goodin, R. E., M. Rein, and M. Moran, eds. 2006. *The Oxford Handbook of Public Policy*. New York: Oxford University Press.
Hajer, M. 1995. *The Politics of Environmental Discourse: Ecological Modernization and the Policy Process*. Oxford: Clarendon Press.
Hajer, M. 2006. Doing Discourse Analysis: Coalitions, Practices and Meaning. In *Words Matter in Policy and Planning: Discourse Theory and Method in the Social Sciences*, eds. M. van den Brink and T. Metze, 65–74. Utrect, Netherlands: Netherlands Geographical Studies.
Hajer, M., and D. Laws. 2006. Ordering through Discourse. In *The Oxford Handbook of Public Policy*, eds. M. Moran, M. Rein, and R. E. Goodin, 251–68. Oxford University Press: Oxford, UK.
Hitch, C. J. 1958. Economics and Military Operations Research. *Review of Economics and Statistics* 40: 119–209.
Houston, S. 2001. Beyond Social Constructionism: Critical Realism and Social Work. *British Journal of Social Work* 31: 845–61.
Jewell, C., and L. Bero. 2006. Public Participation and Claimsmaking: Evidence Utilization and Divergent Policy Frames in California's Ergonomics Rulemaking. *Journal of Public Administration Research and Theory* 17: 625–50.
Jordon, G., and C. Weedon. 1995. *Cultural Politics: Class, Gender, Race, and the Postmodern World.* Cambridge, MA: Blackwell.
Livesey, S. 2001. Eco-identity as Discursive Struggle: Royal Dutch/Shell, Brent Spar, and Nigeria. *Journal of Business Communication* 38: 58–91.
Locker, K. O. 2004. *Business and Administrative Communication*. New York: McGraw-Hill/Irwin.
Osborne, D., and T. Gaebler. 1992. *Reinventing Government*. Reading, MA: Addison-Wesley.
Schon, D., and M. Rein. 1994. *Frame Reflection: Toward the Resolution of Intractable Policy Controversies*. New York: Basic Books.
Steinberg, M. W. 1998. Tilting the Frame: Considerations on Collective Action Framing from a Discursive Turn. *Theory and Society* 27: 845–72.
Stillar, G. F. 1998. *Analyzing Everyday Texts: Discourse, Rhetoric, and Social Perspectives*. Thousand Oaks, CA: Sage Publications.
Suddaby, R., and R. Greenwood. 2005. Rhetorical Strategies of Legitimacy. *Administrative Science Quarterly* 50: 35–67.
Titscher, S., M. Meyer, R. Wodak, and E. Vetter. 2000. *Methods of Text and Discourse Analysis*. Thousand Oaks, CA: Sage.
USCG History. n.d. Retrieved May 4, 2009, from www.uscg.mil/history.
van den Brink, M., and T. Metze, eds. 2006. *Words Matter in Policy and Planning*. Utrecht, Netherlands: Netherlands Geographical Studies.
van Dijk, T. A. 1988. *News as Discourse*. Hillside, HN: Erlbaum.
Wilson, W. 1941. The Study of Administration. *Political Science Quarterly* 56: 197–222.
Yates, J., and W. J. Orlikowski. 1992. Genres of Organizational Communication: A Structurational Approach to Studying Communication and Media. *Academy of Management Review* 17: 299–326.

6

The Rhetorical Legitimation of Organizational Exploration and Exploitation Initiatives

Torsten Oliver Salge and Michael Ian Barrett

This chapter examines the legitimating discourses associated with organizational exploration and exploitation initiatives. Located within the context of a major public hospital organization, we trace the evolution of twenty-nine organizational development projects over time. We categorize these initiatives into two groups as a function of their respective exploration and exploitation orientation. We then draw on rich internal text material to identify intergroup commonalities as well as differences in rhetorical legitimation strategies. Our findings contribute to the field of organizational discourse by advancing our understanding of how actors tailor their rhetorical strategies. Findings equally add to the literature on exploration and exploitation by uncovering the legitimating discourses used by local actors seeking to gain legitimacy for their respective initiative.

INTRODUCTION

Decision makers within organizations have to make far-reaching decisions under conditions of considerable ambiguity as to the course of action that is most likely to entail the desired outcome (March and Olsen 1976).

This situation provides fertile ground for social actors to engage in active strategies seeking to build legitimacy for their preferred course of action (Hirschman 1991; Gamson and D. S. Meyer 1996; Green 2004). Such processes of legitimation are essentially discursive practices, since "the edifice of legitimation is built upon language and uses language as its principal instrumentality" (Berger and Luckmann 1966, 64). Given this close interplay between language and legitimacy (Suddaby and Greenwood 2005), a rhetorical perspective has much to offer for advancing our understanding of legitimation in the context of organizational decision making and beyond. In the field of innovation diffusion research alone, rhetorical approaches have been fruitfully employed not only to develop an overall rhetorical theory of diffusion (Green 2004) but also to empirically examine the adoption of innovative technologies (Heracleous and Barrett 2001), novel organizational forms (Suddaby and Greenwood 2005), and new managerial practices (Green, Li, and Nohria 2009).

Interestingly, this research stream has uncovered considerable variation in the rhetorical strategies adopted. Drawing on a longitudinal field study of electronic trading implementation in the London Insurance Market, Heracleous and Barrett (2001), for instance, highlight the role of competing perspectives resulting from notable differences in the overall argument structure adopted by diverse stakeholder groups. Similarly, Suddaby and Greenwood (2005) observe that proponents and opponents of adopting multidisciplinary partnerships as a new organizational form differ notably in terms of the vocabularies used, the theorizations employed, and the forms of legitimacy appealed to. Going beyond interpersonal and intergroup differences in discursive strategies, Green (2004) as well as Green, Li, and Nohria (2009) point to substantial variation across distinct innovation diffusion stages. Such variation takes the form of differences in the relative importance of rhetorical justifications such as pathos, logos, and ethos (Green 2004), and the extent to which the underlying premises of the central argument are being taken for granted (Green, Li, and Nohria 2009).

While these studies have provided valuable insight, they have focused on a single change initiative—be it a novel information technology, managerial practice, or organizational form. However, we know still relatively little about potential differences in rhetorical strategies across initiatives with distinct practice types (Green 2004). In this chapter, we therefore seek to contribute to filling this theoretical and empirical void. Drawing on rich observational interview and archival data from twenty-nine organizational development initiatives, we compare rhetorical strategies across two structurally distinct project groups. More specifically, we examine how discursive legitimation strategies are being shaped by the extent to which the proposed course of action adds to organizational exploration and exploitation.

The remainder of this chapter is structured as follows. Section 2 introduces a rhetorical perspective on organizational exploration. Section 3 describes the research setting and sets out the data collection and analysis procedures used in this study. Results are then presented in section 4. Section 5 discusses the main findings and highlights important contributions of this study to the literatures on business discourse and organizational learning. We conclude by outlining practical implications and sketching several directions for future studies in what remains a rather under-researched, yet highly fascinating, area.

A RHETORICAL PERSPECTIVE

We outline our rhetorical perspective on organizational exploitation and exploration by drawing on the following interrelated observations. Decision making frequently occurs under great ambiguity as to the course of action most likely to provide the desirable outcome (March and Olsen 1976). This holds not least for the evaluation and selection of exploitative and exploratory organizational development projects (March 1991). Consequently, initiators of such projects have an active role to play in building legitimacy for their initiative (Suchman 1995). The process of legitimacy building in turn is a predominantly rhetorical one, which is thus directly reflected in language (Suddaby and Greenwood 2005).

Exploration and Exploitation

One of the most important strategic choices organizational decision makers have to make consists in allocating financial and human resources to various organizational development initiatives (He and Wong 2004). Perhaps more than other choice opportunities (Cohen, March, and Olsen 1972), investment decisions are subject to substantial uncertainty and ambiguity.

Since March (1991), organizational development and learning initiatives are widely classified as being more or less the ideal type of instances of either exploration or exploitation. Organizational exploration pertains to the discovery of new possibilities through search, experimentation, risk taking, creativity, and serendipity. Organizational exploitation, however, encompasses activities aimed at the refinement of existing certainties through evaluation, modification, implementation, and execution (March 1991).

While both exploratory and exploitative initiatives are essential for organizational survival and performance, they require fundamentally different structures, routines, and capabilities. Organizational exploration is typically assumed to thrive on organic structures, autonomy, and emergence, while mechanistic structures, control, and routinization are believed to be beneficial to organizational exploitation (He and Wong 2004). Returns from exploratory initiatives are often much higher, yet are also more uncertain and more distant in time. Conversely, returns from exploitation are typically more predictable and immediate, yet often less notable. Given their distinct strategic contributions and organizational requirements, exploitative and exploratory initiatives compete for managerial attention and financial resources in form of a zero-sum game, where "more resources devoted to exploitation imply fewer resources left over for exploration, and vice versa" (Gupta, Smith, and Shalley 2006, 695).

Given the expected complementarity of exploratory and exploitative initiatives, organizations are believed to benefit from a balance between exploration and exploitation activities, if they are to achieve sustained superior performance. As Levinthal and March (1993, 105) phrase it, "[t]he basic problem confronting an organization is to engage in sufficient exploitation to ensure its current viability and at the same time, to devote enough energy to exploration to ensure its future viability." This idea has spurred a substantial body of research on how to simultaneously excel at both exploration and exploitation, thereby striving for what has come to be known as organizational ambidexterity (Tushman and O'Reilly 1996; He and Wong 2004).

Faced with considerable uncertainty and ambiguity as to the respective merits of each organizational development initiative and the appropriate mix of exploitative and exploratory projects, decision makers have to engage in complex processes of collective interpretation and negotiation when selecting how to allocate scarce organizational resources among competing initiatives. This situation provides fertile ground for initiators of such projects to engage in active strategies of legitimacy building (Hirschman 1991; Gamson and D. S. Meyer 1996; Green 2004) toward their proposed course of action.

Legitimacy and Legitimation

The field of organization research has a long-standing interest in legitimacy, which has its etymological roots in the Latin term *legitimus*, signifying "lawful" or "in line with the law." We follow Suchman (1995, 574) in defining *legitimacy* as follows:

> Legitimacy is a generalized perception or assumption that the actions of an entity are desirable, proper, or appropriate within some socially constructed system of norms, values, beliefs, and definitions.

Understanding legitimacy as a status conferred by social actors, we concur with Ruef and Scott (1998) that there are multiple sources of legitimation. Deephouse and Suchman (2008, 55) provide useful guidance by suggesting that the "central issue for legitimacy research is identifying who has collective authority over legitimation in any given setting." At the organizational level, state regulators, accreditation agencies, the general media, or other legitimate organizations can fulfill this role as legitimacy-granting agents vis-à-vis individual organizations, structures, or practices (Deephouse and Carter 2005; Durand and McGuire 2005; Deephouse and Suchman 2008). At the intra-organizational level, endorsement by committees or senior executives, who act as project champions (Chakrabarti 1974), often confers legitimacy to a specific initiative or idea.

While legitimacy is conferred by actors with authority over the respective entity (Johnson, Dowd, and Ridgeway 2006), the latter is not without agency in influencing the outcome of this legitimation process (Suddaby and Greenwood 2005). Quite the contrary, organizations and other legitimacy-seeking entities engage in systematic legitimacy management; that is, deliberate actions seeking to influence legitimacy-granting agents (Ashforth and Gibbs 1990; Oliver 1991; Vaara and Tienari 2008). More specifically, Suchman (1995, 586) distinguishes actions targeted at gaining, maintaining, and repairing legitimacy and highlights that "legitimacy management rests heavily on communication [. . .] between the organization and its various audiences." This reiterates earlier observations by Berger and Luckmann (1996, 64), who argue that "the edifice of legitimation is built upon language and uses language as its principal instrumentality."

Discourse and Rhetoric

There is now general agreement that discourse and rhetoric are central to processes of legitimation (Phillips, Lawrence, and Hardy 2004; Deephouse and Suchman 2008). This growing interest in the discursive nature of legitimation comes as part of a wider linguistic turn within the social sciences (Alvesson and Kärreman 2000a; 2000b), which has brought renewed interest to language and texts (Daft and Wiginton 1979).

Discourses can be understood as a structured collection of meaningful texts (Parker 1992). Such texts can take a variety of forms, including but not limited to written documents, verbal accounts, pictures, and other artifacts (Fairclough 1995; Phillips, Lawrence, and Hardy 2004). While discourse analysis and rhetoric share their interest in the role of language and texts in shaping social action, rhetoric is characterized by a clear focus on persuasion and is typically defined as the art of using language as a means to persuade (McCloskey 1983; 1994). In his famous *On Rhetoric*, Aristotle (1991, 13) conceptualizes rhetoric as "an ability, in each case, to see the available means of persuasion." As such, the rhetor—and the rhetorical analyst on that matter—has to consider the particular situation, audience, the genre of text, as well as the credibility of the rhetor (Gill and Whedbee 1997).

Since legitimation is essentially a process of discursive interpretation and negotiation, one would assume discursive and rhetorical studies of legitimation to be manifold. Somewhat surprisingly, though, this is not the case, despite a plethora of scholarly research on legitimacy (Vaara and Tienari 2008). This holds in particular with regard to research that goes beyond the discursive legitimation of organizations. Among the few studies in this research space, Brown (1998), for instance, examines the implementation of a hospital information support system in a major hospital illustrating how individual actors construct narratives to legitimate their actions and interests. Similarly concerned with the implementation of a major IT innovation, Heracleous and Barrett (2001) study the role of discourse in influencing the implementation of electronic trading in the London Insurance Market. While addressing issues of legitimacy only indirectly, they uncover notable differences in the rhetorical strategies used by multiple stakeholder groups. Insomuch as such differences pertain to deep discursive structures, they tend to be relatively stable over time. Creed, Scully, and Austin (2002) study the legitimating accounts deployed by proponents and opponents of antidiscrimination policies. In particular, they examine the use of broader cultural accounts and find that local actors neither plainly import such accounts nor completely tailor them de novo. Their study also reveals that legitimating accounts that mobilize the audience excel at constructing a collective social identity, such that listeners are able to identify themselves with the account. Somewhat similarly, Suddaby and Greenwood (2005) shed light on the rhetorical strategies used by proponents and opponents of a new organizational form consisting in a multidisciplinary professional firm offering accounting as well as legal services. Based on transcribed witness testimonies from public hearings, they uncover substantial differences in the legitimating discourses of proponents and opponents as illustrated by distinct institutional vocabularies and theorizations of change. Vaara, Tienari, and Laurila (2006) investigate the role of media accounts in legitimating a particular organizational act. The latter consisted in the long unthinkable cross-border merger between two previous archrivals in the Scandinavian pulp and paper industry. They focused on legitimation strategies, defined as "specific, not always intentional or conscious, ways of employing different discourses or discursive resources to establish legitimacy" (Vaara, Tienari, and Laurila 2006, 794). Drawing on the work of Van Leeuwen and Wodak (1999), they distinguish and illustrate five distinct legitimation strategies labelled normalization, authorization, rationalization, moralization, and narrativization. Last, Green, Li, and Nohria (2009) trace the discursive process whereby total quality management (TQM) is being legitimated. Concerned with argument structures, they find that the premises of the argument in support of TQM is based on are being increasingly suppressed, as TQM gains in legitimacy.

These studies illustrate that social actors at various levels skillfully engage in discursive practices, by means of which they seek to influence the legitimacy assessment with regard to a specific subject of legitimation. In so doing, they tailor their legitimating accounts to contextual requirements, the expectations of their audiences as well as the nature of their subject of legitimation. As a result, legitimating discourses appear to differ interpersonally; that is, across distinct interest groups (Heracleous and Barrett 2001; Suddaby and Greenwood 2005) as well as temporally, that is across distinct stages in the diffusion of a specific subject of legitimation (Green 2004; Green, Li, and Nohria 2009). Similarly, we expect legitimating discourses to differ as a function of the specific attribute set associated with a particular class of subjects of legitimation.

While this expectation appears highly plausible, little empirical research has sought to understand the extent and nature of such interclass differences (Green 2004). This holds also with regard to the distinction between exploitation and exploration, which is of great theoretical and empirical importance in the fields of organizational learning and strategic management. In this chapter, we seek to address this research gap by examining the legitimating discourses deployed by proponents of exploitative and exploratory organizational development projects. Given the scarcity of organizational resources and the ambiguity of the choice opportunity, initiators will have to engage in skillful strategies to build legitimacy for their project among the top management team. Applying Johnson et al.'s (2006) four-stage model of legitimation, which conceptualizes the latter as a sequence of innovation, local validation, diffusion, and general validation, it becomes apparent that our study concentrates on local validation. Local validation constitutes a type of organizational sense making (Weick 1995) and is thus particularly likely "to result in the production of texts that are widely disseminated and consumed" (Phillips, Lawrence, and Hardy 2004, 642). As such, this stage lends itself particularly well to rhetorical analyses.

In this context, a number of interesting questions appear worth addressing. What are the rhetorical legitimation strategies used by initiators of organizational development projects to gain local validation? To what extent do such legitimating accounts differ among exploitative and exploratory initiatives? What is the nature of these differences? Are there dominant discursive features, which hold for all subjects of legitimation independent of whether they contribute to organizational exploitation or exploration? This chapter constitutes a first step toward exploring these questions. We do so by examining the legitimating accounts associated with all twenty-nine organizational development projects proposed within a major public hospital organization in England during 2007.

Adapting Merton's (1957) distinction, we examine these accounts with regard to their manifest material as well as their latent, symbolic content. The material dimension refers to those discursive elements that are amenable to direct observation, as they are explicitly reflected in the vocabularies present in the text. The symbolic dimension of any legitimating discourse, however, can only be revealed through careful interpretation, as it pertains to latent content—that is implicit meaning (Suddaby and Greenwood 2005). The symbolic dimension thus includes central rhetorical categories, such as the relative importance of pathos, logos, and ethos (Green 2004), the form of theorization of change used (Suddaby and Greenwood 2005), and the type of legitimacy referred to (Suchman 1995).

METHODOLOGY

Research Context

We chose a major public hospital organization in England as the setting for our study. This selection is not least motivated by the fact that public hospitals demonstrate both a pronounced need for external endorsement and a high degree of process formalization. Such organizations hence lend themselves particularly well to the study of discursive legitimation practices.

"Urban," the hospital organization this study is located in, is part of the English National Health Service (NHS). Founded in 1948 with the objective to provide every resident with tax-funded care that is free at the point of delivery (Ministry of Health 1948), the NHS now accounts for nearly 90 percent of English health expenditures. In 2009, a total of 170 hospital organizations provided tax-funded hospital services in England. Each hospital organization manages an average of 2.35 hospitals and enjoys considerable autonomy. This is reflected by its status as an independent entity with its own executive board and annual financial statements. "Urban" is a major urban university hospital with more than one thousand beds, offering the full range of general hospital services as well as a number of highly specialized services. In these specialist areas, it enjoys an international reputation for clinical excellence and attracts referrals from throughout the country.

Data Collection

We followed a year in the history of strategic decision making in this hospital organization. More specifically, we traced the journey of all twenty-nine organizational development initiatives submitted to the investment board between January and December 2007. The investment process at "Urban" is highly formalized and requires all initiatives above a minimum threshold of 100,000 British pounds in capital expenditure or recurring revenue costs to obtain board approval. The overwhelming majority of significant exploration and exploitation initiatives is thus channeled through the investment process.

Proponents of these projects actively sought legitimacy for their respective initiative in a skillful process that can be likened to a theater performance, which is closely guided by texts and stories.

> You can perceive of it as a theatre performance. The staff members presenting their proposal are the actors, who tell a story about how they wish to develop their specific service. They do so against the scenery of an overall service narrative, which sets out the strategy for each major service area. The audience is made up of the members of the investment board, who represent the Trust and ultimately the patient. (interview with an executive at "Urban" on February 6, 2007)

Our data-gathering efforts therefore focused on collecting a wide array of texts salient to the legitimation of all twenty-nine organizational development initiatives.

First, for each project, we collected a copy of the written briefing note, the full proposal and—where available—the project review. This yielded a total of sixty-nine documents with a cumulative length of 171,000 words printed on nearly six hundred pages, corresponding to an average of nearly 5,900 words per project. These texts constitute the main data source for our study and provide a rich account of the discursive legitimation strategies used by agents of organizational development initiatives. As Phillips, Lawrence, and Hardy (2004, 640) point out, "Texts must be distributed and interpreted by other actors if they are to have organizing properties and the potential to affect discourse." This is clearly the case for these texts, which are carefully crafted, circulated within the service area, studied by the investment board, and stored for reference purposes.

Second, we observed some preparatory meetings as well as all seven investment board meetings that took place between January and December 2007. This included six scheduled meetings as well as an extraordinary meeting dedicated to a major infrastructure project. Meetings lasted three hours on average and were recorded through detailed note taking and official meeting minutes.

Third, we interviewed at least one senior project member per initiative, using a semistructured interview guide. Interviews were conducted in temporal proximity to the presentation of their respective project to the investment board. We sought to trace the journey of their project from the inception of the very first idea to its current state, focusing in particular on the strategies used to build legitimacy for their initiative. All interviews lasting slightly more than an hour on average were digitally recorded and fully transcribed.

The participant observation and interviews were central to gaining an in-depth understanding of the respective context each project was located in, as meaning does not solely reside within the text, but also the textual context (Heracleous and Barrett 2001). These insights proved highly useful when interpreting our findings and were as such important elements of the data collection and analysis process (Ricoeur 1991; Van Dijk 1997).

Fourth, we asked two senior executives at "Urban" to assess each project on a number of dimensions. This project evaluation took place in late 2008, yielding complete assessments of all twenty-nine projects undertaken by two key informants with in-depth knowledge of each initiative. While our two informants also assessed the complexity, novelty, and expected success of each initiative, particular emphasis was placed on evaluating the exploration and exploitation. In line with previous research, both constructs were assessed on three distinct dimensions related to the product offered, the market served, and the capabilities possessed (He and Wong 2004). Each dimension was measured on a seven-point Likert-type scale. The specific items used are reproduced in the appendix.

Data Analysis

We proceeded in two steps when analyzing the data collected.

In a first step, we conducted a content analysis of the texts[1]—a common method used in much empirical research on organizational discourse (Sudday and Greenwood 2005; Green, Li, and Nohria 2009). Two research assistants familiar with rhetorical concepts performed the content analysis using a standardized coding frame. This instrument required the coder to assess the emphasis the project team placed on specific categories pertaining to both the material and the symbolic content of their legitimating discourse. We deviated from previous studies (e.g., Suddaby and Greenwood 2005) in that coders were not forced to select a single element that they perceived as dominant. Rather, coders were asked to discuss the discursive emphasis placed on each element, using a six-point Likert-type scale ("not used" to "very important"), which should allow for a finer-grained analysis of discursive differences between exploratory and exploitative projects. As two coders have content analyzed each project, we use the mean assessment for further analyses. Moreover, we asked coders to extract relevant quotes from the original text material to support their specific assessment.

In a second step, we compared the coded legitimation discourses across exploratory and exploitative projects. For this purpose, we had to code each organizational development initiative as either exploitative or exploratory. Conceptualizing exploration and exploitation as two end points of a continuum (Gupta, Smith, and Shalley 2006), we calculated the relative importance of exploration as the ratio between the mean exploration and the mean exploitation score of each project. Each mean score represents the average project assessment of both key informants across all three concept dimensions. Using the median cut-off criterion (He and Wong 2004), we then coded the fifteen projects with the highest relative importance of exploration as exploratory and the remaining fourteen projects as exploitative. We also examined the interrater reliability for this important classification procedure. A project classification solely based on the assessments of informant 1 would have yielded the same classification for twenty-five of the twenty-nine projects (86 percent agreement)., With twenty-three identical project classifications (79 percent agreement), this figure is just slightly lower for informant 2,[2] indicating relatively high interrater agreement.

Having populated the exploitative and exploratory groups, we examined intergroup mean differences by means of Mann-Whitney tests, also known as Wilcoxon rank-sum tests (Wilcoxon 1945; Mann and Whitney 1947). This test procedure is a nonparametric equivalent of the independent samples t-test and enjoys greater robustness, as nonparametric statistics do not rely on distributional assumptions (Siegel and Castellan 1998). The test ranks all observations from both groups, sums the ranks for each group, and examines whether the actual rank sum of each is significantly different from the rank sum expected if all the observations would come from the same distribution. A significant z-statistic therefore indicates that observations from both groups come from distinct distributions and are significantly different.[3] Results from Mann-Whitney tests were largely comparable to t-tests with unequal variances.

Drawing on these quantitative insights, we went back to our rich qualitative data to substantiate and illustrate our findings.

EMPIRICAL FINDINGS

Project Overview

Before describing the sample of development projects, it is worth illustrating our distinction between exploitative and exploratory projects by sketching those two initiatives that occupy the extreme points of the continuum from exploitation to exploration.

The project considered to be most exploitative proposes to introduce a rolling replacement program for all hospital beds to avoid the continuing use of obsolete beds that could cause harm to patients and staff. This proposal is clearly exploitative in that it is targeted at existing services and user groups and builds on existing organizational capabilities. The project considered to be most exploratory proposes to pilot a novel service helping patients with terminal illnesses to live with their condition using music- and art-based therapies and systematic patient education. It is exploratory in that it seeks to create an entirely novel service for a patient group that often falls outside the scope of hospital organizations—an ambition requiring capabilities radically different from those currently possessed by organizational members. Table 6.1

provides an overview of the twenty-nine projects examined for the purposes of this study. The columns labeled "exploit." and "explor." represent the number of exploitative and exploratory projects falling into the respective category.

TABLE 6.1. Overview of Organizational Development Projects (N = 29)

Functional Area	exploit.	explor.	**Project Objective**	exploit.	explor.
Surgery	3	2	Clinical Service Development	2	8
Medicine	3	5	Admin. Service Development	3	4
Diagnostics	3	3	Capacity Expansion	6	1
Pharmacy	1	1	Equipment Acquisition	1	2
Corporate	4	4	Equipment Replacement	2	0
Total Investment / Cost	exploit.	explor.	**Board Decision**	exploit.	explor.
Up to 250.000 GBP	3	4	Accepted	9	9
250.000 to 1 Mio. GBP	4	4	Rejected	2	1
1 Mio. to 5 Mio. GBP	4	4	Returned	3	2
More than 5 Mio. GBP	3	3	Open	1	2

Notes. Organizational development projects presented to the investment board between January and December 2007.

Few systematic differences between exploitative and exploratory initiatives can be detected in terms of functional area, total cost, and the final board decision. That said, it becomes apparent that exploratory projects are typically related to the development of novel clinical or administrative services, while exploitative projects tend to pertain to capacity expansion or equipment replacement.

Material Dimension

Starting with the material dimension of the legitimating discourse, we examine differences and commonalities between exploitative and exploratory organizational development initiatives with regard to the strategic intent, the beneficiary groups, and the underlying project rationale. Table 6.2 presents the medians, means, and standard errors for both project groups along with results from nonparametric Mann-Whitney tests. Differences that are statistically significant at the 10 percent level or more are highlighted in bold print.

Strategic Intent. As for the strategic intent of each organizational development initiative, we examine the extent to which the respective legitimating discourse depicts the proposed project as a response to external threats and opportunities or internal weaknesses and strengths.

TABLE 6.2. Material Dimension of the Legitimating Discourse

	Exploitative Group			Exploratory Group			Mann-Whitney Test	
	median	*mean*	*s.e.*	*median*	*mean*	*s.e.*	*z-statistic*	*p-value*
Strategic Intent								
Threat	1.500	1.250	(0.271)	1.000	1.500	(0.335)	-0.244	(0.807)
Opportunity	**0.750**	**1.143**	(0.361)	**2.000**	**2.133**	(0.353)	**-1.904** *	(0.057)
Weakness	4.500	4.357	(0.161)	4.000	3.767	(0.334)	1.030	(0.303)
Strength	1.500	1.536	(0.380)	0.500	1.267	(0.384)	0.613	(0.540)
Beneficiary Group								
Patient	4.250	4.036	(0.231)	4.000	3.533	(0.418)	0.422	(0.673)
Staff	**2.750**	**2.643**	(0.394)	**1.500**	**1.433**	(0.334)	**2.291** **	(0.022)
Organization	3.500	3.786	(0.179)	4.000	3.933	(0.194)	-0.785	(0.432)
Community	**1.000**	**1.107**	(0.252)	**2.500**	**1.967**	(0.350)	**-1.867** *	(0.062)
Project Rationale								
Economic	2.500	2.250	(0.388)	3.500	3.100	(0.346)	-1.631	(0.103)
Strategic	2.750	2.857	(0.294)	3.500	3.067	(0.308)	-0.532	(0.595)
Clinical	3.000	2.857	(0.269)	3.000	2.600	(0.346)	0.378	(0.705)
Isomorphic	4.000	3.893	(0.268)	4.000	3.233	(0.365)	1.331	(0.183)

Notes. Data: N = 29 (14 exploitative and 15 exploratory). Scales: All variables are measured on six-point Likert-type scales from "not used" to "very important." Mann-Whitney two-sample non-parametric test statistic. *** $p<0.01$; ** $p<0.05$; * $p<0.10$.

Table 6.2 reveals that initiators of exploitative and exploratory projects share the fact that they place the greatest discursive emphasis on internal weaknesses. This finding resonates strongly with previous observations in the public sector. Borins (2000), for instance, finds that the majority of innovation projects in public-sector organizations are driven by internal problems or crises. This also suggests a rather reactive strategic stance, which relies less on the early identification of external opportunities and threats than on addressing critical issues, only once their consequences have materialized at organizational level. This is also reflected in the arguments used to justify the introduction of a proactive service for hospital inpatients with diabetes as a secondary condition:

> The current service is inadequate. The input for inpatients is limited and is provided in a reactive way once problems are identified. An enhanced team will work pro-actively and seek out inpatients with diabetes to ensure their control is not compromised whilst in hospital.

Similarly, it becomes apparent that initiators of exploitative and exploratory projects attach little discursive importance to describing environmental forces—be they opportunities or threats—as a key motivator for their proposal. This observation appears to attest to a rather inward-looking organizational learning and strategizing process. One physician initiating a highly exploratory clinical service development describes his experience as follows:

> I was trying to write the business plan, and about 18 months to two years ago, we got to a point where I knew that Hospital A and Hospital B were going to take activity from us, if we would not take action. All my contacts were telling me the same thing, so I decided that because all my anxiety had fallen on deaf ears, I was going to write a business plan on my own and said: "Look, these are the threats. This is the answer, over to you." They were: "Yes. Yes. Good idea. We must do something" but nothing ever happened . . . they didn't believe there was this threat. (interview with a physician at "Urban" on August 13, 2007)

As for possible differences, we expect the discursive emphasis on external threats and opportunities to be greater for exploratory projects than for exploitative projects. This rests on the observation that organizational exploration consists in the discovery of new possibilities (March 1991), a process that is likely to be inspired by wider trends in the organizational environment. Exploitative projects, however, focus on refining existing certainties (He and Wong 2004), and as such appear more inclined to be driven by internal weaknesses. In line with this expectation, we find initiators of exploratory initiatives to place a stronger rhetorical emphasis on external factors, while initiators of exploitative projects tend to highlight the contribution to addressing internal weaknesses or building on internal strengths. However, the only difference that is statistically significant pertains to the extent to which the strategic intent of a particular initiative is highlighted to consist in taking advantage of an external opportunity. Such discursive emphasis on external opportunities is nicely illustrated by the legitimating account associated with the exploratory proposal associated with a highly innovative intraoperative MRI (iMRI) scanner:

> This would be one of the first iMRI in the UK and would thus enhance our position nationally. There are currently up to 5 iMRI services in Europe and 10 in North America. The facility of iMRI would thus allow us to attract supra-regional referrals and private income.

These insights lead to a first proposition regarding differences in the discursive legitimation strategies associated with exploratory and exploitative initiatives.

> Proposition 1: The more exploratory a project, the more likely its initiators will be to highlight factors external to their organization as part of their legitimating discourse.

Beneficiary Groups. We go on to examine the respective emphasis of legitimating discourses on distinct groups of beneficiaries. Based on a preliminary analysis of the data, we distinguish between four recurring beneficiary groups. These are customers or patients, staff members, the organization as a whole, as well as the wider community the organization is embedded in.

Table 6.2 uncovers substantial differences in the discursive emphasis on these beneficiary groups as part of the legitimating discourses associated with exploitative and exploratory projects. This is reinforced by the significant Hotelling's T-squared test against the null hypothesis that the means for the four beneficiary groups are equal across the exploitative and the exploratory group ($F\,(4, 24) = 3.649, p = 0.018$).

More specifically, we find initiators of exploitative initiatives to place greater discursive emphasis on beneficiary groups in close proximity to the proposed initiative. These include in particular patients and staff members. The legitimating discourses associated with exploratory initiatives, however, reveal a greater emphasis on benefits for the entire organization and the wider community. Differences reach statistical significance with regard to the accent placed on benefits for staff members and for the local community. Exploitative projects are typically concerned with refining existing services rather than with introducing radical structural changes. Their benefits are thus more likely to occur locally. The exploitative proposal to introduce a single-sign-on system, which allows clinical staff to access all IT applications with a single password, is a case in point supporting the particular reliance on local benefits.

> This proposal will increase the ease of access to critical IT applications for clinicians. It will drastically reduce the time it takes clinicians to move between applications whilst treating patients, thereby realizing potential time savings of up to two hours per clinician per day.

The observation that exploratory initiatives tend to highlight a wider and more distant set of beneficiary groups is illustrated by the example of an exploratory epilepsy service, which offers a range of benefits particularly to the wider community:

> This venture would be beneficial to the whole health community, including primary, secondary and social care.

Overall, though, initiators of organizational development projects still place relatively little emphasis on depicting the benefits likely to occur outside organizational boundaries, particularly in the local community. This reflects persistent challenges in the public health care arena to cross the boundaries between secondary, primary, and social care, caused not least by missing economic incentives and distinct professional identities (Ferlie et al. 2005). A clinician closely involved in the aforementioned epilepsy initiative describes this fundamental structural problem as follows:

> It's much cheaper to have less critically ill patients in the community . . . but the community don't want them, because they save money by having them in a hospital. So you have this idiotic conflict that patients are sitting around in hospitals, costing large amounts of money, although they shouldn't be in this place. [. . .] There is no mechanism to negotiate the money between the health care budget and the social services budget. You know money goes into different pockets and they don't talk to each other. So it has to be excluded [from the proposal], but that's frustrating because we can see that there are financial benefits to be reaped outside of that narrow perspective. (interview with a physician at "Urban" on July 26, 2007)

Despite these health-care-specific institutional constraints, our findings suggest that there might be systematic differences between exploitative and exploratory projects with regard to the discursive emphasis placed on various beneficiary groups. Our second proposition seeks to capture this expectation.

> Proposition 2: The more exploratory a project, the more likely its initiators will be to highlight a broader set of beneficiaries as part of their legitimating discourse.

Project Rationale. Preliminary analyses revealed four dominant project rationales to occur recurrently in legitimating discourses. Economic rationales are present when cost-benefit arguments are advanced in favor of a particular initiative. Strategic rationales play a role when arguments evolve issues of competitive advantage and market positioning. Clinical rationales pertain to arguments related to improving patient outcomes or experiences. Isomorphic rationales, finally, evolve around arguments related to the perceived need of complying with established practices in the industry or regulatory norms imposed by central authorities.

Interestingly, we observe that the project rationale most strongly emphasized by initiators of exploratory and exploitative projects is isomorphic in nature. What appears to be at issue here is less mimetic isomorphism, which consists in imitating practices successfully established in other organizations (DiMaggio and Powell 1983), than coercive isomorphism. The latter consists in the need to comply with some practice imposed by an organization with notable authority. In the context of this study, central government as well as regulatory and audit bodies are in the position to exert pressure on the focal organization to meet certain standards. Given the compulsory nature of such regulatory norms, legitimating accounts tend to evoke coercive pressures to create a perception of urgency and inevitability. Such reference to coercive pressures is a particularly salient feature of the legitimating discourse associated with a modernization proposal of the nuclear medicine department:

> The gamma cameras are old, frequently failing and overdue for replacement. Failure to replace the old equipment is likely to cause cancellation of examinations, lengthening of waiting lists, thereby leading to an inability to meet important national targets such as the cancer pathway 18 week wait and various NICE recommendations. The nuclear medicine service at "Urban" is now rapidly losing its status within the nuclear medicine fraternity as leading edge.

Intergroup differences, though, appear to be less pronounced. This is underlined not least by the statistically insignificant Hotelling's T-squared test statistic (F (4, 24) = 1.007, p = 0.423). Similarly, Mann-Whitney tests fail to detect substantial differences at the 10 percent level for all four types of project rationale considered. That said, means and medians appear to somewhat support the idea that initiators of exploratory organizational development projects place greater emphasis on economic and strategic rationales than initiators of exploitative development projects. A number of examples, among which the proposal to develop a highly exploratory patient-level cost-accounting system, substantiate this point:

> This is to support the changing information needs of the Trust and to ensure that the Trust can use patient-level cost and coding information to identify opportunities for improvement and to deliver financial benefits. Externally, it is to allow the Trust to continue leading best practice in these two areas.

Although our analyses did not reveal any statistically significant differences, our anecdotal observations create a plausible case for our third proposition.

> Proposition 3: The more exploratory a project, the more likely its initiators will be to emphasize economic and strategic rationales as part of their legitimating discourse.

Symbolic Dimension

Turning to the symbolic dimension of the legitimating discourse, we seek to identify intergroup differences and commonalities with regard to persuasive appeal, theorization of change, and legitimacy type. Table 6.3 depicts the statistical results of these group comparisons. Again, statistically significant differences are highlighted in bold print.

TABLE 6.3. Symbolic Dimension of the Legitimating Discourse

	Exploitative Group			Exploratory Group			Mann-Whitney Test	
	median	*mean*	*s.e.*	*median*	*mean*	*s.e.*	*z-statistic*	*p-value*
Persuasive Appeal								
Pathos	2.250	2.321	(0.290)	2.000	2.067	(0.396)	0.421	(0.674)
Ethos	**3.250**	**2.786**	(0.290)	**1.500**	**1.733**	(0.308)	**2.561** ***	(0.010)
Logos	4.500	4.357	(0.110)	4.500	4.133	(0.236)	0.023	(0.981)
Change Theorization								
Ontological	2.500	2.286	(0.261)	2.000	1.700	(0.253)	1.633	(0.102)
Historical	2.000	1.679	(0.321)	1.500	1.467	(0.282)	0.421	(0.674)
Teleological	**4.500**	**4.250**	(0.180)	**3.500**	**3.433**	(0.334)	**1.843** *	(0.065)
Cosmological	**1.000**	**1.321**	(0.280)	**2.000**	**2.033**	(0.291)	**-1.833** *	(0.067)
Value-based	1.750	1.964	(0.333)	2.000	2.200	(0.292)	-0.486	(0.627)
Legitimacy Type								
Pragmatic	3.250	2.929	(0.282)	3.500	3.533	(0.260)	-1.557	(0.120)
Moral	2.500	2.643	(0.357)	2.500	2.433	(0.402)	0.419	(0.675)
Cognitive	4.500	4.250	(0.180)	3.500	3.433	(0.334)	0.780	(0.436)

Notes. Data: N = 29 (14 exploitative and 15 exploratory). Scales: All variables are measured on six-point Likert-type scales from "not used" to "very important." Mann-Whitney two-sample non-parametric test statistic. *** $p<0.01$; ** $p<0.05$; * $p<0.10$.

Persuasive Appeal. Classical rhetorical theory (Aristotle 1991) distinguishes among three types of justification or persuasive appeals. Pathos appeals are targeted at the audience's emotions and elicit strong, yet rather temporary, reactions. Ethos justifications seek to create perceptions of moral and ethical rightness, which often results in lasting moral endorsement of a particular subject. Logos appeals pertain to reason and seek to convince the audience of the efficiency or effectiveness of a particular course of action (Green 2004).

Table 6.3 shows that logos appeals constitute the dominant form of persuasion used by initiators of both exploitative and exploratory projects. Such logos justifications seek to link new actions to effective outcomes (Green 2004), and thus fit well with the evidence-based logic dominating the health care field (Dopson and Fitzgerald 2005). Although logos appeals can be found in nearly every legitimating account, its importance is particularly well illustrated by the following argument in support of the proposal for a diabetic foot clinic to prevent amputations among diabetic patients.

A study in the U.S. demonstrated that the presence of a Limb Preservation Service was associated with an 82% reduction in amputations over 5 years, at a time when diagnosed diabetes prevalence increased by 48%. [. . .] A brief cross-sectional review by the community diabetologist has shown that a high proportion (55.7%) of the patients have poor glucose control (8.0+%), at a level likely to reduce healing times thereby increasing cost/demand and likelihood of hospitalization as well as reducing quality of life for the individual patient.

That said, results for Hotelling's T-squared test provide a first indication that exploratory and exploitative projects also differ in their discursive emphasis on specific types of persuasive appeal ($F\,(3, 25) = 2.903, p = 0.055$). In particular, we find ethos pleas to be much more pronounced in the legitimating discourses linked to exploitative than exploratory projects. This finding appears plausible when considering that the exploration of uncharted territories is seldom driven by moral obligation than by strategic opportunity. Conversely, exploitative initiatives, especially in health care contexts, frequently constitute a response to a perceived moral imperative to improve services for patients. The legitimating account associated with an exploitative proposal meant to develop age-adequate facilities for teenage cancer patients substantiates this idea:

Patients over the age of 16 receive their care in the adult ward, where the majority of patients are elderly. These patients in particular miss out on the benefits afforded to children such as facilities for parents to stay, and access to educational facilities, and activities.

We therefore advance our fourth proposition:

Proposition 4: The more exploratory a project, the less likely its initiators will be to engage in ethos appeals as part of their legitimating discourse.

Theorization of Change. Suddaby and Greenwood (2005) uncover that legitimating discourses differ in their theorizations of change, which fall into five classes. Ontological rhetoric depicts change as a result of the inherent compatibility of incompatibility of several entities. Historical justifications present change as a natural, evolutionary progression from the past. Teleological persuasion evokes a perception of change as a necessary step toward achieving some higher objective or grand vision, even if this requires a break with the past. Cosmological theorizations explain change as an inevitable response to some external force or evolution, while value-based theorizations account for change by relating a particular course of action to accepted moral values.

Table 6.3 reveals that teleological theorizations of change play a particularly important role in the legitimating discourses associated with both exploitative and exploratory projects. As such initiators highlight the extent to which their respective project contributes to reaching some final goal or vision (Suddaby and Greenwood 2005). In the health care arena, patient-centered care constitutes such grand vision. As such, justifications in the health care arena often present a particular initiative as contributing to this objective. At the same time, they depart from Suddaby and Greenwood's (2005) ideal type of teleological theorization, as these accounts often advocate incremental rather than radical change. Such teleological theorization is central to the proposal to establish a novel stand-alone facility:

> We are convinced that the development of a stand-alone facility fully integrated with the development of related services, would allow "Urban" to develop the service it wants to—a world class clinical and research unit, leading the way in the UK and Europe in its care across all age groups.

With regard to possible differences in the theorizations of change advanced by proponents of exploitative and exploratory initiatives, Hotelling's T-squared test fails to reject the null hypothesis that the exploratory and exploitative initiatives have identical means with regard to their emphasis on the five theorization types (F (5, 23) = 1.629, p = 0.192). If present at all, intergroup differences are thus likely to be more subtle and only weakly significant. Consequently, Mann-Whitney tests reveal two intergroup differences, which are significant at the 10 percent level.

The first difference pertains to the emphasis placed on teleological theorizations, which appear to be more pronounced in the legitimating narratives related to exploitative projects. As the latter seek to refine existing products, services, and processes, they appear more susceptible to arguments proposing a progression toward some final goal or vision.

The second difference relates to the extent to which the legitimating discourse stresses cosmological theorizations. Cosmological justifications depict the proposed initiative as a response to environmental forces or external trends, which are beyond the immediate agency of the focal actor (Suddaby and Greenwood 2005). Since exploratory initiatives move the organization into uncharted waters, their legitimating discourses appear more likely to rely on outward-looking theorizations of change. This is strikingly illustrated by the legitimating account related to the introduction of a marketing department, which is a highly exploratory undertaking in a hospital context:

> Patient choice at referral was introduced in December 2005. [. . .] 20% of patients surveyed by the Trust indicated that low infection rates would influence them in choosing a hospital. We therefore need to manage messages such as this carefully, differentiating services with no or low infection rates. Although marketing is a new concept for the NHS, a marketing expertise is required to manage such complex messages in a structured and effective way. If we fail to manage this issue proactively in the near future, patients now have the mechanisms and information to choose another provider.

While our empirical findings are not unambiguous, we expect initiators of exploratory projects to rely more strongly on outward- and forward-looking theorizations of change. We thus posit the following as our fifth proposition:

> Proposition 5: The more exploratory a project, the more likely its initiators will be to emphasize outward- and forward-looking theorizations of change as part of their legitimating discourse.

Legitimacy Type. We follow Suchman (1995) in distinguishing among pragmatic, moral, and cognitive legitimacy. Pragmatic legitimacy rests on the self-interested calculations of a specific audience, which concludes that it is in its own interest to support a particular entity. Moral legitimacy is driven less by the self-interests of a particular audience than by a general perception that the actions of a particular entity can be judged as morally the "right" thing to do within a specific value system. Finally, cognitive legitimacy is not the result of either self-interests or moral evaluation, but based on cognitive processes according to which a particular entity is taken-for-granted, that is naturally accepted as necessary or inevitable (Suchman 1995).

Results from Hotelling's T-squared test suggest that there are significant intergroup differences in their respective reliance on distinct legitimacy types (F (3, 25) = 3.277, p = 0.038). Individual differences are most pronounced with regard to pragmatic legitimacy, which appears to be of greater importance in exploratory discourses. While this difference is weakly significant using a two-sample t-test, the Mann-Whitney test statistic just fails to reject the null hypothesis at the 10 percent level. That said, theoretical arguments developed by Green (2004) suggest that novel and potentially contested ideas are primarily in need of pragmatic legitimacy, while moral and cognitive legitimacy become central in later institutionalization stages. Given the greater novelty associated with exploratory projects, we would expect their legitimating discourses to demonstrate a greater emphasis on pragmatic legitimacy. There is some anecdotal evidence in our data, stemming from the aforementioned patient-level costing project, in support of this idea.

> We want to develop our costing and coding teams to allow us to improve the quality and also the accessibility of this information. We also want to be able to use it to identify variations in performance, areas for improvement and therefore deliver these financial benefits to the organization.

Despite the absence of any supporting statistical evidence at this stage, we suggest the following proposition:

> Proposition 6: The more exploratory a project, the more likely its initiators will be to seek initially pragmatic rather than moral or cognitive legitimacy through their legitimating discourse.

CONCLUSION

Previous research has highlighted substantial variation in rhetorical strategies across distinct stakeholder groups (Heracleous and Barrett 2001), interest groups (Suddaby and Greenwood 2005), and diffusion stages (Green 2004; Green, Li, and Nohria 2009). Since little is still known about potential differences in rhetorical strategies across initiatives with distinct types of initiatives (Green 2004), we sought to compare the rhetorical strategies of legitimation used by initiators of organizational exploitation and exploration initiatives. Our study, though exploratory in nature and relatively small in scale, yielded several interesting findings to the following questions: What are the rhetorical legitimation strategies used by initiators of organizational development projects to gain local validation? To what extent do such legitimating accounts differ among exploitative and exploratory initiatives? What is the nature of these differences? Are there dominant discursive features, which hold for all subjects of legitimation independent of whether they contribute to organizational exploitation or exploration?

First, this study revealed a number of commonalities in the legitimating discourses used by agents of exploitative and exploratory organizational development initiatives. These include the strong discursive emphasis placed on internal weaknesses, local benefits, coercive isomorphism, logos appeals, and teleological theorizations of change. Second, we uncovered several material differences in the rhetorical strategies of legitimation associated with exploitative and exploratory projects. Most notably, we found initiators of exploratory projects to place greater discursive emphasis on strategic factors external to their organization as well as on a broader group of beneficiaries. Third, this study pointed to some notable symbolic differences in the discourses of legitimation advanced by initiators of exploitative and exploratory projects. In particular, the rhetorical strategies of legitimation linked to exploratory initiatives demonstrated a significantly lower reliance on ethos appeals and to emphasize distinct theorizations of change.

These findings contribute not least to the literature on organizational exploration and exploitation in the fields of organizational learning and strategic management. Most notably, this study demonstrated that a discursive perspective offers novel insights into the internal dynamics of exploration and exploitation. It advances in particular our understanding of the skillful tailoring of rhetorical strategies by initiators of exploratory and exploitative projects seeking legitimacy for their initiative. These insights are highly complementary to those hitherto gained through simulation and survey studies, which still constitute the dominant methodological techniques in research on exploration and exploitation.

Overall, we believe that our chapter provides a good first step toward building a discursive perspective on organizational exploration and exploitation. However, it is clearly an exploratory study constrained not least by the relatively small dataset at hand. Furthermore, it shares with other single case studies its potentially limited generalizability, as our research is specific to the idiosyncrasies of the English public hospital sector. Further research is thus clearly required, for which our six theoretical propositions might serve as a useful starting point.

This work will not only examine a larger set of project proposals over time but will also draw more intensively on an wider array of texts such as interviews and decision-making meetings. As for the latter, future research could focus on the genres at work. By examining genres, or socially recognized communicative actions (Orlikowski and Yates 1994; Yates and Orlikowski 2002) inherent in evaluation committee meetings, further work could pay closer attention to the context within which the texts are discussed and evaluated. For example, the roles other agents play in the process and the timing and location of the communications, the actual sequence of discursive moves, and the implications genres have for power relations in their enactment (Levina and Orlikowski 2009). Moreover, future research might wish to examine how micro and macro discourses are interrelated. One promising avenue toward this end could consist in considering the role of changing institutional logics within which the legitimating discourses related to specific initiatives are embedded in (Ruef and Scott 1998; Suddaby and Greenwood 2005). The current shift from a "finance-centered" to a "patient-centered" logic in English public health care might serve as a suitable exemplar. Finally, while our study focuses on intraorganizational initiatives, the insights and findings of our work can also be useful in an interorganizational sense.

Future studies examining any of these suggested lines of inquiry will be vital to further developing a rhetorical perspective on the legitimation of organizational exploration and exploitation initiatives.

APPENDIX: ITEMS FOR EXPLORATION AND EXPLOITATION ORIENTATION[4]

Exploration Orientation

(1) This investment project seeks to create an entirely novel service, product, or process.
(2) This investment project seeks to meet the needs of an entirely novel group of service users.
(3) This investment project seeks to develop entirely novel organizational capabilities or knowledge.

Exploitation Orientation

(1) This investment project seeks to improve an already existing service, product, or process.
(2) This investment project seeks to meet the needs of an existing group of service users.
(3) This investment project seeks to build on existing organizational capabilities or knowledge.

NOTES

We would like to thank the hospital organization "Urban" and all staff members involved in this study for the time and energy they invested in supporting our research. We are particularly grateful to the head of planning at "Urban" for facilitating and accompanying this study. This chapter has also benefited much from the excellent research assistance provided by Jack Tunstall and Zheng Yao. Last, we would like to acknowledge the financial support of the Economic and Social Research Council (ESRC Award Number: PTA-031-2006-00317) and St. Catharine's College, Cambridge.

1. We relied primarily on data from the written briefing notes and full proposals, which have the considerable advantage of being directly comparable. That said, we used data from our interviews and from the observed investment board meetings for triangulation and contextualization.

2. Disagreement was most pronounced for projects close to the center of the continuum from exploitation to exploration.

3. As we conduct twenty-three Mann-Whitney tests, we expect to find at least one test statistic that is significant at the 5 percent level purely by chance.

4. All items were measured on a five-point scale, anchored by 1 = strongly disagree and 7 = strongly agree.

REFERENCES

Alvesson, M., and D. Kärreman. 2000a. Taking the Linguistic Turn in Organizational Research: Challenges, Responses, Consequences. *Journal of Applied Behavioral Science* 36: 136–58.

Alvesson, M., and D. Kärreman. 2000b. Varieties of Discourse: On the Study of Organizations through Discourse Analysis. *Human Relations* 53: 1125–49.

Aristotle. 1991. *On Rhetoric*. G. A. Kennedy, trans. New York: Oxford University Press.

Ashforth, B. E., and B. W. Gibbs. 1990. The Double-edge of Organizational Legitimation. *Organization Science* 1: 177–94.

Berger, P. L., and T. Luckmann. 1966. *The Social Construction of Reality: A Treatise in the Sociology of Knowledge*. New York: Anchor-Doubleday.

Borins, S. 2000. Loose Cannons and Rule Breakers, or Enterprising Leaders? Some Evidence about Innovative Public Managers. *Public Administration Review* 60: 498–507.

Brown, A. D. 1998. Narrative, Politics and Legitimacy in an IT Implementation. *Journal of Management Studies* 35: 35–58.

Chakrabarti, A. K. 1974. The Role of Champion in Product Innovation. *California Management Review* 17: 58–62.

Cohen, M. D., J. G. March, and J. P. Olsen. 1972. A Garbage Can Model of Organizational Choice. *Administrative Science Quarterly* 17: 1–25.

Creed, D., M. A. Scully, and J. R. Austin. 2002. Clothes Make the Person? The Tailoring of Legitimating Accounts and the Social Construction of Identity. *Organization Science* 13: 475–96.

Daft, R. L., and J. C. Wiginton. 1979. Language and Organization. *Academy of Management Review* 4: 179–91.

Deephouse, D. L., and S. M. Carter. 2005. An Examination of Differences between Organizational Legitimacy and Organizational Reputation. *Journal of Management Studies* 42: 329–60.

Deephouse, D. L., and M. C. Suchman. 2008. Legitimacy in Organizational Institutionalism. In *The SAGE Handbook of Organizational Institutionalism*, eds. R. Greenwood, C. Oliver, R. Suddaby, and K. Sahlin-Andersson, 49–77. London: SAGE Publications.

DiMaggio, P. J., and W. W. Powell. 1983. The Iron Cage Revisited: Institutional Isomorphism and Collective Rationality in Organizational Fields. *American Sociological Review* 48: 147–60.

Dopson, S., and L. Fitzgerald. 2005. *Knowledge to Action: Evidence-based Health Care in Context*. Oxford: Oxford University Press.

Durand, R., and J. McGuire. 2005. Legitimating Agencies in the Face of Selection: The Case of AACSB. *Organization Studies* 26: 165–96.

Fairclough, N. 1995. *Critical Discourse Analysis: The Critical Study of Language*. London: Longman.

Ferlie, E., L. Fritzgerald, M. Wood, and C. Hawkins. 2005. The Nonspread of Innovations: The Mediating Role of Professionals. *Academy of Management Journal* 48: 117–34.

Gamson, W. A., and D. S. Meyer. 1996. Framing Political Opportunity. In *Comparative Perspectives on Social Movements: Political Opportunities, Mobilizing Structures, and Cultural Framings*, eds. D. McAdam, J. D. McCarthy, and M. N. Zald, 275–90.

Gill, A. M., and K. Whedbee. 1997. Rhetoric. In *Discourse Studies: A Multidisciplinary Introduction*, ed. T. A. van Dijk, 157–83. Beverly Hills: SAGE Publications.

Green, S. E. 2004. A Rhetorical Theory of Diffusion. *Academy of Management Review* 29: 653–69.

Green, S. E., Y. Li, and N. Nohria. 2009. Suspended in Self-spun Webs of Significance: A Rhetorical Model of Institutionalization and Institutionally Embedded Agency. *Academy of Management Journal* 52: 11–36.

Gupta, A. K., K. Smith, and C. E. Shalley. 2006. The Interplay between Exploration and Exploitation. *Academy of Management Journal* 49: 693–706.

He, Z. L., and P. K. Wong. 2004. Exploration vs. Exploitation: An Empirical Test of the Ambidexterity Hypothesis. *Organization Science* 15: 481.

Heracleous, L., and M. Barrett. 2001. Organizational Change as Discourse: Communicative Actions and Deep Structures in the Context of IT Implementation. *Academy of Management Journal* 44: 755–78.

Hirschman, A. O. 1991. *The Rhetoric of Reaction*. Cambridge, MA: Harvard University Press.

Johnson, C., T. J. Dowd, and C. L. Ridgeway. 2006. Legitimacy as a Social Process. *Annual Review of Sociology* 32: 53–78.

Levina, Natalia, and W. Orlikowski. 2009. Understanding Shifting Power Relations within and across Organizations: A Critical Genre Analysis. *Academy of Management Journal* 52: forthcoming.

Levinthal, D. A., and J. G. March. 1993. The Myopia of Learning. *Strategic Management Journal* 14: 95–112.

Mann, H. B., and D. R. Whitney. 1947. On a Test of Whether One of Two Random Variables is Stochastically Larger Than the Other. *The Annals of Mathematical Statistics* 18: 50–60.

March, J. G. 1991. Exploration and Exploitation in Organizational Learning. *Organization Science* 2: 71–87.

March, J. G., and J. P. Olsen. 1976. *Ambiguity and Choice in Organizations*. Bergen: Universitetsforlaget.

McCloskey, D. N. 1983. The Rhetoric of Economics. *Journal of Economic Literature* 21: 481–517.

McCloskey, D. N. 1994. *Knowledge and Persuasion in Economics*. Cambridge: Cambridge University Press.

Merton, R. K. 1957. *Social Theory and Social Structure*. New York: Free Press.

Ministry of Health. 1948. *The New National Health Service*. London.

Oliver, C. 1991. Strategic Responses to Institutional Processes. *Academy of Management Review* 16: 145–79.

Orlikowski, W. J., and J. A. Yates. 1994. Genre Repertoire: The Structuring of Communicative Practices in Organizations. *Administrative Science Quarterly* 39: 541–74.

Parker, I. 1992. *Discourse Dynamics: Critical Analysis for Social and Individual Psychology*. London: Routledge.

Phillips, N., T. B. Lawrence, and C. Hardy. 2004. Discourse and Institutions. *Academy of Management Review* 29: 635–52.

Ricoeur, P. 1991. *From Text to Action*. Illionois: Northwestern University Press.

Ruef, M., and W. R. Scott. 1998. A Multidimensional Model of Organizational Legitimacy: Hospital Survival in Changing Institutional Environments. *Administrative Science Quarterly* 43: 877–79.

Siegel, S., and N. J. Castellan. 1988. *Nonparametric Statistics for the Behavioral Sciences*. New York: McGraw-Hill.

Suchman, M. C. 1995. Managing Legitimacy: Strategic and Institutional Approaches. *Academy of Management Review* 20: 571–71.

Suddaby, R., and R. Greenwood. 2005. Rhetorical Strategies of Legitimacy. *Administrative Science Quarterly* 50: 35–67.

Tushman, M. L., and C. A. O'Reilly. 1996. The Ambidextrous Organization. *California Management Review* 38: 8–30.

Vaara, E., and J. Tienari. 2008. A Discursive Perspective on Legitimation Strategies in Multinational Corporations. *Academy of Management Review* 33: 985–93.

Vaara, E., J. Tienari, and J. Laurila. 2006. Pulp and Paper Fiction: On the Discursive Legitimation of Global Industrial Restructuring. *Organization Studies* 27: 789–813.

Van Dijk, T. A., ed. 1997. *Discourse as Structure and Process*. SAGE Publications.

Van Leeuwen, T., and R. Wodak. 1999. Legitimizing Immigration Control: A Discourse-Historical Analysis. *Discourse Studies* 1: 83–118.

Weick, K. E. 1995. *Sensemaking in Organizations*. London: SAGE Publications.

Wilcoxon, F. 1945. Individual Comparisons by Ranking Methods. *Biometrics Bulletin* 1: 80–83.

Yates, J. A., and W. Orlikowski. 2002. Genre Systems: Structuring Interaction through Communicative Norms. *Journal of Business Communication* 39: 13–35.

7

Introducing British and Spanish Companies to Investors

Building the Corporate Image through the Chairman's Statement

Miguel F. Ruiz-Garrido, Inmaculada Fortanet-Gómez, and Juan Carlos Palmer-Silveira

> Building on these foundations, our challenge is to realize the potential of our portfolio in the coming years and make the most of the strategic positions we have established by being a first mover in key markets. We approach the future with confidence, in the belief that the scale of our operations worldwide and the progressive introduction of new producing assets will form the basis for both near-term performance and the generation of sustained shareholder value.
>
> —CHAIRMAN'S LETTER, BP ANNUAL REPORT AND ACCOUNTS 2003, 4

The corporate image is one of the most important assets of companies to attract investors and shareholders, and annual reports, especially the Chairman's Statement, a common initial section in this document, has become a suitable place to build this image, as shown in the quotation above. The annual report is nowadays one of the most important means of communication among the big companies and their shareholders and potential investors, on the one hand (Lord 2002, 368), and between the firms and the general public, on the other hand (Sydserff and Weetman 2002). Corporate annual reports are required by law by most governments, forming companies to provide shareholders with financial information (Palmer 2009). These reports must be made public so that any potential investor can either ask for a hard copy or download it from the Internet. They help market participants to make informed decisions, assuming they reflect the commercial reality of the reporting firms (Samuels 1993; Al-Razeen and Karbhari 2004).

Skulstad (2002, 50; 2006) claims that even though some chapters of annual reports are required by law, "there are important organizational and linguistic conventions which have developed gradually as a response to communicative purposes." Apart from providing financial data, today's annual reports fulfill an important role as a marketing tool and in the creation of the corporate image (Skulstad 2002, 51). This is mainly done by gaining the confidence of the reader through discourse elements that point at establishing a friendly and open relationship between the writer (company representative) and the reader (company stakeholder). The aim of this chapter is to analyze those discourse elements in Chairman's Statements from Spanish and British annual reports. We will first review the research published in the latest years on annual reports and about its sections. Then, publications on Chairman's Statements and their rhetorical elements will be scrutinized in order to select a model to carry out our analysis of a corpus of Spanish and British Chairman's Statements.

In recent years, there has been a number of studies about the annual reports as reviewed by Lord (2002, 367–89) or the recent two special issues devoted to this topic on the *Journal of Business Communication* (Penrose 2008): many of them have as an aim to give advice on how to write good reports (Cato 1995; Subramanian et al. 1993), whereas others analyze annual reports from a linguistic point of view (Schroeder and Gibson 1990; Myers 1996, 1999; Clackworthy 2000; Rutherford 2005). It is this latter perspective that is of interest for us in this chapter. As said before, the aim of the annual report is to serve as a way to establish some kind of communication between the writer, in this case, the corporate writer (the company), and the reader (the shareholder, the potential investor or the general public) who should get the best possible corporate image of the company (Sydserff and Weetman 2002).

Communication is established in the annual report in a linear way; there is an order of the different parts or sections. Though the financial information is shown from the beginning, a certain number of sections prepare the reader for the usually naked numbers, which appear in tables at the end of the document. These initial sections and their rhetoric have drawn the attention of several linguists. Hyland (1998, 224–45) examines metadiscourse in the CEO's Letter, since it "is widely seen as a promotional genre, designed to construct and convey a corporate image to stockholders." He sustains this "subgenre" within the annual report has strong persuasive characteristics that make it quite different to the other sections of the report. In order to prove his arguments, Hyland (1998) analyzes 137 CEO's Letters, paying special attention to metadiscourse. In his study, this researcher concludes by pointing out the use of personal pronouns as one of the most important devices to personalize discourse and start developing a relationship between reader and writer. However, the opening section of most annual reports is not the CEO's Letter, but the Chairman's Statement. Being in the initial position in most reports, the role of this section in starting a relationship of communication between writer and reader should be the most relevant in the corporate annual report. Several scholars have acknowledged the importance of the Chairman's Statement with studies of British/American companies and European companies' documents. Among these studies we would like to emphasize the ones with a clear international perspective published by Lampi (1992), Gillaerts (1996), Nickerson and De Groot (2005), Skulstad (1996, 2002, 2005), and Garzone (2004, 2005).

Lampi (1992, 127–43) analyzes the Chairman's Statements of annual reports of Finnish and British companies, both in English, since most Finnish companies publish English translations of their reports as part of their internationalization programs. Lampi compares six Finnish and six British companies' reports, and her variables are related to the use of metatext and discourse markers, the structure and the assumptions made about the knowledge of the text shared by the reader and the writer. Though this is presented only as a pilot study, Lampi shows relevant findings in this study. Her conclusions distinguish between two groups of annual reports: on the one hand, the British reports together with the reports of some big Finnish companies with well-established international operations; and a smaller group of Finnish companies that are just entering the global market. She assumes that "the more international the company, the more Anglo-American is the writing in its English Annual Report, and vice-versa, the less experience the company has in international operations, the more does its writing style differ from the Anglo-American pattern" (Lampi 1992, 140). The report written in a language such as Finnish is targeted for a national readership. When it is translated into English, there is a change in the target audience; therefore it should be not only a literal translation but also a rewriting of the text to adapt it to the cultural preferences of a wider, more heterogeneous market.

On the other hand, Gillaerts (1996) analyzes thirty Belgian Addresses to Shareholders identifying a five-move structure. In a similar way, Nickerson and De Groot (2005) analyze and compare ten British Chairman's Statements, ten British CEO's Statements, and ten Dutch-English CEO's Statements or Summaries. These authors compare their resulting six rhetorical moves[1] to Gillaerts's proposal, having some similarities (for example, the layout of a letter). However, Nickerson and De Groot go deeper into their analysis and propose twelve rhetorical strategies,[2] not necessarily bound to any of the moves.

From a slightly different perspective, Garzone (2004) compares two small subcorpora of CEO's Letters generated by Italian multinationals, on the one hand, and other foreign companies (a mixture of European and U.S. companies), on the other. The study is devoted to explaining their differences or similarities in terms of intercultural variables, referring to both the national culture of the parent company and its organizational culture. In her second work (2005), Garzone makes use of a larger corpus of CEO's Letters (derived from European and U.S. multinationals Annual Reports, without distinguishing their origin) with the purpose of verifying their generic integrity. Both studies focus mainly on discourse features, although she also makes reference to the structure of the document. Although Garzone (2005, 194) proposes an obligatory three-move structure, she only adds a brief explanation of the moves as well as mentions an incomplete list of other optional moves and some steps/strategies that can be part of the moves. For our current purposes, she fails to be systematic and thorough in her proposal, and its appropriate use cannot be guaranteed. In table 7.1 we summarize how those authors introduce those moves and strategies.

TABLE 7.1. Gillaerts (1996), Nickerson and De Groot (2005), and Garzone (2004, 2005) Analysis of Moves and Strategies

Gillaerts's 5-Move Structure	Nickerson and De Groot's Rhetorical 6-Move Structure	Nickerson and De Groot's 12 Rhetorical Strategies	Garzone's 3-Move Structure
General assessment Evidence (past) Looking ahead (future) Word of thanks Concluding	Context Financial performance past year Financial performance future Operations Strategy Credentials	Salutation (inclusion) Close (inclusion) Establishing credential Setting the economic scene Providing corporate financial context Providing specific financial performance details Summarizing operational performance in the past Providing detail on the Board Speculating on future performance Providing future objectives Emphasizing a strong workforce Communicating business strategy	Evaluating / commenting on company's performance, trends, and results in the relevant year Providing a narrative of salient facts (events, operations, figures) Illustrating outlook and priorities for the future

Garzone's proposals are not developed enough and consistently to be used in our research. Moreover, she does not relate the linguistic features analyzed to the use of certain rhetorical moves. On the other hand, although Nickerson and De Groot's structure, developed from that of Gillaerts's, shows a high level of complexity, it does not seem to be specific for Chairman's Statements. In contrast, Skulstad (1996, 2002, 2005, 2006) has focused much of her recent research only on the analysis of the Chairman's Statement. Skulstad's research (2002) deals with the rhetorical organization of the Chairman's Statements and on how relationships and identities are established in these documents. Dealing with the rhetorical organization, Skulstad (2002, 65–71; 2005, 75) establishes a move-step pattern, following Swales (1981), which she calls the Relationships and Confidence (RECON) model (see table 7.2).

Furthermore, as said before, Skulstad (2002, 107–21) devotes a chapter of her book to "Establishing Relationships and Identities in Chairman's Statements." In this chapter, she discusses the concepts of involvement and detachment and how these are expressed in the Chairman's Statements. Among the

TABLE 7.2. The RECON Model

MOVE 1: ESTABLISHING A RELATIONSHIP	
Optional Step A	Salutation
Optional Step B	Providing the background for the present scene
Step 1	Summary statement
Step 2	Providing figures describing company performance
Step 3	Selecting aspects of the past financial year
MOVE 2: MAINTAINING CONFIDENCE	
Step 1	Projecting the future by
Step 1A	• Announcing corporate strategies, policies, and objectives and/or
Step 1B	• Predicting the future/looking ahead
Optional Step C	Signaling honesty
Optional Step D	Providing reassurance
MOVE 3: REINFORCING THE RELATIONSHIP	
Step 1	Reviewing board changes (if any)
Step 2	Acknowledging credit to management and employees
Step 3	Closing statement of reassurance
Step 4	Signature

From Skulstad (2002, 71).

devices used to establish relationships and to define identities, this researcher points out the use of salutations similar to those of personal letters ("Dear shareholders"), the use of personal pronouns and their associated possessive adjectives, the introduction of subjective comments, the use of modals and semimodals with a heading function, and the interaction between language and image when photographs are combined with the text in Chairman's Statements. In her conclusion, Skulstad relates all the characteristics of this genre to its functions of establishing identities and relationships as a starting point as well as persuading the reader of the honesty and good work of the company and its employees.

From our point of view, Skulstad's work is the most specifically related to the Chairman's Statement. She proves its validity to analyze these documents and to serve as a framework for further discourse analysis of the elements of the statement. However, she fails to relate both parts of her research; that is, the rhetorical organization with the discourse elements used to establish identities and relationships in the Chairman's Statement. Moreover, she only carries out a preliminary study of the use of the personal pronouns and possessive adjectives in her corpus as elements of interaction between writer and reader. Our aim is to replicate her study with an updated corpus of Chairman's Statements (her corpus was published in 1992 and 1993, over fifteen years ago) in two languages, English and Spanish, paying special attention to the discourse elements used by the authors of these documents in order to establish a friendly and open relationship with the reader.

METHOD

A corpus of fifty Chairman's Statements was compiled by downloading annual reports from the companies' websites found in two Internet addresses, http://londonstockexchange.ar.wilink.com and www.bolsamadrid.es, where we were redirected to the companies' websites or directly to the document.

From the fifty Statements in the corpus, twenty-five belong to UK and twenty-five belong to Spanish companies' annual reports, in English and in Spanish, respectively. (See the appendix for a complete list of the corpus.)

One characteristic of annual reports, as already pointed out by previous research (see Berry 1997), is that there is not just one single author for the whole report, but several. Moreover, various writers may contribute through several revisions to the final version of the document. In addition, there are no specific guidelines on how annual reports should be written. For these reasons, it would seem logical to assume there should be a certain level of heterogeneity in the features of annual reports and their subgenres, even in companies from the same country.

As stated above, a discourse analysis was applied to our corpus. Firstly, we tried to identify the RECON model in the Chairman's Statements in the corpus, and within this structure, some of the discourse elements already identified by Skulstad:

1. The use of personal pronouns and their associated possessive adjectives in the different parts of the Chairman's Statement. Some authors have shown the relationship between the personal pronouns, mainly those of the first person, and the idea of power (see for example, Pennycook 1994, Hodge and Kress 1998, Íñigo-Mora 2004, Čubajevaitė 2006). Berry (1997, 177–88) had already found out that Chairman's Statements make a common use of the pronouns *we* and *I* with the objective of showing power to the readership. Garzone (2004, 2005) also makes clear references to the more frequent use of first-person plural pronouns and possessive adjectives in the foreign documents than in the Italian ones. In fact, she states that "the use of the first personal pronoun [. . .] seems to be aimed to establish a more 'person' corporate identity" (Garzone 2004, 336). In our research, we will observe the use of these pronouns and their associated possessive adjectives, in both Spanish and English, and the contexts where they are found.
2. The use of salutations and words addressing the target reader.
3. The use of personal expressions and comments, such as "I am sure" or "I would like to thank you," considered as stance markers attributed to the writer/author (Biber et al. 1999).

In order to find some of these features, the WordSmith Tools program was used. However, due to the heterogeneity of the texts, especially regarding length and order of the moves, most of the analysis had to be completed manually.

FINDINGS

Our first finding was that not all companies include the Chairman's Statement as part of their annual report, so additional reports had to be found to complete the corpus. Among those that include the Chairman's Statement, several varieties have been observed. Some Spanish companies tend to show a preference for the "Letter from the Chairman," with some associated characteristics, rather than the Chairman's Statement. On the other hand, some annual reports are introduced by the "Message from the Chairman of the Board of Directors," or there are two co-chairmen who share the same message. However, the most extraordinary example we have found is that of the report of the company Anglo American, which turns the Chairman's Statement into an interview.

Personal Pronouns and Their Associated Possessive Adjectives in the RECON Model

Before presenting the results, it should be pointed out that it was not easy to apply the RECON model to the Chairman's Statements in our corpus for several reasons. Although the three Moves seem to be clearly present in most of the texts, the order is not always the one presented in Skulstad's model. Moreover, very often the Moves are interlinked; that is, the author may start with Move 1, go on with Move 2 but then come back to Move 1, proceed to Move 3, and back to 2, or even to Move 1 again. Additionally, the information of some Steps seems only to be slightly different, and it is difficult to allocate in one or the other. This happens in Step 2 and 3 in Move 1; and in Step 1A and Step 1B in Move 2.

Finally, there are parts of the Chairman's Statements in our corpus that do not seem to fit in any of the steps proposed by Skulstad. These parts refer to social policies related to employee welfare, social benefits in the areas where the companies are located, and commitment to the environment. We have classified these as "Social Matters" and have taken into account that this Step can be found when describing the company performance during the year, belonging so to Move 1, or as a policy or objective for the following year, therefore as part of Move 2.

Another part in some Chairman's Statements that does not fit in the provided classification is a short description of the chapters or sections of the report. We have included this as a new Step in Move 3 as "Introduction of the Report," although it is not always located at the end of the Statement.

Apart from these concerns, there are two steps that are not relevant for our purpose in this part of the research, since they cannot include pronouns or possessive adjectives: Optional Step A in Move 1, "Salutation"; and Step 4 in Move 3, "Signature." We will analyze the use of these discourse elements further on. Considering all these factors, the RECON model was adapted, resulting in the following Move-Step scheme (see table 7.3).

Once established the structural model, table 7.4 summarizes the occurrences of the pronoun *we* in the different parts of the Chairman's Statement in English, and what would be the equivalent in Spanish, the pronoun *nosotros* or, since there is a specific form of the verb for first-person plural, also the use of this form.[3]

The tables presented in this section show the number of occurrences and the percentage they represent of the total amount of occurrences in the United Kingdom and Spanish Chairman's Statements.

Due to the excessive amount of data, it would not be appropriate to include here the number of occurrences of *we*, *nosotros*, and the use of the first-person

TABLE 7.3. Modified Version of the RECON Model

MOVE 1: ESTABLISHING A RELATIONSHIP	
Step 1	Providing the background for the present scene
Step 2	Summary statement
Step 3	Providing figures about the past financial year
Step 4	Social matters
MOVE 2: MAINTAINING CONFIDENCE	
Step 1	Projecting the future
Step 2	Providing reassurance
Step 3	Social matters
MOVE 3: REINFORCING THE RELATIONSHIP	
Step 1	Reviewing board changes (if any)
Step 2	Acknowledging credit to management and employees
Step 3	Closing statement of reassurance
Step 4	Introduction of the report

TABLE 7.4. "We" / "Nosotros" or Verb in First-Person Plural in the Chairman's Statements

	MOVE 1				**MOVE 2**			**MOVE 3**				**TOTAL**	**‰**
	S1	**S2**	**S3**	**S4**	**S1**	**S2**	**S3**	**S1**	**S2**	**S3**	**S4**		
UK ChS	26 7.9	25 7.6	94 28.4	22 6.6	57 17.2	40 12.1	9 2.7	18 5.4	12 3.6	26 7.9	2 0.6	331	13.7
Spain ChS	10 4.2	31 13.1	64 27	14 5.9	54 22.8	25 10.6	5 2.1	3 1.3	10 4.2	20 8.4	1 0.4	237	7.1
TOTAL	36 6.3	56 9.9	158 27.8	36 6.3	111 19.6	65 11.4	14 2.5	21 3.7	22 3.9	46 8.1	3 0.5	568	9.8

plural in Spanish in each text and section. However, a summarizing table such as the one presented above, as well as those presented below, do not clearly reflect the actual corpus. On the one hand, the length of the Chairman's Statement is very heterogeneous: the UK corpus ranges from 372 to 3,172 words, whereas the Spanish corpus moves from 483 to 2,724 words. Even though the longest Chairman's Statement is British, the average number of words is considerably higher for the Spanish documents (UK average: 966.24; Spanish average:

1,343.08 words per document). This applies to the length of the Moves and Steps, and consequently to the quantity of words, including pronouns and possessive adjectives in these parts. On the other hand, some of the occurrences found are sometimes distributed in all (or almost all) the documents, and some other times are found mainly in a few texts. For example, of the ninety-four occurrences of the pronoun *we* in Move 1, Step 3, it is found twenty-one times in the statement belonging to the UK report 25 (Unilever) and sixteen times in the statement of report 14 (British Land Company). In the rest of the statements the frequency of *we* in this section is not so outstanding.

If we compare now the data of the British and the Spanish statements, the most relevant result may be the overall difference in the frequency rate in the use of the pronouns *we* or *nosotros*, or the appropriate verbal form in Spanish. This frequency is almost double in the UK Chairman's Statements as compared to the Spanish ones. Regarding the steps where it is most often found, namely in Step 3 of Move 1 (providing figures about the past financial year), and in Step 1 of Move 2 (projecting the future), in the former, the frequency is similar in both languages (28.4 percent in the UK versus 27 percent in Spain), whereas the use in the Spanish statements is considerably higher in the latter (17.2 percent in the UK versus 22.8 percent in Spain). There are also remarkable differences in Move 1, Step 1 (providing the background for the present scene) and in Move 3, Step 1 (reviewing board changes), in which UK documents show a more frequent use of *we* (7.9 percent versus 4.2 percent and 5.4 percent versus 1.3 percent, respectively), and Move 1, Step 2 (summary statement), where it is Spanish statements in which the first-person plural is more often used (13.1 percent versus 7.6 percent). For example:

1. In 2003, *we* saw a continuing commitment to a fully transparent energy market . . . (Centrica, Move 1, Step 3)
2. El esfuerzo realizado en este terreno ha sido especialmente patente en España donde *hemos* incrementado en un 73,5% el número de accesos ADSL con que *contábamos* a finales de 2002, cerrando el ejercicio con 1.660.450 líneas de banda ancha. (Telefónica, Move 1, Step 3)

Next, we will deal with the use of the possessive adjective *our*, or *nuestro/s–nuestra/s* in Spanish.

As can be seen in table 7.5, the total number of occurrences of *our* is larger than the one observed when analyzing *we*, giving the idea that the corporate image provided by the use of the pronoun is not only supported but also co-created by the possessive adjective *our/nuestro/s–nuestra/s*. It can be observed that the greater percentage of appearance of both *we* and *our* concentrate in the same sections (Move 1, Step 3 and Move 2, Steps 1 and 2).

TABLE 7.5. "Our," "Nuestro/s–Nuestra/s" in the Chairman's Statements

	MOVE 1				MOVE 2			MOVE 3				TOTAL	‰
	S1	S2	S3	S4	S1	S2	S3	S1	S2	S3	S4		
UK ChS	25 6.2	37 9.1	153 37.6	19 4.7	59 14.5	40 9.9	4 1	10 2.5	28 6.9	28 6.9	3 0.7	406	16.8
Spain ChS	18 6.2	29 9.9	74 25.4	14 4.9	50 17.2	38 13.1	11 3.8	2 0.7	25 8.6	29 9.9	1 0.3	291	8.7
TOTAL	43 6.2	66 9.5	227 32.5	33 4.7	109 15.6	78 11.2	15 2.2	12 1.7	53 7.6	57 8.2	4 0.6	697	12.1

Comparing the British and the Spanish sources, there is a higher percentage of occurrences of *our/nuestro/s–nuestra/s* in Move 1, Step 3 (providing figures about the past financial year) in both British and Spanish statements, being the British number of occurrences over twice the Spanish one. However, in Move 2, Step 1 (projecting the future) and in Move 2, Step 2 (providing reassurance), the percentage is higher in Spanish statements (14.5 percent versus 17.2 percent, and 9.9 percent versus 13.1 percent, respectively). For example,

3. The Group balance sheet grew strongly from £25.4 billion to £32.2 billion, reflecting the success of *our* lending business . . . (Bradford and Bingley Plc, Move 1, Step 3)
4. Las tres cuartas partes de *nuestro* negocio corresponden a mercados que presentan sectores de crecimiento específicos que estamos en condiciones de aprovechar por *nuestra* capacidad de oferta y de ejecución de proyectos y por *nuestra* presencia internacional. (Indra, Move 2, Step 1)

In the third place, we will present the occurrences of *I/yo* and *my/mi*. In Spanish there is no use of the pronoun *yo* (*I*), so we have considered the use of the verbal form of first-person singular. Since they present a fairly reduced number, we provide the data of these pronouns and possessive adjectives together in table 7.6.

Though we have not distinguished between *I* and *my*, we can state that the pronouns and the corresponding form of the Spanish verb represent over 90 percent of the occurrences. There is a much lower frequency of the use of the first person in singular than in plural, with almost five out of six instances of plural per one of singular (85.8 percent and 14.2 percent, respectively). Even so, in both UK and Spanish Chairman's Statements some steps such as

TABLE 7.6. "I" / "Yo" and "My" / "Mi" and Verb in First-Person Singular in the Chairman's Statements

	MOVE 1				MOVE 2			MOVE 3				TOTAL	‰
	S1	S2	S3	S4	S1	S2	S3	S1	S2	S3	S4		
UK	21	8	7	11	2	3	2	21	30	16	2	123	5.1
ChS	17.1	6.5	5.7	9	1.6	2.4	1.6	17.1	24.4	13	1.6		
Spain	6	7	11	5	8	1	2	2	31	6	5	84	2.5
ChS	7.1	8.3	13.1	6	9.5	1.2	2.4	2.4	36.9	7.1	6		
TOTAL	27	15	18	16	10	4	4	23	61	24	7	209	3.6
	12.9	7.2	8.6	7.7	4.8	1.9	1.9	11	29.2	11.5	3.3		

Step 2 in Move 3 (acknowledging credit to management and employees) still account for a number of occurrences that doubles (or triplicates in Spanish statements) that of *we* and is similar to the occurrences of *our*.

Other steps that also show a more frequent use of the first-person singular are Step 1 in Move 1 (providing the background for the present scene) and Step 1 in Move 3 (reviewing board changes). All in all, Move 3 (reinforcing the relationship), which is not usually the longest, accumulates over 50 percent of the total number of instances of *I* and *my*. For example:

5. *I* would also like to thank them for their contribution to our progress (Land Securities, Move 3, Step 2)
6. Y no *quiero* terminar sin decir a tantas y tantas personas con las que *he convivido y trabajado* a lo largo de estos años, que *guardo* el mejor de los recuerdos y un gran agradecimiento por su compañía, su esfuerzo, . . . (Acciona, Move 3, Step 2)

The Use of Salutations and Words Addressing the Target Reader

As a complement to the analysis of the use of first-person pronouns, we have observed how other expressions are introduced in the text to address the readers directly, and so, to establish a relationship with them. To start with, it should be pointed out that most Statements in our corpus are hand signed[4] by the Chairman (seventeen UK, 68 percent, and twenty Spain, 80 percent), though others just include the name and may add the position or the date of the Chairman without a signature (five UK and five Spain, 20 percent in both subcorpus). There are three UK Chairman's Statements that do not include the signature or name. Moreover, many of the Chairman's Statements show characteristics of a different genre: the formal letter. For example, twenty-five of the samples analyzed, including twenty-two in the corpus of Spanish companies, start with the salutation "Dear shareholders" ("Estimado/s accionista/s," or a similar expression in Spanish). This shift to the epistolary genre is supported in the Spanish documents, as twenty documents include the word *letter* (*carta*) in the title given to the statements: *Carta del Presidente*. Most UK documents (twenty-four) also include a title in their documents. However, they mainly use the word *Statement* or *Message*, whereas the word *letter* appears in just two of them.

Additionally, one of the Chairman's Statements, that of the Annual Report of the company Pearson Plc, not only starts with "Dear fellow shareholders" but also makes frequent use of contractions all over the text, as well as personal anecdotes and informal language such as in the following sentence:

7. The past couple of years have been tough for many businesses, and some of ours have felt the chill. (Pearson Plc)

There seems to be a willingness by the companies to approach the reader in a friendly way in order to enhance their relationship with the company. Even so, as noted above, the Moves and Steps of the adapted RECON model are still present in these documents.

Another way to address the reader directly is by means of the pronoun *you* and the possessive adjective *your* (*usted*, second-person singular and plural of the verb, and *su/s*, referring to *usted/es*). Either one or the other, or frequently both, are found in twelve of the twenty-five UK Chairman's Statements and nineteen out of twenty-five of the Spanish statements, though there are not more than two or three occurrences per text. Skulstad (2002, 109) had already observed that *your* usually collocates with the nouns *company*, *Chairman*, *Board*, and *Directors*, which transmit to the readers the sense of being at their service. This is still valid for our corpus in English, though it should be complemented by other words, such as *investment*, *support*, *goodwill and commitment*, or the words found in Spanish, *aprobación*, *confianza*, *consideración*, which show the contribution of the reader to the company, and which are not mentioned by Skulstad.

You, on the other hand, is very rarely found in metatextual references "in which the reader is referred to other sections of the report," its main function according to Skulstad (2002, 109). However, on several occasions there is a clear willingness by the author to call the attention of the readers and involve them in the company's performance, not only by using the pronoun *you* but also by adding appositions next to it:

8. In stewarding the company for *you, its owners*, . . . (BP, Move 1, Step 2)
9. Finally, we thank *you, the shareholders*, for your continuing support of the company. (Reckitt Benckiser, Move 3, Step 3)
10. Espero seguir contando con la confianza y apoyo de todos *ustedes, señores accionistas*. (Grupo Santander, Move 3, Step 3)

Both *you* and *your*, *usted/es*, *su*, and the second-person form of the verb are found mainly in the first or last paragraphs of the Chairman's Statements, either in Steps 1 or 2 of Move 1; that is, providing the background for the present scene or summarizing the company performance; or in Steps 2 or 3 of Move 3, acknowledging credit to management and employees or closing statement of reassurance.

The Use of Personal Expressions and Comments

Also complementary to the use of the personal pronouns of first person, especially of first-person singular, is the introduction of personal thoughts and feelings, which can also help to establish a more confident and friendly relationship between the chairmen and the shareholders and potential investors of the company. In most of the statements it is common to find expressions such as:

11. As I take over as Chairman, I anticipate many opportunities . . . (Allied Domecq)
12. . . . both bring considerable experience and will, I am sure, make a significant contribution to the Board and the Company. (Reckitt Benckiser)
13. Es para mí una satisfacción presentar a nuestros accionistas el ejercicio 2003. (Abertis)
14. El ejercicio 2003 que tengo el gusto de presentarle en este Informe Anual, . . . (Iberdrola)

These expressions, as already noted about the use of *you* and *your* and before about the use of *I*, are mainly found at the beginning of the statement as an introduction to the background of the report, or at the end, in order to acknowledge credit to management or employees or to provide reassurance.

DISCUSSION AND CONCLUSION

The Chairman's Statement in Company Annual Reports has a very specific communicative purpose, namely to approach the readers, usually the shareholders, and gain their confidence. As well as the defined communicative purpose, the Chairman's Statement has several features that characterize it as a genre. As said above, there is no established pattern for the Chairman's Statement and that leads to a heterogeneity that can be found in the length of the whole document, as well as in the length of each of its sections.

Regarding its structure, it is possible to adapt Skulstad's RECON model to both UK and Spanish Chairman's Statements. However, new Steps have been found in comparison to the model provided by Skulstad, mainly information related to employees' welfare and social benefits for the community where the company is located and their commitment with the environment. This reflects a growing interest both by the companies and by their shareholders in these matters in recent years. Another new Step also found in a few statements is concerned with the introduction of the report. The Chairman's Statement is usually placed at the beginning of the report, and it may be a good section to explain what type of information is included and where. At the same time, by means of this introduction, the Chairman also shows involvement with the whole document and reinforces the corporate image in the company and his own leadership.

In relation to the linguistic elements that define the Chairman's Statement, we have pointed out those that are used in order to fulfill the main communicative purpose of this document; that is, to establish the relationship between writer and reader. Among them, the pronouns and possessive adjectives of the first person play an important role. The most frequent are *we* and *our*, the latter with a higher frequency than the former. Both are used in similar sections; that is, the corporate image they represent is mostly important when providing the figures of the past financial year and when presenting the plans for the next year.

As Pennycook (1994) points out, "'we' is always simultaneously inclusive [including writer and reader] and exclusive [excluding the reader], a pronoun of solidarity and of rejection, of inclusion and exclusion." In this way, *we* represents the company board of directors but also the whole company staff and the shareholders (potential readership of the report). There is a greater power if it is the power of a collectivity, and it has a greater force if it involves the reader.

The pronoun and possessive adjective of first-person singular is much less often used. The author presents himself as the Chairman, with all his authority, but also showing his personal feelings and opinions as an individual in the introduction of the Chairman's Statements, providing the background for the present situation of the company, when he has to inform about changes in the Board and to acknowledge credit to management and employees. The individual role of *I* in the Chairman's Statement suits that of personal correspondence. It is the writer who expresses feelings and opinions showing the magnanimity of his position and the opportunities this position offers to him, such as being grateful for the employees' good work. We think it is necessary to emphasize the relevance of the role of power implied by the use of certain pronouns. In fact, and this is an aspect that will be analyzed in further studies on the topic, the appearance of some marks implying power will help to understand the Chairman's Statements.

Other discourse elements help to create a good image of the company and to establish a good relationship with the reader, such as the use of the second-person pronoun and the possessive adjective. The latter is commonly accompanied by two types of expressions that are used either to show that the company is at the service of the reader in British documents ("your company/ Chairman/Board") or to show the contribution of the reader to the company both in British and Spanish statements ("your investment/support/goodwill and commitment," "su confianza/consideración"). *You* is mainly used to call the attention of the readers and is frequently followed by appositions (*owners, shareholders*), which draw their attention directly.

This pronoun and the possessive adjective, together with some other personal expressions and comments, are found in exactly the same steps as *I* and *my*, trying to establish a close relationship between the writer and the reader at the beginning and at the end of the Chairman's Statement.

Among the outstanding features of the linguistic style of this document, there are some elements in the Statements that seem to show a shift from a statement to a formal letter: handwritten signature in over 65 percent of the statements, and letter salutations (*Dear shareholders*) in most of the Spanish documents, where there is even a change in the title of this document. This variability in the salutations is quite consistent with Garzone's results (2005). Nevertheless, this change of genre to start the corporate annual report may be a tendency for the future in order to personalize even more the first communication between the company and the reader of the report. The main difference between the Chairman's Statements from British and Spanish companies' Annual Reports seems to be this tendency to change the Chairman's Statement into a Letter to the Shareholders, which has been found rather consistently in the whole corpus of Spanish documents. However, further research with a larger corpus seems necessary to corroborate this result.

We have appreciated some differences in the structure and language used in UK and Spanish Chairman's Statements, as well as in the layout. At the beginning of this article we quoted Lampi (1992), referring to the relationship between being more international and writing in a more Anglo-American style. From our results, that statement does not seem to be so clear. In fact, from our reading of the documents, we think that the reason for this may be that the international relations in Spain are biased toward Latin America rather than toward other countries. Therefore, those documents and their authors may keep a more Spanish-speaking countries' style, although further research is needed.

In conclusion, there seems to have been an evolution in the Chairman's Statements in the latest fifteen years; new steps have been added to the RECON model and others do not seem to be clear any longer. This may respond to new interests of the companies and of the shareholders. We have not only identified discourse elements that are used to establish a relationship between the Chairman as the main representative of the company and its shareholders and potential investors but have also observed the functions of these elements in the text and where they are mainly located.

In this article we have only analyzed the language and the implications of the use of certain words/expressions. However, image is becoming more and more important in Annual Reports, as a complement to language (Skulstad 2006, 96–102). Further research will analyze the role of image in relation to language, introducing multimodality in Chairman's Statements.

In an ever-globalizing business world, it would be interesting that companies all over the world could share some common characteristics in one of their most important public documents, the Annual Reports. Within these reports, the Chairman's Statement plays an important role in producing the right atmosphere for a good relationship with the current and prospective shareholders. The results of this research may be of interest to establish some guidelines on how Chairman's Statements should be organized and how discourse elements could be used in order to enhance the writer-reader relationship and to create the appropriate expectations in the reader who needs to understand and sympathize with a document so complex as the Annual Report.

APPENDIX: ANNUAL REPORTS CORPUS

BRITISH ANNUAL REPORTS	SPANISH ANNUAL REPORTS
1. CENTRICA PLC	1. ABERTIS
2. DAILY MAIL AND GENERA TRUST PLC	2. ACCIONA
3. EMAP	3. ACERINOX
4. LAND SECURITIES	4. ACS
5. LEGAL and GENERAL	5. ALTADIS
6. LLOYDS TSB GROUP	6. ARCELOR
7. MAN GROUP PLC	7. BANCO SABADELL
8. NORTHERN ROCK	8. ENAGÁS
9. PEARSON PLC	9. ENDESA
10. ALLIED DOMECQ	10. FERROVIAL
11. ANGLO AMERICAN	11. GAMESA
12. BAE SYSTEMS	12. GRUPO SANTANDER
13. BG GROUP	13. GRUPO BBVA
14. THE BRITISH LAND COMPANY PLC	14. IBERDROLA
15. BP	15. IBERIA
16. BRADFORD AND BINGLEY PLC	16. INDITEX
17. BT	17. INDRA
18. SCOTTISH AND NEWCASTLE	18. METROVACERSA
19. UNITED UTILITIES	19. NH HOTELS
20. WILLIAM HILL	20. RED ELÉCTRICA
21. WOLSELEY	21. REPSOL
22. REUTERS	22. SACYR VALLEHERMOSO
23. RECKITT BENCKISER	23. SOGECABLE
24. TOMKINS	24. TELEFÓNICA
25. UNILEVER	25. UNIÓN FENOSA

ACKNOWLEDGMENTS

This research has been funded by a grant from Generalitat Valenciana (GV05/116) and a grant from Universitat Jaume I–Fundació Caixa Castelló Bancaixa (P1.1A2005-10).

NOTES

1. By "rhetorical move" we mean "predictable patterns of organization" (Swales and Feak 1994, 10).

2. They talk about "strategy" as a synonym of "step," according to the general proposal of genre analysis theory (Swales 1990).

3. In tables 7.4, 7.5, and 7.6, the numbers dealing with the moves and steps show the number of occurrences and its percentage (%) concerning the total of occurrences. Only the final column presents the frequency per thousand words (‰) in relation to the total corpus.

4. The document may be just hand signed, though they tend to appear including the name, the position, and even the date.

REFERENCES

Al-Razeen, A., and Y. Karbhari. 2004. Annual Corporate Information: Importance and Use in Saudi Arabia. *Managerial Auditing Journal* 19: 117–33.

Berry, R. 1997. Pronouns and Power in Company Annual Reports. In *Applying Linguistics. Insights into Language in Education (ILEC)*, eds. V. Berry, B. Adamson, and W. Littlewood, 177–88. Hong Kong: The English Centre. The University of Hong Kong.

Biber, D., S. Johansson, G. Leech, S. Conrad, and E. Finegan. 1999. *Longman Grammar of Spoken and Written English.* Harlow, Essex: Longman.

Cato, S. 1995. The World's 10 Best and 10 Worst Annual Reports. *Chief Executive,* October, 107–39.

Clackworthy, S. 2000. The Value of Reporting in the Information Age. *Management Accounting* 78: 38–39.

Čubajevaitė, L. 2006. Cultural and Linguistic Differences in Using Personal Pronouns: Case of Lithuanian as a Foreign Language. *Kalbotyra* 56: 33–38.

Garzone, G. 2004. Annual Company Reports and CEOs' Letters: Discoursal Features and Cultural Markedness. In *Intercultural Aspects of Specialized Communication*, eds. Christopher Candlin and Maurizio Gotti. Bern: Peter Lang, 311–41.

Garzone, G. 2005. Letters to Shareholders and Chairman's Statements: Textual Variability and Generic Integrity. In *Genre Variation in Business Letters,* eds. Paul Gillaerts and Maurizio Gotti, 179–204. Bern: Peter Lang.

Gillaerts, P. 1996. The Address to the Shareholders in Annual Reports: A Genological Approach. In *1996 European Writing Conferences.* Barcelona: Institut de Ciències de l'Educació (CD-ROM: EARLI Special Interest Group Writing).

Hodge, R., and G. Kress. 1998. *Social Semiotics*. New York: Cornell University Press.

Hyland, K. 1998. Exploring Corporate Rhetoric: Metadiscourse in the CEO's Letter. *Journal of Business Communication* 35: 224–45.

Íñigo-Mora, I. 2004. On the Use of the Personal Pronoun *We* in Communities. *Journal of Language and Politics*, 3: 27–52.

Lampi, M. 1992. Rhetorical Strategies in "Chairman's Statement" Sections in the Annual Reports of Finnish and British Companies. In *Talous ja kieli*, eds. P. Nuolijarvi and L. Tiittula, 127–43. Helsinki: Helsinki School of Economics Publications.

Lord, H. L. 2002. Annual Reports: A Literature Review. *Journal of Technical Writing and Communication* 32: 367–89.

Myers, M. 1996. A Syntactical and Rhetorical Analysis of Selected Annual Reports. Paper presented at the 47th Annual Meeting of the Conference on College Composition and Communication, Milwaukee, Wisconsin, March 27–30.

Myers, M. 1999. The Influence of the Purpose of a Business Document on Its Syntax and Rhetorical Schemes. *Journal of Technical Writing and Communication* 29: 401–8.

Nickerson, C., and E. De Groot. 2005. Dear Shareholder, Dear Stockholder, Dear Stakeholder: The Business Letter Genre in the Annual General Report. In *Genre Variation in Business Letters*, eds. Paul Gillaerts and Maurizio Gotti, 325–46. Bern: Peter Lang.

Palmer, J. C., ed. 2009. *La Memoria Annual: Información y Promoción en la Nueva Empresa Internacional*. Castelló: Publicacions de la UJI.

Pennycook, A. 1994. The Politics of Pronouns. *ELT Journal* 48: 173–78.

Penrose, J. M. 2008. Introduction to the Business Communication of Corporate Reporting: A Special Issue. *Journal of Business Communication* 45: 91–93.

Rutherford, B. A. 2005. Genre Analysis of Corporate Annual Report Narratives: A Corpus Linguistics-based Approach. *Journal of Business Communication* 42: 349–78.

Samuels, J. M. 1993. International Accounting Standards in the Third World: A Synthesis of Six Articles. *Research in Third World Accounting* 2: 19–25.

Schroeder, N., and C. Gibson. 1990. Readability of Management's Discussion and Analysis. *Accounting Horizons*, December 4, 78–89.

Skulstad, A. S. 1996. Rhetorical Organization in Chairman's Statements. *International Journal of Applied Linguistics* 6: 43–63.

Skulstad, A. S. 2002. *Established and Emerging Business Genres*. Kristiansand: Høyskoleforlaget AS–Norwegian Academic Press.

Skulstad, A. S. 2005. The Use of Metadiscourse in Introductory Sections of a New Genre. *International Journal of Applied Linguistics* 15: 71–86.

Skulstad, A. S. 2006. Genre Analysis of Corporate Communication. In *Intercultural and International Business Communication. Theory, Research and Teaching*, eds. J. C. Palmer-Silveira, M. F. Ruiz-Garrido, and I. Fortanet-Gómez, 85–108. Bern: Peter Lang.

Subramanian, R., R. G. Insley, and R. D. Blackwell. 1993. Performance and Readability: A Comparison of Annual Reports of Profitable and Unprofitable Corporations. *Journal of Business Communication* 30: 49–61.

Swales, J. 1981. *Aspects of Article Introductions*. Birmingham: The University of Aston, Language Studies Unit.

Swales, J. 1990. *Genre Analysis: English in Academic Research Settings*. Cambridge: Cambridge University Press.

Swales, J., and C. Feak. 1994. *Academic Writing for Graduate Students*. Ann Arbor: University of Michigan Press.

Sydserff, R., and P. Weetman. 2002. Developments in Content Analysis: A Transitivity Index and DICTION Scores. *Accounting, Auditing and Accountability Journal* 15: 523–45.

8

Benchmarking Organizational Identity

How Who "We" Are Emerges in Organizational Change Discourse

Donald L. Anderson

In recent years, organizational discourse studies have contributed to our understanding of the processes that characterize organizations through examination of spoken and written texts (Grant, Hardy, Oswick, and Putnam 2004). Taking seriously the idea that organizations are systems of meaning formation and interpretation (Putnam and Pacanowsky 1983), researchers have begun to consider the role of language and metaphor (e.g., Illes and Ritchie 1999; Morgan 2001) and narrative (e.g., Czarniawska 1997; Howard and Geist 1995; O'Connor 2000) in organizations. Considering the now-common notion that organizations are socially constructed (e.g., Barrett, Thomas, and Hocevar 1995; Berger and Luckmann 1966), the discourse perspective changes our focus to examine the process of how members work to construct and interpret social reality through dialogue.

Discourse perspectives complicate our notion of an organization in that we no longer view organizations as monolithic "real" entities, but we instead ask how conversations (dialogues) socially construct patterns of meaning in the form of texts that we think of as the organization (Taylor, Cooren, Giroux, and Robichaud 1996). Chia (2002) emphasizes how organizations are social constructions developed from our own social interactions. "Order, form, pattern, identity, predictability and organization are abstractions. . . . Correspondingly, organization is not a thing, but a generic social technology for arresting, fixing, stabilizing and regularizing what would otherwise be a wild, amorphous, and hence unlivable world" (Chia 2002, 866–67). Organizations are also reproduced through discourse and influence our recurrent and regular interpretations and interactions. As Tsoukas and Chia (2002) explain it, "The organization is both a given structure (i.e., a set of established generic cognitive categories) and an emerging pattern (i.e., the constant adaptation of those categories to local circumstances)" (573). Thus the organization both influences our current interactions and sense making, and we also participate in its (re)creation through our interactions. Discourse perspectives offer a fresh way to rethink previous concepts in organizational communication to show how these concepts are discursively constructed, used in dialogue, and supported, negotiated, contradicted, and changed in the process.

Discourse studies have been particularly instructive in a new view of organizational change. Old models of change assume that an organization is a stable, consistent, lasting, durable phenomenon, and that change is the momentary disruption of that stability. Following this assumption, our change management models, books, approaches, and hired consultants recommend that achieving change is best accomplished by "unfreezing" the current organization, making modifications, and then "refreezing" it into its new form (Lewin 1951). Discourse perspectives on change turn this assumption upside down to offer a view of organizational change as a discursive process in which language patterns help members to negotiate and alter underlying meanings. Communication becomes not just an instrumental tool to achieve change, as in previous models, but a process of negotiating meaning that creates what we think of as the organization. Barrett, Thomas, and Hocevar (1995) argue that "crucial to understanding [the change] process are the patterns of discourse through time as organizations achieve stability through patterns of interaction cycles and the evolution of rules for interpreting gestures and utterances" (358–59). The study of organizational change from a discourse perspective has prompted us to investigate how members accomplish change in organized ways, or how members construct the organization in patterned ways in their attempts at achieving change. Organizational members draw upon previous agreed-upon patterns (structures), but also adapt them in creative ways, and it is this adaptation of previous conversations that form what we think of as organizational change (Anderson 2005).

In this chapter I analyze the common organizational practice of benchmarking as a genre of organizational discourse. Through the analysis of discourse excerpts of organizational members at a high-tech corporation, I investigate how benchmarking is patterned discursively and discuss how benchmarking discourse functions for organizational members in the process of organizational change. My argument is that benchmarking contributes to the collaborative evaluation of a collective identity and that as a result, benchmarking discourse opens up a space for negotiating change by confronting organizational members' self-identity with that of another organization. Thus, this study is situated at the intersection of, and attempts to link, the literatures of organizational discourse, identity, and benchmarking. In the next sections I review the recent literature on identity and benchmarking.

IDENTITY AND ORGANIZATIONAL DISCOURSE

A discourse perspective has reshaped our understanding of organizational identity. The concept of organizational identity has most often been defined as the aspects of an organization that remain relatively stable and constant over time (Albert and Whetten 1985). Early concerns with organizational identity conceptualized it as something *held by* an organization, an enduring and widely shared self-concept that could be examined for its relationship to other aspects of the organization and manipulated or controlled. These early views saw identity as a singular, relatively stable entity, but this approach has now given way to new views about identity. In part driven by a postmodern agenda in organizational theorizing that sharply questions the assumptions of coherence and rationality of earlier approaches (Brown 2001), and in part driven by social theory and philosophy that argues that identity is an illusion or myth (Gioia 1998), recent arguments have surfaced regarding the ways in which organizational members manage multiple kinds and levels of identity (e.g., Gioia, Schultz, and Corley 2000; Taylor 1999). Organizational identities may be conflicted, fragmented, and temporary in this revised view.

This latter series of arguments takes the perspective that the element of stability that was proposed by earlier definitions of identity is an achievement derived as an outcome of interactions of organizational members. In this respect, identity is no longer a property of an organization as something it has; rather, identity is an accomplishment as an outcome of a collaborative social process (Ainsworth and Hardy 2004; Hatch and Schultz 2002). Kärreman and Alvesson (2001) concur:

> There is a tendency to loosen up identity in contemporary social science. It is seen as multiple, fragmented, processual and situational, rather than coherent, fixed and stable. . . . The important question is not to investigate which attributes will stay stable, but to study by which means attributes are stabilized and achieved. (63)

Similarly, Gioia, Schultz, and Corley (2000) believe that organizational identity is better conceptualized as a "fluid and unstable concept" (63) in that an adaptable identity helps organizations to achieve change.

If organizational identity is better conceptualized as a "fluid and unstable concept," what we think of as the stability of an organizational identity actually exists as a result of the set of discursive patterns and choices that organizational members make to enact and jointly create it. This view has highlighted the concept of identity work, the process that organizational members enact in order to make sense of, draw upon, create, negotiate, dissolve, or weave identity, since certain actions are seen as more or less appropriate for certain identities (Sveningsson and Alvesson 2003). Organizational members have choices to call upon a certain identity in a certain conversation ("Remember, we're a software company at heart"), and in doing so they highlight it as a resource for the current conversation, but they also simultaneously reproduce and potentially solidify that identity by giving it new "life" in the immediate context. Other members may contradict the called-upon identity ("But we're also a solutions provider") or agree that the earlier identity is an appropriate reference. These multiple interactions can be interpreted as iterations of identity work and provide the foundation for a shared understanding of a collective identity that will influence how a group interprets and acts (Ainsworth and Hardy 2004). Thus organizational identity as a discursive process is an important mechanism for achieving collaboration in organizations. Hardy, Lawrence, and Grant (2005) argue that

> a collective identity, understood as a discursive object, is critically important in achieving effective collaboration. The discursive construction of a collective identity enables participants to construct themselves, the problem, and the solution as part of a collaborative framework in which the potential for joint action is both significant and beneficial. A collective identity also acts as a resource for participants in future conversations. (62–63)

Indeed, discourse perspectives on organizational identity offer us the ability to examine how identities are constructed and reproduced as a foundation for collective action. If this collective identity provides the foundations for a collaborative process of problem identification and resolution, then we might expect that processes such as benchmarking, intended to achieve the latter, may be related to the former as well.

BENCHMARKING

We currently do not know very much about how discourse functions in the common organizational practice of benchmarking. Benchmarking is the common organizational practice of actively searching for best practices, which are those recognized and publicized successful techniques that serve the organization's rational and economic ends. It begins with a seemingly simple question: How is an organization to know how well it is doing unless it knows what its competitors are doing? Spendolini (1992, 9) defines benchmarking as "a continuous, systematic process for evaluating the products, services, and work processes of organizations that are recognized as representing best practices for the purpose of organizational improvement." Benchmarking is a process; that is, it does not take a stance on or advocate any particular best practice or make specific recommendations about any one product design process or organizational structure to adopt (Walgenbach and Hegele 2001). Instead, benchmarking presumes that the preeminent ideas will emerge from careful study of other organizations' results. These ideas can then be put into practice at the home organization. Benchmarking helps organizations to identify and resolve gaps in performance that put them at a competitive disadvantage. Thus, benchmarking's underlying instrumental purpose is organizational change.

Xerox is widely recognized as being among the first major corporation to promote benchmarking, beginning in the 1970s, though terms such as "best practices" and other data collection methods for improving quality appeared much earlier (Walgenbach and Hegele 2001; Yasin 2002). The concept became even more widely known and practiced in the late 1980s after the introduction of the Malcolm Baldrige National Quality Award, winners of which are widely recognized and their data shared publicly. Today, among management scholars and practitioners, benchmarking is seen as almost universally applicable, regardless of size or type of organization (Kyrö 2003), and the practice has such status that there is now an international journal, *Benchmarking*, devoted to its study and practice.

Walgenbach and Hegele (2001) argue that benchmarking can be seen as contribution to the creation of management fashions, as organizational members look within their networks to mine competitive information from one another and adopt the latest management practices. When organizational members conduct benchmarking, they participate in the circulation of management initiatives, languages, and practices that may go in and out of vogue as organizations borrow techniques from one another (Abrahamson 1991, 1996; Abrahamson and Fairchild 1999). Such fashions can be described as "a relatively transitory collective belief, disseminated by management fashion setters, that a management technique leads to rational management progress" (Abrahamson 1996, 257). The study of fashions takes seriously what can be easily dismissed as a consulting industry's attempts to sell the latest craze or fad to an audience searching for any competitive advantage. Abrahamson and Fairchild (1999), for example, note the wax and wane in management techniques such as quality circles, total quality management, and business reengineering. They suggest that these management techniques are preceded by gaps in organizational performances after which these new discourses are adopted. Other findings suggest that recent management fashions require greater resources and have shorter life cycles than in earlier years (Carson, Lanier, Carson, and Guidry 2000), and that there exists only a loose connection between the content of a fashion and its label (Benders and van Veen 2001). Management fashion and studies of the diffusion of management ideas through benchmarking have provided us with a language with which to describe the influence of contemporary discourses of management, their circulation and life cycle.

However, as Newell, Robertson, and Swan (2001) observe, this area of study is relatively new, and we still do not know very much about the process by which fashions such as benchmarking circulate, why some are adopted and others are not, or the rhetorical processes and functions of these fashions. Traditional management perspectives on benchmarking ignore or gloss over these issues in favor of the more instrumental outcomes of benchmarking. As a result, we do not know very much about the "diverse processes by which these rhetorics are socially constructed by heterogeneous groups of actors in specific contexts" (Newell, Robertson, and Swan 2001, 5). In other words, we have only scratched the surface of investigating how organizational members use processes like benchmarking or how they function for organizational members, beyond the most common and surface explanation of information seeking.

This study is one attempt to address that research gap. I consider benchmarking as a speech genre, or a repeated and accumulated pattern of regular speech activity. Such genres consist of similar forms, content, and style that allow participants to recognize that in a given context, a recognizable and familiar kind of speech event is being played out. Genres provide both constraints but also some level of flexibility in that no given instance of speech is a perfect reproduction of a previous action. "Genres carry the generalizable resources of particular events; but specific actions or utterances must use those resources to accomplish new purposes in each unrepeatable milieu" (Morson and Emerson 1990, 291). Thus in any given instance of a genre, something new is created within the confines of the expected pattern. As Fairclough (1992) puts it in his exposition of a social theory of discourse, any given text is an instance of a discursive practice (practices of textual production and consumption) as well as a social practice imbued with ideological meaning and value. Thus, while the text may follow a structure or pattern recognizable to participants, it also provides the occasion for the accomplishment of locally significant objectives and larger social and cultural meanings. In the textual analyses below, I hope to make visible both the pattern and structure of benchmarking as a discursive genre, but also show how benchmarking functioned as an organizationally significant genre.

I take a discourse perspective on benchmarking, a perspective that examines the dialogic process by which benchmarking is accomplished in order to highlight underlying functions of the process for organizational members. This examination of benchmarking discourse proposes that benchmarking functions in several ways that are not explicitly articulated in the current benchmarking literature.

RESEARCH SITE, METHODS, AND MATERIALS

This chapter interprets discourse excerpts from meetings of a project team at a high-tech corporation in the western U.S. "Techco," the name I give to this organization, manufactures products for use in large corporate computing environments. (The name of the organization and the names of speakers in transcripts are pseudonyms.) Just fewer than half of Techco's employees are located at its corporate headquarters, with several thousand employees in offices around the globe, including at a European subsidiary located in London. Techco went through periods of significant turmoil in the late 1990s and early 2000s as revenues stalled and new management was brought in to improve productivity and cut costs.

As one of his final acts before he resigned, the CEO brought in a consulting organization to study Techco and make recommendations that would improve the company's profitability. One of the changes recommended by the consulting group was to Techco's process for forecasting sales demand for its products. In most manufacturing organizations there exist significant incentives to forecast sales accurately. Building more products than customers want means excess costly inventory as the company has already paid suppliers for raw materials that now sit unsold in a warehouse. However, building too few products means that frustrated customers wait weeks or months to receive their orders and thus might decide to purchase elsewhere. The consulting group found that Techco had millions of dollars tied up in excess inventory, and because Techco's forecasting accuracy was so low, manufacturing built products as a preemptive measure against customer dissatisfaction. To remedy this problem, a forecasting project team was put together with representatives from sales, manufacturing, finance, marketing, quality, and product development. The team was given the responsibility to understand the current process and to redesign it to increase accuracy.

I studied Techco as a participant-observer for a twelve-month period of time. With the approval of Techco management, my university's institutional review board, and the project manager, I studied this forecasting team from its first meeting. Attendance and participation varied in team meetings, which generally included about five or six core team members and another eight to ten team members who attended sporadically. For four months the team met almost weekly, and the remainder of the meetings were scheduled as needed. Meetings varied in length from one hour to a full day, and the team granted me permission to audiotape every team meeting. I also interviewed five of the core team members in semistructured one-on-one interviews. In all, I gathered and transcribed over thirty-three hours' worth of team meeting conversation and interviews, and I collected hundreds of pages of documents, such as presentations and e-mail messages. Meetings were transcribed at a moderate level, including hesitancies, nonfluencies, and overlaps, but omitting timing and volume emphases. (A guide to transcription symbols appears in the appendix.) Excerpts from the transcripts that follow have been minimally edited for readability.

The data for this study come primarily from one of the full-day meetings of the team in which team members struggled to understand Techco's current forecasting process. As a part of this meeting, Kevin, the project manager, brought in examples of forecasting processes at other organizations. Kevin had knowledge of these processes from his work at another company before joining Techco, and he told me that he saw it as his responsibility to research the processes of other organizations (both direct competitors and those from other industries) to "teach them [team members] what I knew about best practices and forecasting, to review how other companies do it, and I had some case studies and best practice examples." In the next sections I review examples of how the team engaged in benchmarking discussions and how these discussions functioned for the team.

BENCHMARKING IN THE TECHCO PROJECT

Benchmarking appeared to be a significant practice to the team, as it was discussed at most of the initial team meetings. It also became a frequent topic that the group returned to when it became stuck between choices, with members wondering aloud what other organizations do if they could not come to agreement.

The next two sections describe how these benchmarking discussions played out and how organizational members used them to negotiate opportunities for change. First, I describe the pattern that emerged during benchmarking discussions to illustrate how benchmarking helped members to understand and negotiate organizational identity and current Techco practices. Second, I describe how potential areas for change emerged in the context of benchmarking discussions. Through Kevin's presentations about well-known companies that had been lauded for their practices, Techco's approach became more visible to them as they discussed differences between Techco practices and best practices.

ORGANIZATIONAL IDENTITY AND PATTERNS OF BENCHMARKING DISCUSSION

Organizational identity was negotiated and made meaningful to participants during these explanations of other organizations' forecasting practices. Organizational identity ("Who we are") was brought to light by the team's discussion and evaluation of its typical practices ("What we do") compared to other organizations.

Benchmarking discussions followed a common pattern. First, Kevin would present his research that showed the forecasting process of another organization. Next, team members would frequently either ask questions of Kevin or offer additional detail, which often happened in cases when team members were familiar with the external organization and could offer more information. Finally, the group's discussion would turn to either a rationalization or critique of Techco practices based on this new information.

As an example of how this common pattern played out, consider this excerpt in which Kevin recites the forecasting process of a major competitor by quoting what he had found in an industry publication:

Excerpt 1, tape 2

Kevin: Uh, I found some stuff on [Techco's major competitor]

Michael: The evil empire ((laughter))

Cheryl: Right

Kevin: It's a little old from 95 I got, that's not that old, I thought it was old, "we are obsessed with forecasting" uh this is from an international magazine so it's got an international slant, "each month, 100 salesmen from 14 international districts forecast sales by region and country," so they're doing it monthly, uh, they talk about, "identify all corporate accounts that make up 95 percent of that forecast," so their sales process is at the customer level uh (rolls) up from there, "the forecasts are regularly within 10 percent of actual sales."

Cheryl: Do you know if that's really (at the line item level)

Kevin: I don't know

Larry: I think that's at item level 'cause both sales and type of [product] versus deal I mean the higher you get the more accurate you're gonna be

Cheryl: Absolutely, absolutely

Kevin: "Every 30 days headquarters demands rolling 2 month forecasts from managers in every global region regarding such items as expenses and inventories for the coming month," I don't know if our financial tracking (handles) this, do we measure this on a quarterly basis?

Larry: Expenses and inventory they uh the business groups uh well I don't know what the field, how the field forecasts expenses but I know that (in) the business groups, the expenses are forecasted quarterly, they're forecasted when the quarter is done (   )

((multiple speakers))

228 Larry: I mean every time there's a quarter forecast, that only covers the
229 sales—

230 Scott: But it's a calendar not a rolling

231 Cheryl: Right

Note how the benchmarking pattern is at work here. Kevin begins by presenting data from the competitor in lines 206–213, with Cheryl asking a question about the competitor in line 214. Kevin continues to quote from the article in lines 219–221, and then asks Larry a question about the timing for Techco's expense forecasting. In line 230, Scott clarifies the difference between the Techco competitor's "rolling" forecast (e.g., January to March, then February to April) and Techco's "calendar" forecast (first quarter, then second quarter).

Thus, through a series of turns, Techco's practices are now more visible to the team, and the contrast between Techco and the competitor is becoming evident. Members notice and highlight aspects of Techco practices that are similar to or different from the Techco competitor. In fact, establishing a Techco identity as an important part of what it means to do benchmarking, as well as contrasting itself from its competitor, may have such importance to the benchmarking process that Michael attempts to do this before Kevin even presents the data. By calling the Techco competitor "the evil empire" (line 204), Michael recalls and participates in a long-standing pattern at Techco of insulting this particular competitor. In-group/out-group theorists note that this pattern occurs when a group seeks to develop its own cohesive social identity by pointing to an outside threat or making negative judgments about other groups (Tajfel 1982; Tajfel and Turner 1979). By calling the competitor "evil," Michael not only draws the negative connotation of the competitor and makes the in-group/out-group distinction apparent but he also refers to them as an "empire," indexing the tacit "David vs. Goliath" knowledge that many at Techco had, knowing that the competitor was many times larger.

As the meeting continued, Kevin presented some of his research on "Company P." Prior to this, Kevin has had an extended turn, in which he explains Company P's practices in depth:

Excerpt 2, tape 3

133 Kevin: Their forecasting is in monthly quantity not a quarterly quantity
134 and uh they had a planning group that was responsible for developing all
135 the production plans, they held a lot of different measurements but the
136 key measurement is hitting the production plan uh product is scheduled
137 on time, on time. Um, and that's more of a daily type production schedule
138 function as opposed to a one point

Jay: They're repetitive? (Repetitive) manufacturing?

Kevin: uh, I (   ) Michael, do you know?

Michael: No, um, but I think [as a company in industry X] what they're trying to do they're trying to maximize the longest batch times as possible, sorta what they can do, so, they do have—what's interesting with [Company P] I think is around—they have capacity issues. So they they try to allocate ca- the business groups are competing for capacity so they try, then they do—they allocate capacity across plans worldwide, we don't—today we don't have that issue, I hope someday ((laughter))

Cheryl: Yeah to be in that (   )

Scott: When you say repetitive, you mean volume?

Jay: Yeah

Michael: Mass customization

Jay: Pushing volume

Scott: Yeah

Jay: Where I push it is what I decide on a monthly (   )

Kevin: On the allocation part though we do have a- allocating capacity we do have a problem with allocating key materials, is that true?

Michael: At the component level so we can build to finished goods

Cheryl: Right, component level right

Michael: We consume components because of building to a finished goods strategy

Kevin: So, so how does that happen? How do we if there's a part that has limited supply we're only gonna get 500 of 'em, how do we allocate that across product?

The same pattern is at work in this example, and note that again, as much as they use it to learn about current industry practices in forecasting, the structure of the benchmarking conversations results in the group turning to a discussion of its own current practices. "We" and "They" phrasings appear frequently. After Kevin presents the competitive practice (lines 133–138), the group's attention turns to understanding this organization through Techco eyes. Michael helps to make sense of Company P's ability to manage manufacturing capacity (lines 146–147) in terms of Techco practices related to the allocation of capacity, drawing a distinction between the two organizations.

Some organizations have difficulty meeting demand because of the complexity involved in the availability of raw materials, lengthy cycle times in the manufacturing process, or large customer demand. Michael's point in this excerpt is that particularly the last challenge in this list is, in most respects, not a bad problem to have. Michael's point draws a knowing laughter because of the group's shared understanding that Techco is having financial difficulty.

Kevin's comments (lines 155–156) function in a similar way to draw parallels between Company P practices and Techco practices, that both organizations share a challenge in allocating or organizing how key parts or manufacturing capabilities are used. Thus Kevin is trying to show similarities between Techco and Company P, but Michael works again in lines 157 and 159 to show a difference between the two organizations. Michael answers Kevin's question about Techco manufacturing capacity by concurring that components are indeed allocated but that the two company strategies differ, with Techco building products to a "finished goods" or warehouse location from which products can be taken once sold. This strategy, Michael argues, is what causes the "problem" that Kevin is referring to (the lack of certain components at certain times). Michael's underlying message is that this would not necessarily be a problem, however, if another strategy were to be chosen. In lines 155–163 Kevin, Cheryl, and Michael are beginning to make sense of how Techco practices operate, now noticing the source of Techco's problems in light of how Company P operates. The distinction between the two organizations is now more evident.

Through the benchmarking discussions, a diverse group of organizational members who do not ordinarily work together co-construct what work life is like at Techco during the forecasting process. Each has knowledge of certain parts of the forecasting process. Like the news bill meetings in Kärreman and Alvesson's (2001) study of a newspaper editorial office, the benchmarking discussions made organizational identity visible as Kärreman and Alvesson note that this is where "vital aspects of how people frame and synchronize collective action are played out" (Kärreman and Alvesson 2001, 80). A shared identity is building through these discussions, with Techco becoming gradually characterized as a smaller company, unlike its competitors, having made different strategic choices, experiencing financial problems, and with some forecasting process steps that are confused or causing difficulties.

The seemingly simple and coherent way that other organizations go about forecasting was contrasted with what Techco employees experience day-to-day as a disjoined process. Other organizations' practices were made coherent and simple through Kevin's extended turns at presenting them as well as through written PowerPoint slides that explained an entire organization's practice in one utterance. We lack any of the insider context from a member of the benchmarked organization, making their decisions appear firm, bold, reasonable, decisive, and somehow more correct, whereas by contrast, Techco practices were represented by many participants throughout many utterances, making them appear more fragmented, ad hoc, and chaotic than the comparison organization. These discursive practices helped to create a sharp contrast between the two companies and thereby make Techco practices more explicit to members. It also caused angst and confusion among Techco employees, who often summarized Techco practices and Techco as a whole in a single statement: "This place is so messed up."

Hearing Company P's forecasting practices prompted the group to discuss and compare Techco practices. At first this might appear a "natural" reaction to learning about a forecasting methodology that seems foreign, but this seemingly natural behavior also has an identity function. It is both an effect of and contribution to the construction of Techco's identity boundaries between itself and other organizations. Benchmarking discussions make identity and organizational practices visible in that members' cultural assumptions of "the ways things are done around here" are confronted by both the practices and values of another organization. Thus, it is in this context that "members jointly tell themselves and each other, under the pretext of a more instrumental topic: this is our shared universe, this is how we are" (Kärreman and Alvesson 2001, 80).

By and large, Techco team members do not recognize that best practices are themselves rhetorical presentations, constructed for the benefit of the *represented organization* (or that organization's self-presentation in industry publications) as much as for *Techco* use in comparing organizational practices. (The same could be said for Kevin's choices to bring in these particular examples in order to bring out certain topics of discussion, a point he made in our interview but did not share with the rest of the team.) Instead, these benchmarking discussions served as identity work dialogues with members collaboratively evaluating how Techco's practices compared to organizations largely viewed as superior. These were also boundary-creating activities, delineating the Techco organization from the outside world. While members explicitly pointed to benchmarking as a method for understanding others (a common belief, see Spendolini 1992), it also served an important internal identity function as it made the Techco organization visible to project team members.

Thus the first function of benchmarking discourse was to construct a shared Techco organizational identity so that Techco's unique approach to the forecasting process was visible to project team members. A part of this function was also evaluative—how Techco's process should be evaluated in light of the benchmarked organization. This led to a second function of benchmarking.

BENCHMARKING AND THE NEGOTIATED LANGUAGE OF CHANGE

Benchmarking served a second, and related, function in that by discussing Techco's differences the group not only negotiated which Techco practices needed to be changed but also how the group would talk about them. In any process, there are many possible sources of ideas for change. Organizational members may conclude that the process is taking too long because of customer complaints, because too many decisions are being revisited, or because there are not enough people working to move the process forward quickly, and they may generate solutions based on these conclusions. As would be expected, the Techco team used benchmarking to generate these possible sources of change and often picked up on the language of the benchmarked organization in their identification of subjects for change. Consider, for example, how this worked as a direct repetition of a single word in excerpt 1 above. Kevin's statement that Techco's competitor used a "rolling" forecast (line 219) is repeated by Scott to distinguish Techco's practice of a "calendar, not a rolling" forecast (line 230).

In several of the benchmarking discussions, the team began to explicitly question or negatively evaluate Techco practices, suggesting that the benchmarked organization provided a superior process. In other cases, participants stressed the differences among the benchmark organization and Techco, noting that differences in industry, organization size, budget, or any of a number of other significant differences meant that the benchmark organization's practices should not be taken seriously at Techco. This began a period of persuasion and negotiation, a practice that opened up (or closed down) a space for change by focusing the group's attention and concentrating the dialogue on certain aspects of Techco's practices.

The following excerpt shows a typical example of this practice, where Jay (a sales consultant) points to an organization that does a five-quarter rolling forecast:

Excerpt 3, tape 2

Jay: A company that I talked to, a very large high-tech company, they have six full time (employees) forecasting, and uh I've got some more answers, we'll see it another day and they do uh five quarters rolling five quarters rolling and uh everybody's comp plans associated with the process, they have just like 25% (variable compensation)

Cheryl: How much?

Jay: 25% and they're a very very large high-tech company

Scott: And and this is something we can talk about later and if you don't know the answer, how do they balance short-term forecast accuracy

Jay: I, I don't know that

Scott: But if they're when we're talking out fro- four five six quarters um the natural tendency is to base accuracy based on current quarter versus four and five quarters out and at the ( ) we're talking about, the current quarter is somewhat meaningless so somehow we need to figure out how to balance short versus long term

Jay: I mean I would imagine I mean without any data my (gut) answer is is the farther out the less (right) we are but the closer in we then (it's) the quarter out, not the quarter (Scott: yeah, right quarter out) you're in. We're very light, (Scott: right) we're stuck in the quarter you're in

Scott: And that's why I asked, that's why I asked

Jay: And in reality I don't know, I don't know

Scott: And so if we've got examples of companies that are doing compensating I'd be curious to understand how they balance those two uh

Kevin: Yeah, let's go dig into that

Of note initially is Jay's repetition of the size of the organization (lines 274 and 280) to build the credibility of its practices. This point plays upon Techco's beliefs that larger organizations are more likely to have better practices to study and also reminds the team about the size of Techco by comparison. Jay, Scott, and Kevin appear to agree here that Jay's example offers something useful for the team to investigate in two subject areas: forecast timing/accuracy and compensation. Jay and Scott concur that Techco's practices in focusing on the current quarter offer a "light" alternative to what appears as a more robust process of a five-month rolling forecast. Both of Jay's benchmarking practices survive the subsequent discussion here as the team recognizes these as possible areas of change at Techco. (To see how the team later discussed compensating sales executives for accurate forecasts, see Anderson 2005.)

Another excerpt from another all-day team meeting helps to illustrate how benchmarking preceeded a negotiation process of topics for change. This excerpt focuses the group on the topic of inventory "ownership," meaning who in the process has the responsibility for the accuracy of the company's inventory (and ultimately its cost). Kevin explains who owns inventory at the benchmark organization, Company Q:

Excerpt 4, tape 7

Kevin: At [Company Q], capacity is allocated to the business groups and they decide the production schedule with the goal to maximize profitability then manufacturing is measured on meeting the production plan. Uh, and the production plan of course is driven by the business groups, and the business groups end up owning the finished goods inventory.

Jackie: Should we uh make comments here?

Kevin: Sure.

Jackie: Because one of the things that I see is a big disconnect is who owns the finished goods inventory? Um, and what I sense is that manufacturing is so incented to make sure they end up with zero that there's no consideration for a blue bird, I'm sure everybody knows that term, and that's real concerning, and I think that's a big issue, and I see that as conflicting goals, we're talking you know, sales would like, and again we'll get into this as to how, you know, it's a guess, right, I mean forecasts are educated guesses, you know we'd like to see some sort of safety stock, but that's in, you know, contrary to where manufacturing is coming in, where they're measured, so that's a big issue with me, I assume we'll talk about it 'cause I think it's a big issue, I don't know if anybody shares my- ((multiple speakers))

Tom: Actually though I believe that the business groups own finished goods, however the metrics ((pause)) No? No, isn't that true?

Jackie: No

Larry: Uh, the way it's supposed to be is the business groups supposedly owns the DOF [demand on factory]

Cheryl: Right

Larry: And I think manufacturing owns finished goods, but I think one of the big issues is there's no ownership period, whether it be DOF, or finished goods, I mean by ownership I mean you can say yeah, I own it, but you know what stake he has in the ground on it.

Jackie: Well, I was I was under the impression that people in manufacturing at least in manufacturing management had MBOs or you know compensation based on what levels of inventory they had. That that you know that they're incented to keep those as low as possible, whereas the field is incented to try and pull in everything they can pull in, forecasted or not forecasted, and to me that's just that's just a problem

Cheryl: And I can give you some direct feedback on that, because we do come under the manufacturing umbrella, we do have a high level dollar

> value of finished goods and it's certainly not zero, but we will add all the various locations and products together you know it could be minimal in one area maybe higher in another, and we made some recent very recent changes to uh not be as conservative in our inventory levels but we've not defined what those levels are, so that's an open action but I agree, and the OEMs the struggle we have there is because they are so unique? Not always real feasible to be able to rework those without considerable cost, as we're trying to balance, so, but I agree with you we need to have agreement on who is the real owner and then also set targets around what's most important.

In this excerpt we see the combination of the benchmarking pattern, identity work discourse, and the negotiation of which elements of the forecasting process to change. Kevin's review of Company Q introduces three topics that participants weave together in subsequent turns at talk: measurement of manufacturing, inventory levels, and ownership of the final inventory. Kevin's initial statement about business group ownership at Company Q in line 394 gets picked up by other speakers eight different times as they repeat the words "own/owns," "owner," or "ownership" in the subsequent dialogue (lines 397, 408, 412, 414–416, and 434). Jackie's first contribution quickly contrasts Company Q's ownership practices with those of Techco, identifying it as an area of concern, and Techco's practices emerge through a series of turns between Jackie, Tom, Larry, and Cheryl. At the end of this excerpt, both Larry and Cheryl support Jackie's statement that there is some level of confusion with ownership of the forecast at Techco. Kevin clarified the practice at Company Q, which led to a group dialogue about the lack of the same level of clarity at Techco.

Next the negotiation process begins. What is negotiated here are what Techco practices ought to be, and by implication, Techco identity. Jackie's initial statement proposes that the group pick up on higher inventory levels and how to measure manufacturing as possible topics for change. Early discussions on how the forecasting process worked in manufacturing characterized it as incoherent, inconsistent, and full of gaps and unclear responsibilities. Here, however, those earlier impressions are contrasted with the sense Cheryl gives that there is more coherence than it might appear. The extended turn, firm language such as "we will add," "we do have a high dollar value," and "we made some recent changes" help to make current Techco practices sound as straightforward and as well thought out as those from Company Q. Note that Cheryl's use of "we" here can be heard as referring to manufacturing, not Techco as a whole, fracturing the cohesive organizational identity seen in earlier excerpts.

While it might be that Cheryl is defending her department in response to what can be heard as an attack on her department from Jackie, she counters

Jackie's suggestion that the group take up "safety stock" of inventory as a possible item for discussion, but she concedes the need to define a clear set of responsibilities for the process and target inventory levels. Cheryl's concession here paints a picture of Techco practices as being as consistent and coherent as those from Company Q, with a few well-defined opportunities for change (clear ownership and targets) that the group will later take up. By the end of the discussion, of the three topics that Kevin had introduced, these two survive the negotiation and remain as possible subjects for change.

DISCUSSION AND CONCLUSIONS

In this chapter I have argued that benchmarking, when seen as a discursive dialogic process, functions in several unique ways not addressed by the current literature on benchmarking. Benchmarking functions as one of a number of discursive processes that call upon and contribute to organizational identity. It served to temporarily stabilize the fleeting and day-to-day work environment into standardized and routinized practices that Techco members could then see as available to them as objects for change. By discussing the routines of another organization, Techco members began to hear how their routines, and thus their implicit shared worldview, sound different when seen from another perspective. They adopted and tried out new languages from other organizations to hear how they would sound within the framework of their own organization. The practice of benchmarking is thus a means by which organizational identity and stability are negotiated and constructed but which also provides an opportunity to categorize possible changes and brainstorm them in light of a newly learned language. In this case it provided the forecasting project team the opportunity to critique organizational practices, which became the topics for future discussions of change.

Understanding a group's use of benchmarking is significant because it provides a view into how the group sees itself. A discursive perspective on benchmarking calls our attention to how benchmarking is the bringing together of two organizations into dialogue. It pits two practices against one another in a "test" of sorts (Bakhtin 1984), which Bakhtin refers to as "dialogized heteroglossia." Benchmarking forces organizational members to "regard one language (and the verbal world corresponding to it) through the eyes of another language" (Bakhtin 1984, 296). Morson and Emerson (1990, 310) describe what Bakhtin means by this:

> When languages enter into dialogue, complex changes take place. . . . To begin with, a language that has entered into dialogue with another language, especially if that dialogue concerns the topic or experience to which the language

> is specifically adapted, loses its "naivete." It becomes self-conscious, because it has seen itself from an alien perspective and has come to understand how its own values and beliefs appear to the other language. When it is used subsequently, such a language can no longer directly and unself-consciously talk about its topic as if there were no other plausible way of doing so. The language begins not just to speak, but to hear how it sounds; it not only represents the world, but imagines itself as the object of representation.

In this regard, other organizations' practices act as languages. It is through these competitive "best practices" that organizational members see their own organizational "selves" and immediately begin to notice and assess the differences between the two organizations. Putting the organizations in dialogue becomes a "critical interanimation of languages" (Bakhtin 1981, 296) that now demands "actively choosing one's orientation among them" (Bakhtin 1981, 296). When organizational members choose their own language over the "other" language, they rationalize and defend theirs; when they choose the "other" language, they become critical about their own. The isolation of a world in which organizational members experience Techco practices alone is now confronted by an outside world that causes them to reexamine, question, and/or validate Techco practices.

The current benchmarking literature promotes the analysis of data; that is, the collection, interpretation, and analysis of data for the purposes of comparison. Content is privileged. As a result of this examination of benchmarking at Techco, I would propose the enhancement of this perspective by noting that perhaps content is less vital than it may appear on the surface. It may not matter as much which data get collected if organizational members have the opportunity to analyze the data by seeing it in identity terms in order to form the basis for an effective collaboration in the accomplishment of change.

If it is true that organizational change occurs "when one way of talking replaces another way of talking" (Barrett, Thomas, and Hocevar 1995, 370), organizational members proposing changes must hold discussions where they are able to consider how language will change as organizational practices change. Based on the conversations at Techco, I believe that benchmarking provides a genre for this "trying out" of new languages. Benchmarking introduces new language choices into the organization, and in doing so, confronts the organization with another point of view on the world. Benchmarking, understood as a process of identity work, works as a practice for achieving organizational change because it opens an internally focused organization to another organization's language, and thus its worldview. Members were forced to acknowledge this difference and to examine their own choices as an outsider would. At Techco, (as Bakhtin would put it), once "the ideological systems and approaches to the world that were indissolubly connected with these languages contradicted each other and in no way would live in peace and quiet with one another . . . the necessity of actively choosing one's orientation among them began" (Bakhtin 1984, 296).

TRANSCRIPTION KEY

Transcripts in the chapter use these conventional transcription symbols. Transcripts use punctuation not as grammatical symbols but instead to indicate intonation.

?	Question mark: Rising intonation
.	Period: Falling intonation
[ ]	Brackets indicate content changed by the author to protect anonymity
,	Comma: Brief pause
-	Dash: Halting or cut-off speech
( )	Empty parentheses: Inaudible segment of talk
(word)	Text in parentheses indicates transcriptionist doubt
((laughter))	Double parentheses describe nonspeech activity

REFERENCES

Abrahamson, E. 1991. Managerial Fads and Fashion: The Diffusion and Rejection of Innovations. *Academy of Management Review* 16: 586–612.

Abrahamson, E. 1996. Management Fashion. *Academy of Management Review* 21: 254–85.

Abrahamson, E., and G. Fairchild. 1999. Management Fashion: Lifecycles, Triggers, and Collective Learning Processes. *Administrative Science Quarterly* 44: 708–40.

Ainsworth, S., and C. Hardy. 2004. Discourse and Identities. In *Handbook of Organizational Discourse*, eds. D. Grant, C. Hardy, C. Oswick, and L. L. Putnam, 153–73. London: Sage.

Albert, S., and D. A. Whetten. 1985. Organizational Identity. *Research in Organizational Behavior* 7: 263–95.

Anderson, D. L. 2005. "What You'll Say Is . . .": Represented Voice in Organizational Change Discourse. *Journal of Organizational Change Management* 18: 63–77.

Bakhtin, M. M. 1981. *The Dialogic Imagination*. Austin: University of Texas Press.

Bakhtin, M. M. 1984. *Problems of Dostoevsky's Poetics*. Minneapolis: University of Minnesota Press.

Barrett, F. J., G. F. Thomas, and S. P. Hocevar. 1995. The Central Role of Discourse in Large-scale Change: A Social Construction Perspective. *Journal of Applied Behavioral Science* 31: 352–72.

Benders, J., and K. van Veen. 2001. What's in a Fashion? Interpretative Viability and Management Fashions. *Organization* 8: 33–53.

Berger, P. L., and T. Luckmann. 1966. *The Social Construction of Reality*. Garden City, NY: Doubleday.

Brown, A. D. 2001. Organizational Studies and Identity: Towards a Research Agenda. *Human Relations* 54: 113–21.

Carson, P. P., P. A. Lanier, K. D. Carson, and B. N. Guidry. 2000. Clearing a Path through the Management Fashion Jungle: Some Preliminary Trailblazing. *Academy of Management Journal* 43: 1143–58.

Chia, R. 2002. *Essai*: Time, Duration and Simultaneity: Rethinking Process and Change in Organizational Analysis. *Organization Studies* 23: 863–68.

Czarniawska, B. 1997. *Narrating the Organization.* Chicago: University of Chicago Press.

Fairclough, N. 1992. *Discourse and Social Change.* Cambridge: Polity Press.

Gioia, D. 1998. From Individual to Organizational Identity. In *Identity in Organizations: Building Theory through Conversations*, eds. D. A. Whetten and P. C. Godfrey, 17–31. Thousand Oaks, CA: Sage.

Gioia, D., M. C. Schultz, and K. G. Corley. 2000. Organizational Identity, Image, and Adaptive Instability. *Academy of Management Review* 25: 63–81.

Grant, D., C. Hardy, C. Oswick, and L. L. Putnam. 2004. Introduction: Organizational Discourse: Exploring the Field. In *Handbook of Organizational Discourse*, eds. D. Grant, C. Hardy, C. Oswick, and L. L. Putnam, 1–36. London: Sage.

Hardy, C., T. B. Lawrence, and D. Grant. 2005. Discourse and Collaboration: The Role of Conversations and Collective Identity. *Academy of Management Review* 30: 58–77.

Hatch, M. J., and M. Schultz. 2002. The Dynamics of Organizational Identity. *Human Relations* 55: 989–1018.

Howard, L. A., and P. Geist. 1995. Ideological Positioning in Organizational Change: The Dialectic of Control in a Merging Organization. *Communication Monographs* 62: 110–31.

Illes, L. M., and J. B. Ritchie. 1999. Change Metaphor: Grappling with the Two-headed Organizational Behemoth. *Journal of Management Inquiry* 8: 91–100.

Kärreman, D., and M. Alvesson. 2001. Making Newsmakers: Conversational Identity at Work. *Organization Studies* 22: 59–89.

Kyrö, P. 2003. Revising the Concept and Forms of Benchmarking. *Benchmarking: An International Journal* 10: 210–25.

Lewin, K. 1951. *Field Theory in Social Science.* New York: Harper and Brothers.

Morgan, J. M. 2001. Are We "Out of the Box" Yet? A Case Study and Critique of Managerial Metaphors of Change. *Communication Studies* 52: 85–102.

Morson, G. S., and C. Emerson. 1990. *Mikhail Bakhtin: Creation of a Prosaics*. Stanford: Stanford University Press.

Newell, S., M. Robertson, and J. Swan. 2001. Management Fads and Fashions. *Organization* 8: 5–15.

O'Connor, E. S. 2000. Plotting the Organization. *Journal of Applied Behavioral Science* 36: 174–92.

Putnam, L. L., and M. E. Pacanowsky, eds. 1983. *Communication and Organizations: An Interpretive Approach*. Beverly Hills, CA: Sage.

Spendolini, M. J. 1992. *The Benchmarking Book*. New York: AMACOM.

Sveningsson, S., and M. Alvesson. 2003. Managing Managerial Identities: Organizational Fragmentation, Discourse and Identity Struggle. *Human Relations* 56: 1163–93.

Tajfel, H., ed. 1982. *Social Identity and Intergroup Relations*. Cambridge: Cambridge University Press.

Tajfel, H., and J. C. Turner. 1979. An Integrative Theory of Intergroup Conflict. In *The Social Psychology of Intergroup Relations*, eds. W. G. Austin and S. Worchel, 33–47. Monterey, CA: Brooks/Cole.

Taylor, B. C. 1999. Browsing the Culture: Membership and Intertextuality at a Mormon Bookstore. *Studies in Cultures, Organizations, and Societies* 5: 61–95.

Taylor, J. R., F. Cooren, N. Giroux, and D. Robichaud. 1996. The Communicational Basis of Organization: Between the Conversation and the Text. *Communication Theory* 6: 1–39.

Tsoukas, H., and R. Chia. 2002. On Organizational Becoming: Rethinking Organizational Change. *Organization Science* 13: 567–82.

Walgenbach, P., and C. Hegele. 2001. What Can an Apple Learn from an Orange? Or: What Do Companies Use Benchmarking For? *Organization* 8: 121–44.

Yasin, M. M. 2002. The Theory and Practice of Benchmarking: Then and Now. *Benchmarking: An International Journal* 9: 217–43.

9

Narratives of Diversity in the Corporate Boardroom

What Corporate Insiders Say about Why Diversity Matters

John M. Conley, Lissa L. Broome, and Kimberly D. Krawiec

Over the last generation, the concept of diversity has become commonplace and taken-for-granted in discourses ranging from law to education to business. In higher education, for example, it is hard to imagine a faculty job search or a student admissions discussion that was not heavily laden with talk of diversity, in the sense of the representative inclusion of women and racial and ethnic minorities in a group or organization. In this paper we present the results of an interview-based study of the discourse of diversity in a particular business setting: the corporate boardroom. Our principal observation is that—thirty-one years after the Supreme Court's *Bakke* decision introduced the term into public discourse—corporate insiders appear not to have arrived at a master narrative to explain the pursuit of diversity on boards of directors. Instead, their accounts stress a variety of factors and feature few concrete examples.

The racial, ethnic, and gender makeup of corporate boards has recently become the subject of intense public focus in many countries, including the United States. In Norway, for example, gender representation on corporate boards has become a matter of government mandate. Legislation enacted in 2006 required that roughly 40 percent of public company board seats be held by women by 2008 (Reiersen and Sjafsjell 2008). As of January 2008, women held close to 38 percent of board seats at Norwegian public corporations, the world's highest percentage. The news prompted claims of victory from the legislation's advocates, as well as charges of quotas, window dressing, and divisiveness from opponents. In the United States, by contrast, the makeup of corporate boards has been left to market forces and private advocacy efforts. Dozens of groups are dedicated to promoting board diversity, by measuring it, studying it, or providing training or mentoring to potential female or minority board members (e.g., Alliance for Board Diversity 2008).

By some measures, the level of gender, racial, and ethnic diversity on U.S. public company boards has increased markedly over the past few decades. For example, in 1993 some 51 percent of Fortune 500 firms had no women on the board (Catalyst 1993). By 2008, that percentage had fallen to 13 percent (Catalyst 2008). In 1973, 93% of Fortune 1000 companies had no minority directors (Fairfax 2005). That percentage had declined to 24 percent by 2004 (Fairfax 2005). By other measures, however, progress has been slow and has leveled off. For example, the percentage of Fortune 500 board seats held by women increased only from 9.6 percent in 1995 to 12.4 percent in 2001 to 15.2 percent in 2008 (Catalyst 2005, 2008). Minority representation on Fortune 100 boards increased, barely, from 14.89 percent in 2004 to 15.42 percent in 2006 (the most recent year for which we found data), but Hispanic and African American males actually lost ground (Alliance for Board Diversity 2008).

Given these changing boardroom demographics, many researchers have attempted to explore the possible rationales and motivations for board diversity efforts (reviewed in Broome and Krawiec 2008, 432–35). They include theories that board diversity addresses fairness concerns; that firms seeking board diversity are accessing an untapped talent pool; that female and minority board members reduce agency costs; that a more diverse board possesses more and better information; that diverse boards are more likely to engage in constructive dissent; that a diverse board conveys a credible signal to relevant observers of corporate behavior; and that board diversity is a meaningless public relations maneuver, generating neither real costs nor real benefits for shareholders. There is no consensus among researchers on the critical question of whether board diversity improves firm performance (Broome and Krawiec 2008).

The research reported here does not address psychological motivations, or the actual effects of diversity on board behavior, or the business performance outcomes that may or may not stem from board composition. Our question is a more direct one: what do the protagonists *say* about the significance of diversity? That is, what narratives (or, synonymously, stories or accounts) do board members, executives, government officials, and others produce when asked to explain whether and why diversity matters on corporate boards?

NARRATIVES AND STORIES

Scholars in many discourse literatures (including the frequently overlapping fields of sociolinguistics, linguistic anthropology, conversation analysis, and other forms of discourse analysis) tend to use the terms *narrative*, *story*, and *account* interchangeably (e.g., Ewick and Silbey 1998; Conley and O'Barr

1990). Narratives have been described as "everyday communication devices that create interpretive contexts for social action" (Bennett and Feldman 1981, 7). As Patricia Ewick and Susan Silbey (1998, 242) put it, "Storytelling is a conventional form of social interaction, among the ways we come to know each other, encounter the larger world, and learn about its organization." More specifically, "[i]n everyday social situations people use stories as a means of conveying selective interpretations of social behavior to others" (Bennett and Feldman 1981, 7). In form, a story typically "provides for the development, climax, and denouement of action in the context of a defined collection of actors, means, motives, and scenes" (Bennett and Feldman 1981). In effect, "a story not only focuses attention and judgment on certain key behavior (and the actors' relations to it), it also has the capacity to constrain a clear understanding about the significance of that behavior" (Bennett and Feldman 1981). Narrative can be used to configure past, present, future, and hypothetical experience (Ochs and Capps 2001) as well as to explain causation; Cheryl Mattingly (1998), paraphrasing Aristotle, argues that narrative "imitates action and experience through clarification and condensation, revealing causal connections between motive, deed, and consequence which also allows a moral reading of events."

A great deal has been written about the social, strategic, and rhetorical practices that characterize everyday storytelling. An early and still influential model of narrative structure is that of the sociolinguist William Labov (1972). Labov characterized a narrative as a sequence of "clauses" that match up with a sequence of "events which (it is inferred) actually occurred" (Labov 1972, 360; see Johnstone 2001). The narrative clauses fall into several functional categories, including the abstract or summary; the orientation, or introduction of time, setting, and characters; the complicating action clauses, which recapitulate events leading up to the climax; the result or resolution; one or more evaluation clauses, which permit the narrator to comment on the story; and a coda, which announces the end of the story. Elaborating on the Labov model, the linguist Wallace Chafe (2001, 677) has proposed "a ubiquitous schema for narrative topic development" that consists of summary, initial state, complication, climax, denouement, final state, and coda.

The various discourse literatures emphasize the social aspect of stories. The anthropologist Charles Briggs (1996, 14) writes that "the manner in which stories are presented and used is often contingent upon their being framed as embodiments of shared beliefs and understanding." Relatedly, "narratives do not simply describe ready-made events; rather, they provide central means by which we *create* notions as to what took place, how the action unfolded, what prompted it, and the social effects of the events" (Briggs 1996, 23). Narratives, in other words, comprise a "process of social construction" (Briggs

1996). In examining this process, it can be useful to think of storytelling as a metadiscursive practice, as the production of "discourses that seek to shape, constrain, or appropriate other discourses" (Briggs 1996, 19). Any given narrative is not only shaped by its own discursive context but can also build upon, incorporate, and reformulate prior discourses.

The fact that a member of a cultural group analyzes and interprets the world in a particular way does not, of course, permit one to make strong claims about what other members are thinking or doing. Nonetheless, the study of narratives can support a limited but significant kind of generalization. If members of a group repeatedly tell a similar story about an event or phenomenon, then it may be reasonable to characterize it as a master narrative: an account that achieves accepted, taken-for-granted, hegemonic status in the relevant group (Conley and Conley forthcoming). Through continual retelling, elaboration, and negotiation in a particular speech community, a master narrative can become *the* story of an event or other phenomenon, at least until challenged and replaced.

In this study we have collected narratives about the meaning of diversity in the selection and functioning of corporate boards of directors. (We acknowledge, of course, that as interviewers we are the coproducers of these narratives; see, e.g., Briggs 1996.) To date, we have interviewed thirty-six people around the United States who have a direct interest in the topic. Most are or have been directors of publicly traded companies; others include lawyers, consultants, and advisors of various sorts, and government regulators. We used an informal snowball technique, starting with subjects with whom we had some direct or indirect connection, and then branching out as subjects introduced us to others. In this qualitative analysis we make no claim about the representativeness of our sample.

The interviews have ranged from one to two hours in length, with two of us participating. At least one of us has been physically present for all but two of the interviews, which were done by telephone at the request of the subjects. We worked from a short list of general topics that we made sure to cover in each interview, but we encouraged the subjects to elaborate, digress, and introduce new topics as they saw fit. The subset of topics that are the subject of this paper are whether director diversity is important; if so, why; and whether the subject can give examples of director diversity making a difference in some respect.

We made audio recordings of all of the interviews. The recordings were transcribed by a professional transcription service, and we have verified and corrected the transcripts. The three of us conducted qualitative analysis of the tapes in conversation analysis-style discussions. But because our focus here is on topic and content rather than conversational details, we have chosen not to present the level of transcribing detail found in conversation analysis papers. First, we have rendered the subjects' speech in standard English spelling and punctuation rather than phonetically; thus, these transcripts say *weren't you* and *you can get* where a conversation analysis transcript might contain *werenchu* and *ya c'n get.* Second, we have eliminated many of the nonverbal elements, including the timing of pauses, the details of overlapping speech, and most nonverbal utterances. We recognize that we may be eliminating linguistic features that some readers would find useful, but we conclude that these compromises are appropriate to promote broad accessibility.

LEWIS POWELL AND THE ROOTS OF THE DIVERSITY NARRATIVE

Where did the concept of diversity come from, and why might it be important? The word *diversity* has roots in Middle English. But the contemporary usage that concerns us entered legal discourse—and seems to have entered general public discourse[1]—in Justice Lewis Powell's 1978 opinion in *Regents of University of California v. Bakke* (U.S. Supreme Court 1978), which dealt with a race-conscious admissions program at the UC-Davis medical school. The regularity with which it is repeated and relied on in higher education and other contexts suggests that the Powell narrative has become a kind of master narrative of diversity.

In *Bakke,* a Supreme Court majority voted to strike down UC-Davis's program as contrary to the Fourteenth Amendment's Equal Protection Clause and a federal civil rights statute, but it could not agree on a single opinion. In an opinion signed by no other justice, Powell, a member of the majority, asserted the proposition that race could be *a* factor in university admissions, because of the value of diversity. Recounting the university's argument in support of race-conscious admissions, Powell wrote (U.S. Supreme Court 1978, 312–14):

> The atmosphere of "speculation, experiment and creation"—so essential to the quality of higher education—is widely believed to be promoted by a diverse student body . . . it is not too much to say that the "nation's future depends upon leaders trained through wide exposure" to the ideas and mores of students as diverse as this Nation of many peoples.
>
> Thus, in arguing that its universities must be accorded the right to select those students who will contribute the most to the "robust exchange of ideas," petitioner invokes a countervailing constitutional interest, that of the First Amendment. In this light, petitioner must be viewed as seeking to achieve a goal that is of paramount importance in the fulfillment of its mission.

> It may be argued that there is greater force to these views at the undergraduate level than in a medical school, where the training is centered primarily on professional competency. But even at the graduate level, our tradition and experience lend support to the view that the contribution of diversity is substantial.
>
> Physicians serve a heterogeneous population. An otherwise qualified medical student with a particular background—whether it be ethnic, geographic, culturally advantaged or disadvantaged—may bring to a professional school of medicine experiences, outlooks, and ideas that enrich the training of its student body and better equip its graduates to render with understanding their vital service to humanity.

Justice Powell and the parties apparently adopted this definition of diversity from an amicus curiae brief submitted by Harvard, Columbia, Stanford, and the University of Pennsylvania in support of the University of California's position. Powell cited the brief later in his opinion in describing the kind of race-conscious admission program that would survive constitutional scrutiny (U.S. Supreme Court 1978, 316, 322–23):

> In recent years Harvard College has expanded the concept of diversity to include students from disadvantaged economic, racial and ethnic groups. Harvard College now recruits not only Californians or Louisianans but also blacks and Chicanos and other minority students. Harvard College now recruits not only Californians or Louisianans but also blacks and Chicanos and other minority students. Contemporary conditions in the United States mean that if Harvard College is to continue to offer a first-rate education to its students, minority representation in the undergraduate body cannot be ignored by the Committee on Admissions.
>
> In practice, this new definition of diversity has meant that race has been a factor in some admission decisions.

But Powell found the UC-Davis medical school's application of the concept to be unconstitutional because it amounted to little more than a quota system (U.S. Supreme Court 1978, 315):

> It may be assumed that the reservation of a specified number of seats in each class for individuals from the preferred ethnic groups would contribute to the attainment of considerable ethnic diversity in the student body. But petitioner's argument that this is the only effective means of serving the interest of diversity is seriously flawed. In a most fundamental sense the argument misconceives the nature of the state interest that would justify consideration of race or ethnic background. It is not an interest in simple ethnic diversity, in

which a specified percentage of the student body is in effect guaranteed to be members of selected ethnic groups, with the remaining percentage an undifferentiated aggregation of students. The diversity that furthers a compelling state interest encompasses a far broader array of qualifications and characteristics of which racial or ethnic origin is but a single though important element. Petitioner's special admissions program, focused solely on ethnic diversity, would hinder rather than further attainment of genuine diversity.

To return to the original *Bakke* quote, Justice Powell's argument for diversity—his foundational narrative, as it were—emphasizes two themes: the general value of "wide exposure" and the specific contribution of diversity to the educational process. Future "leaders" must be exposed "to the ideas and mores of students as diverse as this Nation of many peoples." Even at the graduate and professional level, with its emphasis on specific competencies, it is important that students not be kept "in an academic vacuum," "in isolation from the individuals and institutions" with which they will interact as professionals. With respect to process, Powell argues that diversity contributes to the "robust exchange of ideas." In medical school, a particular student's background, "whether it be ethnic, geographic, culturally advantaged or disadvantaged," may be a predictor of, or proxy for, "experiences, outlooks, and ideas that enrich the training" of fellow students and enhance their "understanding" as they enter a career of service to humanity.

The exposure part of the narrative has rarely elicited any objection; it seems self-evident that it will be better for students to be exposed to different kinds of people. The process component is potentially more problematic. Is the exchange of ideas really more robust if there is racial diversity in the classroom? If so, how does that come about? Is race a reasonable proxy for differences in "experiences, outlooks, and ideas"? Do students think or speak differently because of their racial backgrounds? Is it appropriate for teachers to assume that they do, or encourage them to do so? One can make a plausible case either way: that race is fundamentally important, or that the robustness of the exchange in a particular class depends almost entirely on the diligence and personalities of the individual students.

It should be noted that Justice Powell's diversity narrative is lacking one element that many nonlawyers might include in theirs: social justice. Powell says nothing about pursuing diversity as means to compensate for past injustice or simply to do something "right." The reason is probably legal: because there was no evidence of current discrimination at UC-Davis, a remedial or compensatory rationale would have been inappropriate.

In 2003, in two cases involving race-conscious admissions policies at the University of Michigan, *Gratz v. Bollinger* (U.S. Supreme Court 2003a) and

Grutter v. Bollinger (U.S. Supreme Court 2003b), the Supreme Court noted that the Powell opinion had become a cornerstone of university admissions policies nationwide. The business world had certainly taken notice of the *Bakke* narrative as well, as evidenced by General Motors and 3M's filing of amicus briefs in support of the University of Michigan.

BAKKE IN THE BOARDROOM?

Against this background, we wondered at the outset whether our subjects might invoke the Powell master narrative in the corporate board context. As a logical matter, the Powell argument for diversity translates well into the boardroom. If "leaders" should be exposed to the "ideas and mores" of the country's "many peoples," then why make an exception for corporate leaders? Moreover, the essence of the boardroom should be discussion and debate (although corporate chief executives might well have a vested interest in suppressing such debate). If the various forms of diversity that Powell mentioned actually do make the classroom exchange more robust, then might one expect the same effect in the boardroom? In addition, the social justice rationale that Justice Powell did not advance might be relevant as well. In choosing their members, boards are not constrained by the equal protection and antidiscrimination laws that governed the university's conduct in *Bakke.* (They are, however, constrained by a vaguely defined legal requirement that they act in the best interests of the corporation's shareholders; for example, they may not seek to enrich themselves at the expense of the shareholders, or take other actions that would diminish the value of the company.) Might they take into account past exclusionary practices as well as a general sense of right and wrong?

As will be seen in subsequent sections, the Powell narrative did not dominate our interviews. Nonetheless, we did hear distinct echoes of *Bakke.* Some subjects also added the justice rationale that Justice Powell had left out. Perhaps not coincidentally, two of the most vivid examples were full-time academics, people who have lived in the *Bakke* environment. One of the two, a white woman who is a university professor and experienced board member, even described the Powell rationale as an academic perspective, making reference to specific experiences on campus. Whereas Justice Powell wrote of diverse "experiences, outlooks, and ideas," she spoke of "different perspectives and different experiences."

TEXT 1

Q: Well, tell us more about [identifying material deleted] why you all [the board members] thought that [diversity] was a good idea.

A: Well, I guess I thought it was a good idea for two reasons—one, because it's justice, and two, most importantly, it makes sense for business. As a former CEO said, "I hate to see a board that has only on it the people I went to prep school with." And it's exactly true. Diversity in gender and race I think of as a proxy for different perspectives. And if you don't have different perspectives on a business, you're really missing a lot. Business case for it. It adds something. And it clearly does at [the company's] board meetings.
Q: Tell us how it adds.
A: Well, you put your finger on one thing, the difference between academics' and business people's perspective. I'm on a campus [identifying material deleted]. And so I hear about [diversity] from [academics] . . . I think because of socialization, I don't believe it's biological, most women have different experiences in our culture and bring to it something different. African Americans, Hispanics, Asian Americans. I mean, I think people have different experiences, and they bring it to the board meeting, and different knowledge.

The second subject, a white man who has been a business executive, a board member, and an academic, gave a similar account, stressing demographic proxies for "different points of view."

TEXT 2
Q1: You mentioned the right reasons [for diversity]. What are the right reasons?
A: Well that you appreciate that different points of view collectively will get to a better overall answer. That you appreciate that there are points of view that you wouldn't have because of your race or your economic status or your industry background that you wouldn't have that you need to have and that you need to take into account so and then just it's the morally right thing to do so I think boards get it on all those counts. Many of them do.

But justifying this Powell-like narrative—explaining precisely how difference can make a difference—is apparently as challenging in the corporate world as in higher education. In both interviews we asked immediate follow-up questions, and both subjects acknowledged difficulty in illustrating theory with reference to practice. The female academic responded with a single instance, admittedly not "a bold example."

TEXT 3
Q: Can you think of any anecdotes or concrete examples of "I [name deleted] said this, and maybe that was a contribution that I could make that my male counterpart could not make or would be unlikely to make?"
A: Well, I don't, I can't think of a bold example. I can give you one good example, which was several years ago. We have a group that does research on

issues of interest to us, and they presented several scenarios in which the wage earner was always the man. When a board member raises her hand and said, "This is not what life is any more," they pay attention. I'm surprised senior management didn't catch it before it even came to the board, because they do rehearsals and all that sort of thing. But they didn't. I think the presence of a critical mass of women means that there's likely to be a critical mass of women in anything we do, and certainly minorities.

The man struggled to avoid stereotyping:

TEXT 4

Q1: Can you elaborate on points of view? I mean to what extent do you think somebody's race or somebody's gender predicts a different kind of point of view?

A: Well you can't other than to say stereotypically you might see some of that fulfilled but when people of color are on a board, part of the reason they're on a board is to represent the point of view of people of color so I don't know whether that's stereotyping. I mean that's why they're there. You know? You don't want me to represent them. I can't. So I'm not sure quite how to answer your question.

But as we invited elaboration in a different way, he hit upon the subtle example of succession planning—subtle in the sense of not "cause and effect." That led him into a rumination on gender differences in awareness and sensitivity that was evocative of Carol Gilligan's *In a Different Voice* (1982):

TEXT 5

Q: Can you think of any anecdotes of things being discussed around the board table where you think because there was a woman or a person of color that you heard a point of view that was different than you would have otherwise heard or that was helpful in making a decision?

[Long pause]

A: When we talk about succession planning which every board does, it's in the boards that I've been on where there was a person of color, that person always spoke up about the need for greater progress in the management ranks for people of color and that would be, that kind of gets to your point too. That's not unexpected. It's welcomed that they do it. The issue that I raise gets raised and the point gets made well we've just got to overcome that and work harder and get more of our share of this limited pool than other folks do and so I think that's influential. I've never been on a board where the board will say let's do this and management will go okay we'll take that on board and put it on our agenda. It doesn't work like that. You know? It's more you let it be known that you think

> that this is important and then a meeting or two later it shows up on management's agenda so it's not going to be as cause and effect as you might imagine in a faculty meeting. There are other instances where in that spirit of men are from Mars and women are from Venus that and probably after we're all dead it will be accepted and okay to talk about the differences between the sexes and not pretend that everybody is exactly alike but there will be discussions about how do the typical employees feel or react in the organization and I don't know that may be slightly more than average, women will comment on issues of culture and staff acceptance or staff issues and by staff I mean at all levels.

Two elements of this account stand out. The first—the "limited pool" story—is one that we have heard on a number of occasions. The point, made here in the context of racial diversity, seems to be that there are currently relatively few experienced, high-level minority executives, and that companies that emphasize diversity will get more than their share of this talent, to their ultimate benefit. The second element is that there are fundamental differences between men and women in the way they approach business problems. The speaker suggests that is politically incorrect to talk about those differences now, but they are real and can make a positive contribution to the board environment. Other subjects talked around this issue, but none addressed it so forthrightly.

BUSINESS STORIES OF DIVERSITY

We now turn to the other diversity narratives we heard in our interviews. With the exception of the male academic already quoted (who, as we noted, had extensive business experience as well), all of the speakers in this section come from business and government. Elements of the Powell narrative appear, but other issues are also prominent. Overall, no coherent master narrative emerges. And regardless of content, our subjects' theories of diversity almost always prove difficult to illustrate with reference to practice. We next review several of these accounts, organized by principal theme. We begin with several versions of *Bakke's* "robust exchange of ideas" theme, and then discuss stories of diverse directors' personal experiences, the possible role of board diversity in sending signals to employees and other audiences, and the always-elusive "business case" for diversity. We conclude with a sharp if cynical summary of the diversity issue by an experienced corporate lawyer.

Analogs to Bakke's "Robust Exchange of Ideas"

A number of our subjects advanced theories of why boardroom exchanges are—or at least *should* be—more productive when a board has race and gender diversity. We saw relationships between these narratives and Justice Powell's "robust exchange of ideas" story. Our subjects' accounts tended to focus not on any specific affirmative benefits, but rather on the desirability of avoiding what some called "group think." Here again, concrete examples were hard to come by.

The most succinct statement of how boardroom communication improves came from a white female director of a manufacturing company, who said that diversity "makes for a richer conversation. It's not just all about the good old boys then." A shareholder proxy advisor (a white male) took the theory a step further, implying that diversity might predict viewpoint and tying diversity to risk avoidance:

TEXT 6
It started off as a small cadre of clients but I think it's grown over time, view diversity through that prism that it really genuinely is a way of reducing risk by encouraging a divergence of viewpoints in the board room.

Absent this "divergence of viewpoints," according to the same source, a board faces the prospect of "group think," which he explicitly identifies as a form of risk:

TEXT 7
I think people know especially on the risk side that whenever you get anything involving sort of group think, everybody in the room having the same background, group of experiences and so forth that that is an absolute breeding ground for risk, for problems to occur.

Another, superficially similar version of this basic account came from a white male director of a technology company:

TEXT 8
Q: You mentioned your own efforts to diversify boards at other companies you've been in. What do you see as the advantages to a company of an other-than-white-male board?
A: Well I think it brings an entirely new perspective to the thinking of a board. It creates a very positive dynamic and [laughs] you're right; I've sat on boards where all of us were silver haired males and the dynamic is different from when you have minorities and women on boards so I guess I just feel that there's more creative vibes going on [laughs] if you're on a board where there's different thinking and different channels of thinking.

We described Text 8 as "superficially similar" to the robust exchange story because, despite the semantic similarity between Justice Powell's "experiences, outlooks, and ideas" and this speaker's "different thinking and different channels of thinking," it was not entirely clear that this speaker was telling the same story. He could have been invoking a literature often taught in business schools that suggests that a major benefit of diversity derives from an effect on group dynamics that may not be related to the experiences of the participants (for overviews of this general literature see Jackson, Joshi, and Erhardt 2003; Williams and O'Reilly 1998; Milliken and Martins 1996). For example, the presence of diverse people in the boardroom could lead to conflict, dissent, or an erosion of deference to traditional authority and, consequently, more vigorous and skeptical debate. But as this director strived to provide an example of this "entirely new perspective" at work, the similarity between his theory and Powell's became clearer. He gave an elaborate account that moved from general observations to a specific instance from a company where he had formerly worked in an executive capacity:

TEXT 9

Q1: Can you give us maybe a real or a hypothetical example of what that dynamic is like? For those of us who haven't been there it's hard to visualize how the dynamic changes from the silver-haired males to the more diverse group.

A: I think one causal effect of the dynamic being different is that the base experience level of most of the males, the seasoned males, has been channeled in a similar direction. It's an old, classic hierarchy of organization which is, I think, rapidly becoming outmoded. It's very outmoded now and a way of thinking that is driven by this basic chain of command thinking and I believe that women who have joined boards and who've joined management in fact later than men and who bring a different value system, I think in a different way they can actually think more creatively. Most of my good marketing people in the food business, really good marketing people, were women because they I think better understood our primary consumer who happened to be women [laughs] and I just think there's a different thought process, a different way that they solve problems or attempt to talk through a problem. With minorities I've not had as much exposure with minorities. I've had only one Oriental direct report in my businesses and I've had maybe a half dozen African Americans but what I found valuable is they have a different way of thinking in a social structure. They actually bring you thought channels that you would never even think about or even broach in a meeting as it relates to not only their segment of the population but to the interaction between the segments of the population and people just, if they're not challenged to think about things like that they don't [laughs] so [name of an African American

> female director] was a classic example. She actually brought us new ways of thinking about how to approach the minorities where we had in many instances, some of the [company's restaurants] were located in predominantly African American areas [identifying information deleted] and she just gave us a lot of great insight into what stimulates an African American family to experience [the company's style of restaurant]. It was very valuable.

Note the elements of this fascinating account:

- "Seasoned males," shaped by their experience, engage in "basic chain of command thinking." That is, the usual suspects—experienced white males—tend to approach corporate issues in the same way.
- Women, by contrast, "bring a different value system"; "in a different way they can actually think more creatively." They approach problems in fundamentally different ways—a less colorful version of the point made in Text 5 that "men are from Mars and women are from Venus."
- In the food business, perhaps because women better understood the consumer, he observed "a different thought process, a different way that they solve problems or attempt to talk through a problem." This seems to be an illustration of his notion of different value systems and thinking more creatively. As such, it is strikingly trivial, apparently relating to little more than women's experience as shoppers.
- In his admittedly limited experience with minorities, he has found "they have a different way of thinking in a social structure." He continued in this anthropological vein, noting that this way of thinking "relates to not only their segment of the population but to the interaction between the segments of the population." The point seems to be that minorities have different social experiences that lead them to different insights about individual and group relations.
- But the single example he provided is of an African American director advising the board on how to market restaurants to African Americans. Is this the "entirely new perspective" that director diversity promises?

Female and Minority Directors Describing Their Own Experiences

When asked to describe their own experiences, many of our female and minority respondents make it clear that they have not been treated like spokespersons; in the words of a white female director, "I do not believe at all that by sitting in a chair I am speaking the woman's point of view." A few others have embraced that role. All make it clear that they have not been treated as tokens, regardless of whether they take on the mantel of "spokesperson." Some retell elements of the *Bakke* story, but is difficult to discern from their accounts just how their race or gender has contributed to boardroom discourse.

An African American man strongly rejected tokenism:

> **TEXT 10**
> **Q:** How does, given that there's sort of this unwritten rule [just described by the subject] that we'd like at least two minorities on the board, how does that impact the dynamic in the board room? Do you feel like you are a quota or a token or do you—
> **A:** Oh, no. No. Other than knowing that, and I'm not sure, well, I guess the other directors do, it doesn't have an effect on me one way or another. I'm a director and I'm there to do a job and when issues of diversity come up I don't necessarily feel that I'm the one that's got to bring it to the floor.

When asked about the value of his diverse background, he endorsed the proposition in the abstract. But the example he gave had less to do with the "robust exchange of ideas" than with leveraging his personal contacts for marketing purposes:

> **TEXT 11**
> **Q:** Does the experience of someone who is a racial minority or is a woman, does that experience, in and of itself add something, assuming of course that the skill set that is necessary is there?
> **A:** Yeah, I think it does. When [a large bank] acquired [a local bank in a city with a large African American population] there was considerable concern across the community that [the local bank] had been the "family bank" that everybody knew and if you wanted to start a business you went to [the local bank] and you could get some money and that kind of thing. So people were very comfortable but there was an awful lot of concern about what was gonna happen when the marquee no longer said [the local bank] and it changed over to [the large bank]. And [an African American female director] and I were both able to be helpful to [the large bank] because we knew people in that market who [the large bank] folks could go talk to, to allay those kinds of fears. And that worked well. I think that given the skill sets of everybody are the same, the experience and background and kind of things you know that you can bring to the table are beneficial to boards.

An African American woman who has been a board member as well as a consultant began with a statement (Text 12) that leaves the listener unclear about exactly why she thinks race and/or gender diversity affects the boardroom, but then quite clearly invoked the *Bakke* "ideas and experiences" narrative in her later statements (Text 13).

TEXT 12

Q: What do you think it is then about the diverse board that helps the company to do better and helps them—

A: I think people ask complex and different, I think people do, now am I seeing that if you look there and all of us look alike and we all do the exact same thing, the likelihood is we're not challenging each other. We're not saying look let's think about this, think about that, what about this, what about that, I think it's a richer conversation that occurs that then says broader, open this door, take the blinders off, let's consider a lot of different kinds of things as we think about this.

At another point in the discussion, in response to essentially the same question, she spoke in considerable detail from both the board member and consultant perspectives. Her emphasis shifted several times during the course of the account. She began by speaking of the totality of her experience ("a whole complexity") as a Southern, African American woman who went to a historically black college. She next focused on her gender, distinguishing her experiences from those of "an African American guy." She then condemned race- and gender-based affirmative action as "racist and sexist," and finally concentrated on the value of professional experience and "competencies."

TEXT 13

Q: Well do you think it's important to have race and gender diversity on boards?

A: Yeah I do and not just for the race and gender. I bring a whole complexity of what I bring to the table. Having grown up in the South, being an African American, having gone to an African American college, I mean the question I may ask that I may ask is totally different from the question the guy may ask and it could be an African American guy but he's had a whole different set of complex experiences too but even more so I do think and I do firmly believe this, boards should not be doing social engineering. You know? Now having said that, do I think it's beneficial? Absolutely, but not for the sake of having an African American, not for the sake of having a woman and being able to say we've got ours. That doesn't work for me. That in and of itself is racist and sexist in my opinion. You don't want that. You want, is this person a technology expert, a logistics expert, do they have government relations; I mean there's something. We do a grid on a board and we look to see what are the gaps, what competencies would be beneficial for them and then in my opinion then you look broadly and in looking broadly we also look for diversity in this process.

The Signaling Theory

Several of our subjects argued that boards should be representative of various constituencies, including communities, customers, shareholders, and employees. They did not seem to be saying that board members should represent demographic groups in the sense of being prepared to answer the "so what do you guys think about this?" question. Rather, their accounts emphasized using board composition to send positive signals about the company to particular groups. Except in the case of employees, the specific reasons for doing this were stated with less clarity than the basic principle. Text 14 is a statement by a white male banking regulator. He discussed representation of communities, customer bases, and workforces in a meandering account that did not distinguish board members and employees. He concluded with an argument for gender diversity that mixed an experience-based marketing expertise rationale with a signaling theory:

TEXT 14

The rap on banks has been traditionally that they were, as one of my [board] members so colorfully puts it, "They were male, pale, and stale." And in truth for many of our banks the composition of a bank board is very much like the composition of the local Chamber of Commerce Board, certain church boards. They're social institutions of cities and towns of various sizes and there are strengths to that and there are weaknesses. The strengths are that you have cohesion and a certain sense of reflecting broadly held values of the community. The weakness is that you don't, boards can become inbred, in-, hidebound, inbred, and can fail to take into account changes that are going on in their communities. Plus, in the case of women, I have tried to point out to banks that more than half the people in their markets are women, this has also been pointed out by a member of our [board]. A classic situation where one bank was asked, "Well, how many people in your market are women?" The poor guy said like 25 percent, [laughter] which means he needed a little mathematical or sociology, sociological training. And no joke, women still, although the effects of increased and lawfully increased equality in the workplace may mean that women's life spans don't [laughter] exceed them so much in the future, but as I understand there's still a demographic trend that women live longer and to the extent that there is, there are residual wealth in estates and there's real money that's held by women who are widows or living alone, as a lot of it is. And if you go into the average bank if you look at who's working in plain view of everyone, the representation of the bank to the community is often female. It's sensible to me that you would want to have someone who is a working woman on a board, at least one, to point out to the rest of the board what it's like—what the life of their employee—many of their employees is like.

The Elusive Business Case

Several of our subjects mentioned aspects of what can be termed a "business case" for diversity—that diversifying a board leads to better financial performance by the company. In the succinct words of the just-quoted banking regulator, "I believe it [board diversity] is also a business imperative." But citing evidence was a more difficult proposition. The same regulator continued:

TEXT 15

Q: Have you observed any difference in business performance between boards that have no diversity and the boards that do?

A: I haven't yet, but I haven't studied it really well. I will say I think this is the kind of thing you'd have to look at over a long period. And I say that because many banks which realize they need to diversify are in an interesting place in their corporate development, it's almost like adverse selection. As they begin to diversify things may get worse for awhile. I don't mean worse, they just may have slowed down.

This equivocation was especially interesting because it is presumably part of this person's job to be aware of indicators of bank performance. Equally interesting was this comment by a white male executive with a proxy voting advisory service, whose job is clearly to be aware of boards' impact on earnings. His rhetoric is technical, as is his explanation for the dearth of evidence—a lack of good data.

TEXT 16

It's been discussed from time to time I think and again one of the things we always look at in [analysis] is going to the empirical data and trying to find some sort of indication of an impact on either financial performance and/or mitigation of risk and I think it's only been fairly recent that we've started to see some studies focusing in particular on gender diversity that has started to indicate there may be an economic element connected with it and so that could probably increase the likelihood that it will get stronger consideration going forward . . . I'd have to go back and check as to whether we've actually run the regressions using diversity as a factor before. I doubt that we have because that's our other problem is getting good data.

The male academic quoted at the beginning of this section shared this uncertainty, and he doubted that it would ever be resolved:

TEXT 17

Q: Do you think over the long term board diversification is going to affect company performance in any tangible way?

A: Well tangible way means that you could do some research and show first of all a correlation and then a connection between diversity and performance. I don't think you're going to get—
Q: Twenty-five years from now our successors won't be able to show that?
A: Well I think there's just so many other variables that you're not going to get a sample size big enough to tease it out.

By contrast, a white female director of a manufacturing company treated the business case as a hope rather than a reality that is hard to prove:

TEXT 18
Q: Do you think there's a case to be made that diversity is related to company performance, diversity at the board level has some ties to corporate performance?
A: I hope so. I mean I'd love to have that. I'd love to have a researcher make that case to show that that's true.

When asked for existing evidence that diversity impacts performance, she began on an affirmative note. But she seemed to say nothing more than that the company must be better because the board was pushing diversity:

TEXT 19
Q: Do you have any qualitative or even anecdotal sense of situations where you thought we're doing something because of our board diversity that makes the company better, is going to make the company perform better? I just wonder what your instinct is on that.
A: My instinct on that is yes we are doing something because we're pushing our senior colleagues on the diversity issue that we want to see and this is not just [names another female director and an African American male] doing this.

We also asked about a different kind of business case for diversity: whether shareholders would insist on it. Some of our respondents rejected this proposition, and a white male director with broad experience dismissed it out of hand:

TEXT 20
Q: Do shareholders care about board diversity or the composition of the board in general?
A: They really don't. You would hope they would. Major institutional shareholders really care about having people on boards who've had board experience with other companies and who have experience in sector.

Summing Up

A striking summary of why companies pursue board diversity came from a white female director who also has years of experience providing professional advice to corporate boards. The specific topic was why one particular board had sought diversity. Her account suggests that the business world does not have a well-reasoned diversity rationale—in fact, the question of rationale is never even discussed:

> **TEXT 21**
> **Q:** When you guys were looking for another director and came up with [a diverse director] and diversity was one but not the only metric [according to the subject], why was that on the list of metrics? What was articulated about what benefit might come to [the company] from having some more diversity in terms of race or gender on the board?
> **A:** I suspect you haven't gotten many introspective answers on that because, in fact, you're never going to have a board that will honestly question whether or not there is a value associated with that. And people will accept it and move on. Everybody says the same thing because, again, I'm in board rooms a hundred times a year and I hear the same discussion. And what they say is we have skill sets that we want and if we can find a diverse candidate who fulfills them without sacrificing the skill sets that we're looking for that would be terrific. And the analysis doesn't go any further. It just isn't discussed. So anything I tell you about why I think diversity adds value is going to by [my] thoughts not because it was a topic of discussion. [Sentence that identifies company deleted.] So to the extent we're talking about sort of that wide swath of middle America then it's nice to have a board that is in some respects emblematic of that but we've never discussed it.

CONCLUSION

Our relatively small sample of interviews (thirty-six) provides no evidence of the emergence of what might be reasonably called a master narrative of board diversity. One plausible candidate—a business version of Justice Powell's *Bakke* narrative—appears from time to time. Our subjects have mentioned their beliefs that diversity creates a "richer conversation," "an entirely new perspective," "different points of view," and "a very positive dynamic." But it is a theoretical narrative without concrete detail, a story without substance. When invited to elaborate, subjects have digressed into instances that had little to do with race or gender, and in fact have often distanced themselves from demographic variables. The few specific examples that they have presented seem almost trivial, as in the case of the African American female director who advised the company on the restaurant dining preferences of black families. We heard nothing specific about diversity contributing to the kind of high-level strategic thinking that is the presumed province of corporate boards. Significantly, none of our subjects expressed anything more than a hope that diversity would correlate with business performance. Overall, our subjects tell a story that amounts to little more than "it seems like the right thing to do."

An obvious final question is why this is so. Why do our subjects, on the one hand, affirm board diversity as a goal while, on the other, they offer little substantive justification for pursuing it? Perhaps the *Bakke* narrative has achieved a broad but shallow victory, a discourse-level hegemony that has few consequences for thought or action. Recall the lawyer's comment in Text 21 that "you're never going to have a board that will honestly question whether or not there is a value associated with [diversity]." That is, in the years since *Bakke,* genuflecting in the direction of diversity has become a routine part of polite and politically correct discourse. This has correlated with a modest increase in women and minorities on boards, though their representation may have reached a plateau. But, to judge by our sample, business people do not seem to be thinking very hard about the concept of diversity, and so have not come up with a coherent narrative about why it is important.

A related possibility is that our subjects did engage in some introspection about diversity, but at a general moral level. They may think that diversifying boards is a good thing for a variety of moral reasons: compensation for past discrimination, promoting equal access to opportunity, or making the company a fairer place. On a practical level, they may identify some potential positives, including signaling to employees and other audiences and, perhaps, the elusive "richer conversation." At the same time, they may see few if any negatives. Against the recent background of corporate scandals and disaster in the financial sector, one might well ask, How could anyone else do worse?

All this, however, is speculation about motive. The linguistic evidence we have collected neither proves nor refutes any particular hypothesis. We are left, rather, with the absence of a coherent and consistent narrative about boardroom diversity. Given the way that the *Bakke* story has penetrated higher education and public discourse more generally, it is striking that no analogous master narrative seems to have evolved among the corporate elite.

NOTES

Financial support for this project was provided by the Fulfilling the Dream Fund: North Carolina Consortium, the Z. Smith Reynolds Foundation, and the Pogue Foundation Fellowship.

1. This generalization is based on our own review of published sources. The use of "diversity" (with the meaning we discuss here) seems not to predate, but to explode thereafter.

REFERENCES

Alliance for Board Diversity. 2008. *Women and Minorities on Fortune 100 Boards*, http://www.elcinfo.com/downloads/docs/Final_1_22_08.pdf.

Bennett, W. L., and M. S. Feldman. 1981. *Reconstructing Reality in the Courtroom: Justice and Judgment in American Culture.* New Brunswick, NJ: Rutgers Univ. Press.

Briggs, C. L. 1996. Introduction. In *Disorderly Discourse: Narrative, Conflict, and Inequality,* ed. C. L. Briggs, 3–40. Oxford, UK: Oxford Univ. Press.

Broome, L. L., and K. D. Krawiec. 2008. Signaling through Board Diversity: Is Anyone Listening? *Cincinnati Law Review* 77: 431–64.

Catalyst. 1993. *Women on Corporate Boards: The Challenge of Change,* http://www.catalyst.org/file/227/women_on_corporate_boards_the_challenge_of_change.pdf.

Catalyst. 2005. *2005 Catalyst Census of Women Board Directors of the Fortune 500,* http://www.catalyst.org/file/9/2005%20wbd.pdf.

Catalyst. 2008. *2008 Catalyst Census of Women Board Directors of the Fortune 500,* http://catalyst.org/file/242/08_census_wbd_jan.pdf.

Chafe, W. 2001. The Analysis of Discourse Flow. In *The Handbook of Discourse Analysis*, eds. D. Schiffrin, D. Tannen, and H. E. Hamilton, 673–87. Malden, MA: Blackwell Publishing.

Conley, J. M., and W. M. O'Barr. 1990. *Rules versus Relationships: The Ethnography of Legal Discourse.* Chicago: University of Chicago Press.

Conley, R. H., and J. M. Conley. 2009. Forthcoming. Stories from the Jury Room: How Jurors Use Narrative to Process Evidence. *Studies in Law, Politics and Society* 49, 25–56.

Ewick, P., and S. S. Silbey. 1998. *The Common Place of Law: Stories from Everyday Life.* Chicago: University of Chicago Press.

Fairfax, L. M. 2005. The Bottom Line on Corporate Board Diversity: A Cost-Benefit Analysis. *Wisconsin Law Review* 2005, 795–854.

Gilligan C. 1982. *In a Different Voice: Psychological Theory and Women's Development.* Cambridge, MA: Harvard University Press.

Jackson, S. E., A. Joshi, and N. L. Erhardt. 2003. Recent Research on Team and Organizational Diversity: SWOT Analysis and Implications. *Journal of Management* 29: 801–30.

Johnstone, B. 2001. Discourse Analysis and Narrative. In *The Handbook of Discourse Analysis*, eds. D. Schiffrin, D. Tannen, and H. E. Hamilton, 635–49. Malden, MA: Blackwell Publishing.

Labov, W. 1972. *Language in the Inner City.* Philadelphia: University of. Pennsylvania Press.

Mattingly, C. 1998. *Healing Dramas and Clinical Plots: The Narrative Structure of Experience*. Cambridge: Cambridge University Press.

Milliken, F. J., and L. L. Martins. 1996. Searching for Common Threads: Understanding the Multiple Effects of Diversity in Organizational Groups. *Academy of Management Review* 21: 402–33.

Ochs, E., and L. Capps. 2001. *Living Narrative: Creating Lives in Everyday Storytelling*. Cambridge: Harvard University Press.

Rose, C. 2007. Does Female Board Representation Influence Firm Performance? The Danish Evidence. *Corporate Governance* 15: 404–39.

Sjafsjell, B., and H. B. Reiersen. 2008. Report from Norway: Gender Equality in the Board Room. *European Company Law*, No. 4, http://papers.ssrn.com/sol3/papers.cfm?abstract_id=1139604.

U.S. Supreme Court. 1978. *Regents of University of California v. Bakke*. *United States Reports* 438: 265–421.

U.S. Supreme Court. 2003a. *Gratz v. Bollinger*. *United States Reports* 539: 244–304.

U.S. Supreme Court. 2003b. *Grutter v. Bollinger*. *United States Reports* 539: 306–94.

Williams, K. Y., and C. A. O'Reilly. 1998. Demography and Diversity in Organizations: A Review of 40 Years of Research. *Research in Organizational Behavior* 20: 77–140.

10

Going Green

How Organizations Use Narrative to Build Commitment to Environmental Values and Action

Daphne A. Jameson and Judi Brownell

Historically, U.S. industries have valued the environment as a resource to be used, not protected. Mining companies extracted coal, copper, and other minerals for manufacturing. Paper companies cut down forests. Energy companies drilled for oil and gas. Manufacturers disposed of toxic chemicals by dumping them into rivers. Influenced by the biblical precept that humans had dominion over the earth, businesses treated the natural world as a kingdom to be conquered and subjugated.

The rise of the environmental movement in the second half of the twentieth century gradually led to the growth of a different philosophy: that business and industry should protect and nurture natural resources, not overuse and deplete them. Several catalysts led to this shift in public perceptions. The publication of Rachel Carson's *Silent Spring* in 1962 alerted people to the damage that pesticides and pollution had done. The oil embargo in the early 1970s led consumers to want automobiles with more gas efficiency. Environmental organizations, such as the Sierra Club and Nature Conservancy, grew in membership and visibility. In 1970 the U.S. government created the Environmental Protection Agency, which began to restrict commercial and industrial practices. In the late 1990s, Vice President Al Gore interwove warnings about global warming into political discourse, culminating with the documentary *An Inconvenient Truth* and a Nobel Peace Prize in 2007.

In responding to the public's evolving attitudes and concerns, business and industry faced not only public pressures to become more proactive in environmental protection but also financial pressures to do so without sacrificing profits. In transforming themselves into so-called green organizations—those that avow commitment to practices that do not harm the environment—businesses have had to learn to engage and persuade constituencies who often have different and sometimes diametrically opposed interests.

This chapter reports on a study of how organizations in one industry—lodging—have approached the pressures to become "green" and reconciled them with evolving corporate values. Specifically, we studied environmental texts, a term we define to mean written and visual discourse through which organizations promote values and actions related to protecting nature or achieving sustainability, a balance between the depletion and renewal of natural resources. We sought to answer two questions. First, we wanted to learn how organizations use environmental texts to tell a story that will create shared meanings and develop a collective understanding of and commitment to environmental values and action. Second, because the success of such efforts is by no means assured, we wondered how contradictions and discrepancies might undermine the persuasiveness of environmental texts and thus diminish organizational ethos, a new concept that we define as identity built on deeply held values and credibility demonstrated through action.

We start by situating our study within previous explorations of the connections between environmentalism and the language, rhetoric, and narrative that make it possible. Then we explain how we applied narratology—a narrative theory and methodology drawn from literary and cultural studies—to business discourse. Next, we present our findings, showing how organizations created narrative structures based on three contrasting story lines, each with multiple possible author-reader relationships. We close by discussing how narrative balance among story lines may influence organizational ethos—an impact that has important implications for all organizations that seek to engender commitment to environmental values and action.

SITUATING OUR STUDY

Interest in issues of environmental values and action has grown as the public's expectations for responsible practices have increased and pressures to conform to new standards and controls have moved the agenda to the center of boardroom tables. Of course, a disconnect often exists between values and action. Most corporations avow commitment to environmental values in official policy statements and, sometimes, in advertising. Developing business practices and new initiatives to support those values requires hard decision making and persuasive communication with a variety of audiences to engender support. Some previous research has explored the link between environmental values and action.

Motives for Taking Environmental Initiatives

Researchers have identified a range of motives for environmental initiatives, from regulatory compliance to competitive advantage, from public pressures to ethical considerations, from individual values to top management directives. For example, in a study of firms in the United Kingdom and Japan, Bansal and Roth (2000) concluded that personal values and the degree of individual discretion to act on environmental problems contributed to a firm's ecological initiatives. Sharma (2000) showed how managers faced significant ambiguity in understanding key environmental issues and identifying the concerns of multiple constituencies. Fineman (1996) argued that green initiatives are motivated by emotional meanings such as guilt and shame; managers in environmentally sensitive companies were not operating from a personal moral code about the environment but from a perceived obligation to perform the required duties of their roles.

The Role of Language, Discourse, and Symbols

Scholars have also explored how organizations develop a collective understanding of environmental values through the use of language, discourse, and symbols. In creating a model of socioecological responsiveness, Johnson and Macy (2001) contrasted and connected different stakeholders' expressed principles. Harris and Crane's (2002) study of management values revealed that confusion regarding definitions led to gaps between a company's espoused environmental position and its actual management practices. This study also suggested that the public's actions had a strong symbolic power and persuasive effect in molding managers' actions. Fineman (1996) found that a strong culture characterized by formal documents homogenized values, selling the language of commitment to members rather than shaping it from their experiences. While the common corporate language enabled organizational members to share an environmental focus, customers' responses were the standard for determining action. Strong cultures sold the "language of care" (493) and encouraged adoption of emotional scripts that might simply have been skilled performances. Starkey and Crane (2003) addressed the power of language and metaphor in environmental discourse, noting that language carries norms and values implications; framing organizations as the "planet's stewards," for example, had a much different effect from acknowledging their "compliance with environmental codes" (231).

Applications of Narrative and Rhetorical Theories to Environmental Texts

Only a few studies have used narrative and rhetorical theories to elucidate complex environmental issues. Starkey and Crane (2003) described the narrative basis of the evolutionary epic as a means for what they called the "reenchantment" of sustainability. Livesey (1999) examined the rhetorical and discursive aspects of McDonald's green alliance with the Environmental Defense Fund and analyzed the rhetorical strategies the corporation applied in its efforts to create a green public image. She concluded that inside accounts of green initiatives are needed and that collaboration between business and the environmental community is more complex than the business literature portrays. Analyzing the rhetoric used in environmental disputes by deconstructing documents produced by Royal Dutch/Shell and its critics, Livesey (2001) demonstrated how the corporation's communication symbolically both influenced and constructed its external audiences. Her study of ExxonMobil's discourse (2002) contrasted the value of rhetorical versus discourse analysis in business communication research. Other than Livesey, however, few scholars have taken up the challenge that Bullis (1997) issued: to explore how communication functions in the relationship between business and the natural environment, recognizing that cultural assumptions often color our understanding of that relationship.

In this chapter we seek to add to the body of knowledge that Bullis (1997) envisioned by approaching the issues that Livesey (1999, 2001, 2002) studied from a different theoretical perspective: narratology. Specifically, our study sought to answer the following research questions:

1. How do organizations in the lodging industry use the narrative aspects of environmental texts to try to create shared meanings and develop a collective understanding of and commitment to environmental values and action?
2. How might contradictions and discrepancies undermine the persuasiveness of these environmental texts and thus diminish organizational ethos; that is, identity built on deeply held values and credibility demonstrated through action?

APPLYING NARRATOLOGY TO BUSINESS DISCOURSE

To explore these research questions, we used an interpretive methodology to apply a narrative theory to a contemporary organizational issue. Specifically, we used textual analysis to apply the theory of narratology to the question of how organizations develop collective understanding of and commitment to environmental values and action. Interpretive methodology was appropriate because our goal was not to test hypotheses about how organizations could best gain support for environmental initiatives but instead to explore the broad range of linguistic, narrative, and rhetorical approaches that organizations have used in their efforts to establish collective values related to environmental action. An interpretive methodology allowed us to analyze the rich language and imagery through which organizations seek to draw diverse constituencies into collective understanding and commitment.

Hospitality as a Research Context

The hospitality industry, which encompasses lodging, food service, travel, tourism, entertainment, and real estate, is a good site for studying the phenomenon of environmental action for several reasons. First, hospitality is a major economic force, one of the world's largest industries. In the United States alone, lodging revenues exceeded $139 billion in 2007 (Smith Travel Research 2008), while tourism sales rose to $740 billion (American Hotel and Lodging Association 2008). Environmental action in this industry size has the potential to make a significant impact. Second, the hospitality industry faces bigger hurdles than do others in securing attention and support for environmental efforts. To make compelling appeals is challenging because the hospitality industry is a less direct consumer of natural resources than manufacturing and heavy industries. Because hospitality businesses affect the environment in such a seemingly ordinary, low-impact way, it is a bigger challenge to convince constituencies, such as employees, customers, investors, and owners, that environmental action is necessary and to secure their commitment. Our study focused on one major segment of hospitality, lodging, because compared to other industry segments, hotels and resorts were early adopters of environmental initiatives. Many properties instituted energy-saving programs in the 1980s and have broadened these efforts in recent years.

Narratology as a Theoretical Framework

The framework for our study was narratology, a narrative theory that originated in literary studies and subsequently has been applied to cultural studies. Narratology explores how stories originate and why different versions of the same story create different effects. Narratology describes complex relationships among several levels of narrative, explains how these interact, and in so doing provides a sound basis for interpretation of meaning and divergences in meaning. The first level of narrative, called the *fabula*, is the broad universe of all possible materials related to a particular theme or subject from which a story could be derived. The second level consists of the materials actually shaped into one particular *story*, which we define as a logically or thematically connected sequence of events involving one or more characters. The third level of narrative is a *text*, by which we mean the concrete instantiation of a story in a particular medium with specific language, visual images, or combinations thereof.

Narratology emphasizes that the broad universe of materials can yield multiple stories, and each story can yield multiple texts. Consider the following example from the lodging industry. Drawn from the broad universe of materials related to Marriott International's concern about social and environmental issues, one story concerns how the company created a partnership with the Brazilian government to help protect part of the Amazon rain forest. This story has been recounted in many specific texts in a variety of verbal and visual media, including press releases, internal memos, a social responsibility report, annual reports to shareholders, advertising, web pages, Facebook postings, videos, a blog by the Chairman and CEO, news articles, commentaries by external sources, etc. A narratological study might trace the origin of the materials, the evolution of the story, the divergence among the texts, the impact of different media choices and combinations, or other elements of the narrative discourse.

As the framework for our study, narratology offered several advantages. First, it directly links to the significance of our research question. An important underlying belief of narratology is that "language shapes vision and worldview, rather than the other way around" (Bal 1997, 19). If this is the case, then the language that the hotel industry used did not merely persuade constituencies to agree with corporate values but in fact shaped those values. Second, narratology recognizes that functional, rhetorical discourse (e.g., reports, meetings, advertising, websites) is equal in importance and complexity to literary and artistic discourse. The domain of narratology includes verbal texts, such as novels and business reports; visual texts, such as paintings and architecture; and hybrid texts that combine both verbal and visual elements, such as films and commercials. Though narratology has most often been applied to aesthetic texts, such as literature, it can also be applied to nonaesthetic texts, such as news articles and organizational documents. Bal (1997, 220) says that "like semiotics, narratology applies to virtually every cultural object. Not that everything 'is' narrative; but practically everything in culture has a narrative aspect to it, or at the very least, can be perceived, interpreted as narrative."

Textual Analysis as a Methodology

One primary methodology is associated with narratology: textual analysis. Narratology uses textual analysis as a humanities-oriented rather than social-science-oriented process (Boje 2001). Bal (1997) describes narratology as providing a heuristic tool. For her and other narratologists, textual analysis involves close reading as performed in literary and rhetorical criticism rather than quantitative analysis of linguistic features. Narratologists consider their primarily role in intellectual inquiry to be critics, reflecting their acknowledgment of subjectivity as natural and even desirable. The word *subjective* in this sense does not mean whimsical, idiosyncratic, or unsystematic; instead, subjective refers to the significance placed on human understanding and interpretation of phenomena.

We chose textual analysis as the methodology for our study not only because of its compatibility with and traditional linkage to narratology but also because textual analysis is especially well positioned to answer research questions like ours (Bargiela-Chiappini, Nickerson, and Planken 2007). Texts are officially sanctioned, authorized expressions of organizational values and goals. Though a discrepancy between official texts and organizational practice often occurs, one must understand the avowed organizational values before studying the discrepancies with actual practice.

Another important reason that textual analysis is a valuable methodology for this and other business discourse studies is that most written business texts live on to become historical records and legal documents. They create organizational and institutional accountability that oral business communication does only when it is recorded and retained. For this reason, texts create heightened awareness of moral and ethical values as well as legal obligations. A final reason for our choice of textual analysis is that it opens a window for organizational researchers onto an important temporal phenomenon: Most texts are planned, not spontaneous discourse. Thus they differ cognitively from informal conversations, meetings, and other interactions common to organizational life.

Collection of Environmental Texts

The data for this study consisted of a corpus of 135 texts created by ninety hotel-industry organizations in order to explain or promote environmental values or action. Over a period of years, we had collected environmental texts from the hospitality industry. In this study the main criterion for including a text was that it must directly and specifically address one or more environmental values, practices, policies, or initiatives in hotels, resorts, or other types of commercial lodging. The organizations that produced these texts included public and private corporations, individual hotel and resort properties, professional and trade associations, hotel-employee labor unions, industry-oriented publishers, hospitality consulting groups, and government tourism offices. Most organizations had headquarters in North America, but some were in Europe or Asia. Many operated throughout the world; the major lodging companies are global. Almost all documents were in English, but some included parallel translations in French, German, Spanish, Turkish, Chinese,

Japanese, or other languages. We included only the English texts in our study. The genres represented in the corpus of texts included customer and client communications, employee communications, reports, press releases, web pages, manuals, announcements, newsletters, articles, guidelines, and corporate social responsibility statements and reports. Many documents included visual elements, such as photos, charts, and logos. We included both the verbal and visual elements in our study. We used a broad corpus of texts in this study because we wanted to explore stories, symbols, and themes that cut across specific audiences and genres.

Limitations and Future Options for Study

Our methodology has several limitations, but each suggests further research opportunities. Because our theoretical framework is from the humanities, we did not attempt to collect a representative sample that mirrored a target population. Instead, using the approach of literary and cultural studies, we gathered a wide range of materials that shared a common subject matter and theme—in this case, environmentalism. A subsequent study might use scientific sampling to answer additional questions, such as how frequently companies used each of the narrative structures we discuss. Another study might focus on environmental narratives in a particular genre, such as corporate social responsibility reports, or on narratives aimed at a particular audience, such as franchisees or investors.

In addition, though, our choice to study planned, edited written discourse has several advantages, which we have mentioned, but there is a downside. Spontaneous oral discourse about environmental values, which could be gathered by recording meetings, interviews, or conversations, would provide different insights about how organizations inculcate environmental values and make decisions about environmental initiatives. Such data, however, were beyond the scope of our current study.

Finally, our study's focus was textual criticism rather than what in literary studies is called "reception"; that is, a focus on the readers who receive, process, and use texts. A future complementary study might apply such methodologies as protocol analysis, surveys, ethnography, or interviews to determine how readers respond to environmental texts. While valuable, these methods were beyond the scope of our current study.

Data Analysis Process

We divided our data analysis into three stages, using an inductive sequence that moved from text to story to fabula, the three levels of narrative posited by the theory of narratology. First, using linguistic concepts, we analyzed each text, including both verbal and visual elements. Second, using concepts drawn from literary criticism, we developed the major story lines through which the texts attempted to persuade readers about environmental values and action. Third, using rhetorical concepts, we connected these storylines to the fabula to discover to what extent the storylines synchronized with the broad universe of all materials related to the environmental narrative. Figure 10.1 depicts this sequence. Our intent in combining concepts from linguistics, literary criticism, and rhetoric was to enrich our analysis by using a variety of perspectives.

Textual Analysis Stages

	Stage 1		**Stage 2**	**Stage 3**
Narrative level	Texts		Stories	Fabula
Concepts	Linguistic		Literary	Rhetorical
Analytical categories	<u>Verbal</u> Agents Actions Symbols	<u>Visual</u> Agents Actions Symbols	Implied author Implied reader	Narrative fidelity Narrative probability

Figure 10.1. Stages of textual analysis.

Stage 1: Explicating the individual texts. The first stage of analysis included two subparts that focused on verbal, then visual, textual features. Using a linguistic approach, we reviewed each text at the sentence level, identifying agents (grammatical subjects); actions (grammatical predicates); and symbols (metaphors and other imagery). The purpose of the linguistic analysis of agents was to determine from what point of view the text was presented. The term *point of view* refers to the human consciousness whose vision informs a piece of discourse. To discover each text's point of view was important in our analysis because focalization, the angle of vision, is the most important element by which an author transforms raw narrative materials into a shaped story. The linguistic analysis also revealed what sorts of actions each text described or proposed and whether these were primarily situated in the past, present, or future. It was important to know this temporal dimension of each text because we would later use this information in determining how the time sequence related to each story line. The identification of symbols in each text was important because persuasion depends not only on logical argument but also on emotional conviction, which is often embedded in verbal and visual imagery, metaphor, and symbolism.

After having analyzed the verbal features of the texts, we next turned our attention to the visual components. Organizations often use what Boje (2008) has called visual storying to create narratives that reveal much about organizational values and beliefs. We defined "visual" in this study as encompassing photos, drawings, charts, and other objects included in a text; we excluded the visual aspects of words, such as font design. Of the texts we studied, about three-fourths included visual as well as verbal features. We identified the same three elements—agents, actions, and symbols—in the visual features of each text as in the verbal components. Not all texts included all three. An example of an agent would be a hotel housekeeper as shown in a photo, making a bed. The action, in this case, would be making a bed, which might be considered a subset of a broader action of serving customers. An example of a symbol would be a green tree in a program logo to represent the environment.

Stage 2: Extrapolating the story lines from the texts. In the second stage of our analysis, we used the data from the first stage as the basis for identifying major story lines in the corpus. By "story line" we mean a coherent series of actions performed by characters in order to advance a particular goal or resolve a particular problem. The actions need not be presented chronologically, though a chronology is implied. The word *characters* denotes an important distinction between real people and fictionalized ones or abstract, collective constructs, such as *guests*, *employees*, or *Hyatt*. Narrative theory stresses that the people projected in a text are never the same as the live people to whom the text refers. An organizational document is an artifact: a representation of reality, not reality itself.

In this stage we applied the methods of literary criticism and the concepts of narrative theory to organizational texts. Building on the linguistic approach of the first stage, this second stage focused on larger units of language beyond the sentence level. We identified the narrative structures of each individual text: the components that implied or directly stated a series of actions that had been, were being, or would be performed by people, either individually or collectively, for some purpose. In this case, the purpose was related to some environmental initiative or other type of action, though the relationship could be positive or negative; that is, either supporting or criticizing the initiative.

We then grouped the texts into categories related to focalization, the narratological concept of the perspective from which each story was told (Bal 1997; Fludernik 2009; Genette 1980). Inevitably, stories are shaped according to who narrates them from a particular point of view and to whom they are narrated. We used several criteria from narrative theory to determine what pattern of focalization each text used. The first criterion was the identity of the implied author. The implied author, as distinct from the live human being who actually created the text, is a constructed identity, sometimes entirely fictional even in nonfictional texts (Booth 1961). For instance, the president's letter that opens a report to investors often constructs a textual identity for the president that differs in personality, character, and style from his or her actual self. All texts have implied authors whether or not they are identified by name or associated with real people: The implied author is the person that the author wants readers to imagine talking to them.

The second criterion we used to determine focalization was the identity of the implied reader (Iser 1974; Iser 1978). According to narrative theory, texts construct an ideal reader who may differ from actual readers in motivations, values, and ethics. For instance, investment prospectuses convey the assumption that readers are knowledgeable, careful, rational investors, but that is not always true (Jameson 2000). The concept of the implied reader refers not only to the qualities that texts attribute to readers but also to the roles readers are invited to play as active interpreters of the meaning of the text (Eco 1984; Tompkins 1980).

The distinctions between live and implied authors and between live and implied readers are important because, as phenomenological criticism has emphasized, what engages readers is the encounter with a human mind, "the sense not merely of a human hand behind the work but of a human consciousness informing it" (Slatoff 1970, 94). This quality is as essential in nonliterary as in literary texts (Jameson 2004). To engage readers and establish credibility, a text must project the personality, intelligence, and character of both an implied author and an implied reader. As Boje (2008, 209) has emphasized, there is "no such thing as story neutrality." To instill environmental values and build commitment to related initiatives and other actions, organizations must create texts that use implied authors and implied readers to build credibility and conviction.

Through an iterative process, we grouped the individual texts into story lines. We identified these by cross-comparing the patterns of focalization with the grammatical predicate patterns of the texts, which we had identified in the first stage of analysis. This process thus matched the textual identities of people with the action representations related to temporal dimensions: past, present, or future.

Stage 3: Contrasting the fabula with the story lines. In the third stage of our analysis, we compared the major story lines to the fabula to determine their significance. Fabula refers the raw materials of narrative: the broad universe of facts, details, and ideas related to a particular theme or subject from which a story could be drawn. In this case, the fabula includes the hotel industry's economic, social, and political situations that existed during the period in which the corpus's texts were produced from 1990 to 2009. From this array of facts, events, situations, and other contextual elements, the writers and designers who developed the stories chose what to include and what to exclude. We used historical and contemporary news reports in major media and the hospitality trade press to identify the fabula.

By contrasting the story lines with the fabula, we sought to discover the significance of the narratives. Specifically, we wanted to identify any contradictions or discrepancies that might affect the persuasiveness of the texts in convincing readers to believe in environmental values or to take actions related to environmental initiatives. The main purpose of the texts in this corpus was not aesthetic but rhetorical: to influence readers to believe in values and act on them. Theories of rhetoric can provide important insights for management communication studies (Hartelius and Browning 2008), and narrative is often intertwined with rhetoric, as Kearns (1978) showed in his study of rhetorical narratology.

To contrast the story lines with the fabula, we therefore turned to rhetorical concepts, specifically Walter Fisher's (1987) ideas of narrative fidelity and probability. By the term *fidelity*, Fisher refers to the extent to which a narrative is verifiable in terms of the external world. By *probability*, he means the internal consistency of the argument implied in the narrative. Both fidelity and probability contribute to the believability of a narrative and the ethos of the organization that created the narrative. Fisher argues that people make decisions more often based on narrative reasoning than on logical reasoning. If narratives, such as the hotel-industry texts in this study, can meet the tests of fidelity and probability, then they have a better chance of achieving their rhetorical purposes: to infuse values within the organization, to ensure collective commitment to those values by internal and external constituencies, and to transform values into action. However, an organization's ethos can easily be compromised or subverted by contradictions within the story or discrepancies between the story and the fabula. Such is the power and potential impact of narrative discourse in organizations (Jameson 2001).

MOVING FROM TEXTS TO STORIES TO FABULA

Our research questions asked how organizations use narrative to try to create shared meanings and collective commitment to environmental values and action and how contradictions and discrepancies in such texts might undermine their persuasiveness. By analyzing the texts in terms of linguistic, narrative, and rhetorical features, we found that several language elements affected meaning in important ways.

In this section we present the findings of our analysis. First, we describe the focalization categories of narrative structure that established relationships between texts and readers and, by extension, between organizations and their constituencies. Then we show how the patterns of focalization led to three major story lines that the organizations used to inculcate values and motivate action: the environmental story, the financial story, and the service story. Finally, we contrast the story lines with the fabula, the universe of all possible elements that stories might have contained. Figure 10.2 illustrates the relationships we uncovered. The discrepancies between what a story includes and what it excludes have important implications for the credibility of the texts and, more broadly, of the organizations themselves.

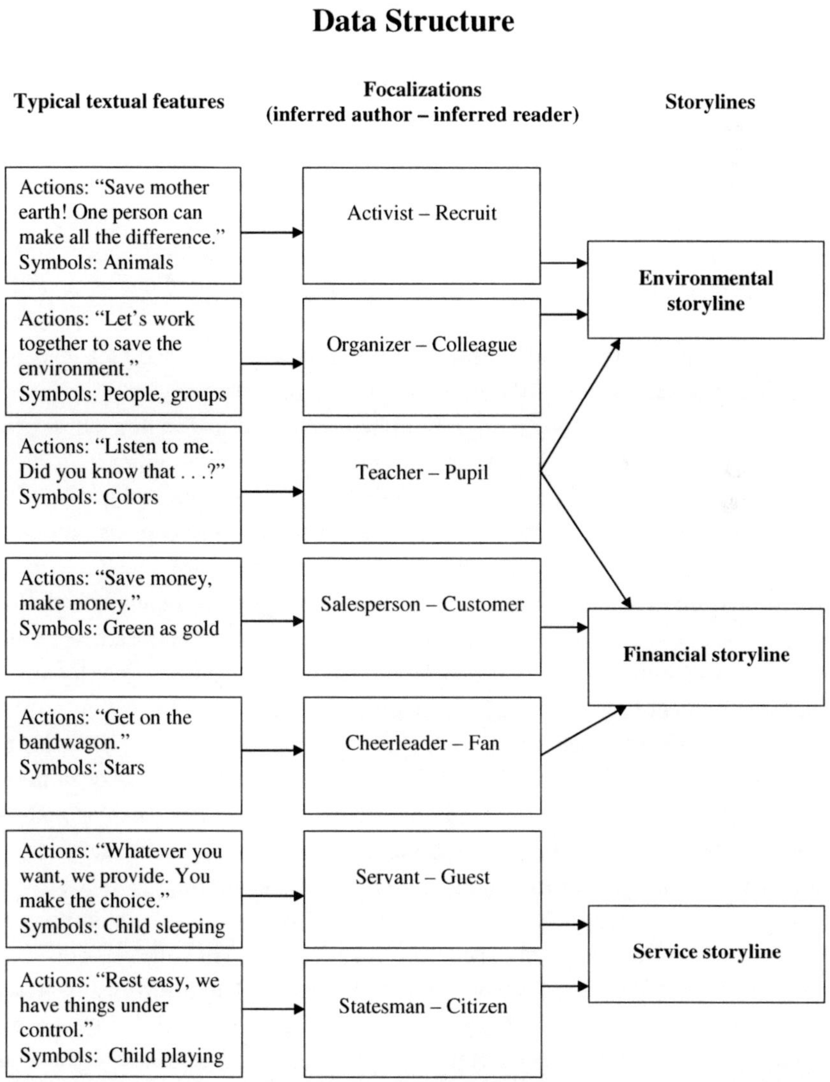

Figure 10.2. Data structure.

Patterns of Focalization in the Texts

Based on an analysis of the linguistic structure of each text, in particular the grammatical subjects and predicates, we identified seven focalization patterns that helped texts create shared meaning about an organization's environmental values and action. Each pattern conveyed a distinctive relationship between the implied author and the implied reader. For each focalization pattern we describe one or more paradigmatic examples of texts that use this narrative structure.

Texts may construct the implied author and implied reader either explicitly or implicitly. Explicit methods include direct revelations about motivations (e.g., to save money, save time, or achieve success), language that conveys character or personality, and assertions about beliefs and values. Often, however, the construction of the implied author and reader is more subtle. A text may establish parallels between textual and real identities, use symbolism that signifies character and values, or offer clues about how to best understand a text. Whether constructed explicitly or implicitly, the implied author and implied reader can influence readers' beliefs, attitudes, and values. The depiction of implied authors and readers thus has the power to influence real readers' specific actions taken in response to organizational texts.

Activist-recruit. In many texts the implied author portrayed himself or herself as a committed and determined environmental activist communicating with potential recruits. Such texts concentrated on environmental goals, with little or no acknowledgment of the business context, purpose, or potential financial impacts. These texts mentioned neither costs nor savings but instead highlighted environmental imperatives, using imagery, metaphors, and slogans drawn from the broader environmental movement. For instance, some texts asked readers to "save Mother Earth" and "think globally, act locally." The grammatical structures and language choices stressed individual power and efficacy; for instance, in the assertions that "you can change the world" and "one person can make all the difference." Directed either at customers or hotel line staff who implemented environmental programs, such as housekeepers, this choice of vocabulary flattered readers while at the same time conveying the urgency of individual commitment and action.

One of the most widely used environmental programs in hotels, Project Planet, exemplified the activist-recruit focalization. The guest-room brochures and cards described the program's rationale as "an effort of this hotel to protect the environment through conservation of water and decreased use of detergent." The texts asked hotel customers voluntarily to reuse sheets and towels throughout their stay and to signal their intent to the housekeeping staff. The cards were adapted linguistically to meet the needs of international clientele, with parallel texts in six languages (English, Spanish, French, German, Chinese, and Japanese) and other translations available upon request. In many locations the hotel workforce had a large proportion of immigrants, so the multiple translations helped these materials motivate not only customers but also housekeepers who looked at these texts many times each day. The visual symbolism of the Project Planet materials complemented the verbal rhetoric. Each text included vivid photos of the natural world, most centering on wildlife. Hotels could choose materials with either mountain or shoreline landscapes.

In the script of the Project Planet video-training materials for the housekeeping staff, the actor portraying the general manager asserted that "this important hospitality environmental initiative is all about conserving our earth's natural resources for future generations." The reference to "future generations" positioned the program's environmental goal as especially relevant to employees who have children. A reference to "easing the burden on your community's water treatment facilities" also suggested an environmental impact with some local benefit. However, neither the print materials nor video script alluded to the hotel's saving money or making money by reducing labor, energy, or supply costs. Environmentalism was not associated with profits.

Texts that focalized the implied author as an environmental activist who was recruiting the implied reader often had spiritual overtones conveyed both through verbal and visual symbolism. For instance, Hotel 1, a new environmentally oriented hotel brand opened in late 2008 by Starwood Capital, described its purpose as "to feed the soul and nourish the planet." Project Planet's materials were filled with Eden-like landscapes that conveyed reverence and awe. What was excluded from texts with the activist-recruit focalization was any hint of commercial motivation. In this expression of corporate values, the narrative structure distanced organizations from efforts to save or make money. Thus, this narrative structure was a means of promoting environmental altruism.

Organizer-colleague. Whereas texts that use the activist-recruit focalization emphasized individual commitment and action, a related approach emphasized groups more than individuals. In texts of this type, the implied author played the role of an organizer trying to convince readers to join a team of colleagues or friends in order to work on an environmental project. The social relationship was primary; the environmental cause was secondary. The language used to convey this relationship between implied author and implied reader stressed "we" and "us," with themes such as "Let's work together to save the earth," "Together we can make a difference," and "Thank you for being part of our environmental team." In these types of texts, the environmental programs often had specific names, for example Clean Up the World or Environmentally Conscious Hospitality Operations (ECHO), to underscore the idea that the reader would be joining a specific group with a clear identity and membership.

The visual symbolism that supported the appeal to social belonging depicted not landscapes and wildlife but people: partners working in groups for environmental causes or initiatives. Marriott's 2008 Corporate Social Responsibility report exemplified this approach. The opening letter from the chairman and chief executive officer, J. W. Marriott, Jr., introduced the environment as a "signature issue" on which the corporation collaborated with employees, hotel owners, developers, franchisees, suppliers, customers, clients, charitable organizations, and industry groups, such as the International Tourism Partnership. Of the twenty photos in the report, not one featured landscapes or wildlife; instead, each one showed people in action, working together on environmental and other social initiatives. These photos symbolized the organization's collective commitment to shared values.

Texts with an organizer-colleague focalization sometimes promoted large-scale projects and ambitious goals. The Green Marriott website, for instance, announced that the centerpiece of the company's environmental strategy was to protect the endangered Amazon rain forest. Specifically, Marriott promised to work with partners to raise $6 million to fund an environment management plan for 1.4 million acres in the Juma Sustainability Reserve. In describing this goal, the text's implied author asked the company's employees and customers to join in partnership with the corporation, the Brazilian government, and the Amazonas Sustainable Foundation. The rationale for this geographically and culturally distant program was that protecting the rain forest compensated for the corporation's energy use; the text discussed how the corporation had calculated its "carbon footprint" and gave readers a way to calculate their own footprints. The metaphor of a footprint to signify a technical calculation about energy consumption made the concept seem more accessible and human. By offering readers the footprint calculation option, the text provided an immediate participation mechanism as a way for readers to understand and personalize the rationale behind a corporate value.

There was a subtle but important difference in the actions sought in texts with different focalizations. Whereas the implied author as activist asked recruits to "save" the planet or "rescue" endangered animals, the implied author as organizer merely requested colleagues to "protect" the environment, "preserve" the earth, and "respect" nature. These less forceful verb choices implied that the corporate value involved less dramatic action. Fairmont Hotels' Green Partnership brochure developed this more moderate meaning by stressing the theme of commitment to "environmental stewardship" through a "quest for sustainable solutions." The choice of the word *stewardship* signified responsibility, and the word *quest* connoted a quasispiritual journey into the unknown.

An important way that some of the texts attempted to inculcate the corporate value of environmentalism was to involve readers in an immediate quest. The internal website text of Thayer Lodging's Sustainability Standards Program exemplified this approach well. Thayer, a privately held real estate investment company, owns and manages hotels under the flags of Marriott, Hilton, and others. Writing to the company's managers, the corporate executive in charge of the sustainability initiative expressed the idea that both goals and methods in other companies' so-called green programs were ambiguous. So he provided rationales and resources for environmental initiatives and encouraged his managers to "Try them. Do as many as you can. There is no one right way to be green." He depicted the program as a quest for the best ways to "conserve or protect the environment" and empowered his managers to try different approaches without worrying that all must succeed. The symbolism of the quest for knowledge, the openness to new ideas, and the reassurance that the company was headed in the right direction all served to signal to the company's managers that they belonged to a creative team of people engaged in important work. In sum, texts with an organizer-colleague focalization developed commitment to organizational values by creating a social context, participation options, and symbolic reinforcement.

Teacher-pupil. A different narrative structure through which organizations tried to inculcate values used an educational approach. The implied author addressed the implied reader as a pupil. The underlying assumption of this category of focalization was that if readers understood the facts, they would voluntarily choose to act in a way that the organization wanted. The implied author, therefore, did not need to advocate so explicitly or to use such dramatic imagery and symbolism, as did other types of implied authors. Rather than urging readers to "save Mother Earth" or to "join together with us to preserve nature," these texts asked readers simply to listen and learn. Narration always involves an implied distance between author and reader, and this distance can be physical, intellectual, emotional, or related to some other human dimension. The implied author as teacher spoke as an expert who had amassed information that the pupil needed; the intellectual distance between teacher and pupil was greater than that between activist and recruit or between organizer and colleague.

The texts created by the International Tourism Partnership (ITP) exemplified the teacher-pupil focalization pattern. Founded in 1992 by Great Britain's Prince Charles, the ITP is composed of corporate members, comprising the major hotel chains and travel companies from throughout the world. Its purpose is "to inspire global leaders in the travel and tourism industry on a noncompetitive platform, to share knowledge and resources, develop policy and actively implement programmes and initiatives that have a positive impact on social, economic and environmental issues." The emphasis on avoiding competition is significant because other programs promote environmental initiatives as means of winning competitive advantage. The ITP has promoted high-level summit meetings about tourism-related policy and produced practical guides that companies can use for environmental initiatives.

Going Green: Minimum Standards Toward a Sustainable Hotel, an ITP manual for hotel managers, used the teacher-student focalization to provide concrete advice. The implied author playing the role of a teacher started by posing the question "What does it mean to be a sustainable hotel?" and then answered that question by explaining the concept and developing detailed steps that managers could take. The implied author taught a lesson about the "triple bottom line" of economic, social, and environmental management; the text symbolically reinforced the tripartite concept with a logo of three colored circles, green where they overlapped, signifying that sustainability—greenness—requires attention to all three elements. The text explained that environmentalism involves two goals: to decrease hotels' negative impact on ecosystems and cultures and to increase hotels' positive contributions by conserving biodiversity, preserving culture, and developing communities. To make these broad, abstract goals concrete, the text suggested that hotel managers take seventy-three steps, which were grouped into six categories and expressed in imperative verb forms as directives. The systematic process and detailed instructions, as well as the prescriptive tone of the implied author, mirrored an educational setting. Readers were asked to play the role of humble pupils listening attentively to a knowledgeable teacher and then following instructions carefully.

Texts that used the teacher-pupil focalization pattern often tried to build commitment to environmental initiatives by stressing the environment itself, especially what damage had already occurred and what managers could do to reverse that situation. However, texts with the same focalization pattern sometimes took a quite different approach: the teacher educating pupils about the financial impact of environmental initiatives. In texts that used this narrative structure, the implied author provided information about the ways in which environmental initiatives saved money by lowering existing business costs or, in some cases, actually made money by creating new business opportunities: new services, products, markets, or pricing strategies. These texts sought to motivate readers by invoking profit opportunities rather than or in addition to environmental altruism.

Of course, an approach to instilling corporate values based on their financial impact is not well suited to all constituencies and would backfire if misapplied. However, some texts in our study used this focalization pattern, especially when their goal was to influence operations managers, whose success depended directly upon lowering costs and discovering new profit opportunities. Some of the extensive print materials distributed by the "Green" Hotels Association (GHA) exemplified this type of teacher-pupil focalization. Founded in 1993, the GHA is a group of several hundred hotels that are interested in environmental initiatives. In its membership materials, the GHA foregrounded the financial rationale for environmental action by emphasizing the goals of "saving you money . . . making you money." The association collects and distributes to its members extensive information about all types of environmental initiatives. The GHA texts were well balanced, containing extensive information about both the environment and the financial impact of environmental initiatives.

One section of the 151-page *Membership Conservation Guidelines and Ideas* manual was devoted to statistics related to the impact of environmental programs in the lodging industry. The implied author as teacher gave a wealth of specific data and concrete examples about the financial savings derived from environmental programs. The sources were documented, some from research organizations, some from publications, some from company reports, some from GHA surveys. The implied author as teacher asked readers to use the information to convince others, including owners, management, staff, guests, and the media. Perhaps because the GHA sought to amass as much information as possible and distribute it to its members, this text lacked visual symbolism: no photos, drawings, or diagrams. The text did include a simple logo consisting of green fern leaves. The association recommended that members fly the association flag, on which the green fern leaves were surrounded by the slogan "A green hotel . . . committed to help save our planet."

As a color, green has a double meaning in the United States and other countries whose currency is green. For this reason, the verbal or visual references to the color green sometimes expanded symbolic meanings to suggest ambiguity between commitment to the natural world and to making money. Some of the texts that stressed a profit motive for environmental action capitalized on this color symbolism.

Salesperson-customer. Several other focalization patterns approached commitment to environmental values and action through profit more than altruism. The implied author played the role of a salesperson who overtly attempted to convince the implied reader, in the role of a client or customer, to adopt environmental programs. This narrative structure had an intensity similar to that of the activist-recruit structure but differed in that the focal point aimed inward, not outward. The implied author as salesperson stressed the direct benefits to the implied reader and his or her organization rather than to an abstract, distant concept: the environment. As in all sales discourse, the language in the salesperson-customer narrative structure highlighted what readers got, not what they gave. In an article entitled "Green Is the New Gold in Lodging," for instance, a hospitality consulting firm flatly stated that "environmental sustainability is much more about making money than saving the planet."

The press kit of Project Planet, an environmental initiative endorsed by the American Hotel and Lodging Association and used in thousands of hotels worldwide, aptly illustrated the salesperson-customer focalization pattern. The press kit reaches two audiences: hotel managers who are considering using the program and journalists at trade publications who are writing about the program. The text contained a four-page press release followed by thirty-three additional documents, including magazine and newspaper articles, testimonial letters from hotel managers, and comment cards from hotel customers. In the press release, the implied author as salesperson foregrounded the "enormous financial benefit to the hotel industry" and gave a hypothetical calculation that eleven thousand hotels with 1.4 million rooms could save $55 million per year by using the program. Each of the thirty-three subsequent documents introduced a new implied author and new information, including examples of how much individual hotels had saved. For instance, one property reduced the average room-cleaning time from twenty-six to sixteen minutes. Another increased occupancy 25 percent after marketing itself as a "green" hotel. Another reported savings of $121,000 per year. The executive housekeeper of a Crowne Plaza enclosed detailed daily records for three months showing exactly how the hotel saved money. Together, this compendium provided strong evidence that the Project Planet program worked well.

The Project Planet press kit was a striking example of what Mikhail Bakhtin (1981, 1986) called hybridized, dialogic narration. Texts, whether literary or nonliterary, are social spaces. The Project Planet text was hybridized in that it embedded thirty-four different subtexts and juxtaposed multiple linguistic styles used by the implied authors who wrote the press release, articles, letters, and comment cards. The text was dialogic in that the overall meaning arose from the tension and contrasts among the language and ideas of the implied authors. Though all were positive about the Project Planet program, they had different perspectives and reported different results, challenges, and experiences. The opening press release set the stage, but the thirty-three following subtexts enriched the meaning and determined to what extent readers would be convinced to support environmental initiatives. By combining the multiple perspectives and language of the many implied authors, the text fulfilled a social purpose by reflecting human relationships and negotiating the meaning and significance of environmental values.

Cheerleader-fan. Another focalization pattern that contributed to texts' creation of shared meaning about organizations' environmental values was similar to but less intense than that of the salesperson-customer pattern. In this narrative structure, the implied author became a kind of cheerleader, encouraging readers to be active fans of environmental initiatives and celebrating the financial successes of those who did. Whereas the implied author as salesperson emphasized individual monetary benefits as a rationale for environmental action, the implied author as cheerleader emphasized normative behavior that conformed to that of a peer group as a rationale. The texts we studied created this social perspective by offering a wide array of concrete examples that showed what other hotels were doing and then encouraging readers to join the crowd.

Many state-sponsored environmental initiatives, such as Florida's Green Lodging Program, used this narrative structure. Florida's materials included success stories of hotels that had met the requirements to be designated "green" and thus received the program's benefits, which were stated in financial terms: saving money by cutting costs, receiving free technical assistance to help save even more money, reaching new target markets whom the program logo would attract, gaining free advertising on the program website, and becoming qualified to hold events for state agencies and departments, which the governor's executive order required to use green-designated hotels whenever possible. As a state whose economy depends on tourism and some of whose ecosystems are fragile, Florida has a special incentive to encourage hotels and resorts to transform environmental values into concrete action.

One vivid example of the cheerleader-fan focalization pattern occurred in *Our Planet*, an internal environmental newsletter produced for several years by Six Continents Hotels, a corporation that in 2003 was split into the InterContinental Hotels Group and a separate retail division. Six Continents had over three thousand hotels, including the brands Holiday Inn, Crowne Plaza, and InterContinental. A typical issue of *Our Planet* included several dozen short feature articles celebrating how individual properties were putting corporate environmental values into practice. Most articles were accompanied by photos that recognized the achievements of employees, managers, and owners. A sixteen-page issue published in 2001, for instance, included twenty-five such photos, so that the text as a whole visually symbolized the large group of colleagues with whom the implied reader was asked to join. A four-page feature story introduced the winners of the company's Conserve Our Planet Award and depicted their environmental efforts at the Holiday Inn Resort Sharjah in Dubai, United Arab Emirates. By highlighting the efforts of hotel owners and management companies, as well as line employees and managers, *Our Planet* expanded the symbolic "crowd of fans" who cheered the company's environmental efforts. Yet *Our Planet* balanced the social appeal with substantial, detailed financial information. Articles discussed the impact of environmental initiatives on profits and reported that some hotels had "spectacular results" in lowering costs and enhancing profitability. *Our Planet* exemplified what Boje (2001) calls "antenarrative": a nonlinear, interactive, polyphonic type of organizational storytelling. As a theatrical type of social discourse, antenarrative seeks to draw readers into a cast of characters and involve them in action (Boje and Rosile 2003).

In summary, both the salesperson-customer and cheerleader-fan focalizations shifted attention from the environment itself to the financial impact of environmental initiatives, but they did so by using different emphases. Whereas the former highlighted the individual benefits, the latter used a stronger social appeal and emphasized becoming part of a worldwide team that achieved financial benefits through environmental action.

Servant-guest. While discussing environmental initiatives, some narrative structures redirected readers' attention toward service rather than the environment itself or the financial impact. Several guest-room communications, for instance, were written from the perspective of a humble servant whose only goal was to provide guests with whatever they desire. Rather than asking guests to save the planet by conserving water and energy, the implied author as servant stressed that the hotel was giving guests what some asked for: the option to reuse linen and towels rather than having them automatically replaced every day. Wyndham's Earthsmart communications, for instance, used this focalization pattern: "At Wyndham, we know that many of our guests are interested in helping to protect the natural resources of our planet. That's why we've instituted a new program—Earthsmart." A variation was to stress the quality of the linens, bed, and pillows, which many hotels had upgraded since Westin introduced the Heavenly Bed program in 1999. The texts of guest communications that used this focalization pattern contained a request that guests let housekeeping know when they desired new linens and towels. The grammatical structure of such requests, usually conditional verbs ("if you would like the linens replaced") signified that it was purely the guest's choice. Texts with the servant-guest focalization pattern often had strong visual symbolism, such as Hampton Inn's photos of a beautiful blond child peacefully asleep on crisp white linens. Thus, texts with the servant-guest focalization redirected attention away from the environment to the individual guest's preferences and concurrently conveyed the symbols of luxury and service while suggesting that guests voluntarily decline such luxury and service.

Statesman-citizen. A final narrative structure that we discerned in the texts was similar to the servant-guest focalization pattern but with a stronger emphasis on a group's collective benefit rather than an individual's. In this approach the implied author was like a statesman, a distinguished leader who was writing to citizens of the community and who served them. Often the implied author was named and pictured: the chief executive officer, chairman, president, or another high-level executive. In this situation it is especially important to distinguish between the live person and the implied author in the text, for these may differ greatly in style, personality, tone, and sometimes even ethics and values. The implied author is always a constructed identity. The implied author as statesman typically created substantial distance between himself or herself and readers to convey authority and command. Yet the purpose was service: to reassure the implied reader as citizen that the situation was under control and that the organization was healthy in terms of its environmental philosophy, programs, and results. The emphasis was on the organization as a whole more so than the individuals within it.

Hilton Hotels' sustainability materials exemplified this focalization pattern well. In an opening letter, the chief executive asserted that responding to environmental change as a value created the opportunity for leadership and service. The CEO broadened the concept of sustainability when he wrote that the company's responses to environmental challenges would determine "the sustainability of our future lifestyles, the sustainability of our communities as we know them, and ultimately the sustainability of our planet." Sustainability, for him, referred first to human lifestyles and only later to the more common focus on the natural environment. He lowered readers' expectations of short-term results, writing that "our true success in building a sustainable business will be judged by future generations, not in quarterly reviews." This passage alluded to the initial start-up costs of environmental initiatives, which can be quite high, and thus helped establish his frankness and thoughtfulness. He promised that the company would be "prudent and deliberate" as it transformed itself through implementation of environmental values. In the environmental mission, commitment, and policy statements that followed the CEO's letter, the theme of service and leadership opportunities continued, and the texts stressed that "each and every" team member had an important role to play in implementing the environmental mission and strategy. In short, the implied author presented himself as a reliable, forward-looking leader who served those in his organization as well as the larger community, industry, and society.

Story Line Structures Built on the Focalizations

After identifying these seven patterns of focalization in the texts, we had partially answered our first research question. By choosing different focalization patterns, organizations signaled different reasons to accept, believe, and act on environmental values. Each pattern built a different relationship between the implied author and implied reader and, by extension, between the organization and its intended audience. Next, we considered how the patterns of focalization helped build larger narrative structures: story lines, which we defined as coherent series of actions performed by characters in order to advance a particular goal or resolve a particular problem. The word *characters* in this definition encompasses the inferred author, inferred reader, and the representations of any other people depicted in the texts—the fictional identities that the narrative constructed, not to be confused with the real blood-and-flesh people. We identified the story lines by cross-comparing the patterns of focalization to the actions expressed in the texts; in this way we matched the textual representations of people with the representations of actions each had taken, were taking, or would take in the future. The grammatical predicates of sentences in the texts, which we had identified in the first stage of analysis, expressed these actions and their temporal dimensions.

We found that to increase commitment to environmental values and participation in related initiatives, most texts used one of three story lines, which we called the environmental story, the financial story, and the service story. Only a few texts combined more than one story line. In this section we discuss each story line and show how it used symbolism to meet readers' emotional needs related to environmentalism and how it balanced the individual with the group in order to gain commitment from different types of readers. Figure 10.3 shows the resulting narrative structures.

The environmental story line. Some organizations tried to create shared meanings and develop a collective understanding of and commitment to environmental values and initiatives by creating a story line that presented a

Focalizations and Narrative Structures

<table>
<tr><th></th><th>Individual Focalization</th><th>Group Focalization</th></tr>
<tr><td>Environmental Storyline</td><td>Activist – Recruit</td><td>Organizer – Colleague</td></tr>
<tr><td></td><td colspan="2">Teacher – Pupil</td></tr>
<tr><td>Financial Storyline</td><td>Salesperson – Customer</td><td>Cheerleader – Fan</td></tr>
<tr><td>Service Storyline</td><td>Servant – Guest</td><td>Statesman – Citizen</td></tr>
</table>

Figure 10.3. How focalizations create narrative.

series of actions directly related to the environment. Typical actions were to honor the earth, to make sacrifices for it, to join environmental programs, and through them to compensate for past excesses in the consumption of water, energy, and other resources. This story line used the activist-recruit, organizer-colleague, or teacher-pupil focalization pattern. Motivated either by guilt or by idealism, the implied reader as recruit, colleague, or pupil would take these actions—honoring, sacrificing, joining, and compensating—in the immediate future if the implied author as activist, organizer, or teacher was convincing. This story line often appeared in texts whose primary intended audiences were customers, line employees, or the general public.

The symbolism associated with the environmental story line often had a spiritual dimension and sometimes a religious overtone. Several programs used the word *spirit* in their names; for instance, Marriott's Spirit to Preserve, and built upon that imagery. Some texts depicted acts of sacrifice, such as employees volunteering their time for philanthropic projects or customers declining full-scale luxury and service. Other texts used the metaphor of the "quest" to link environmental action to the Arthurian legend of the search for the Holy Grail. Sometimes the story included a moral dimension, invoking guilt by mentioning the wasteful habits through which people had sinned against the earth. Some stories interwove Native American imagery by anthropomorphizing Mother Earth as a character in the story and conveying a sense of obligation to her. Radisson Hotels even quoted and used imagery from Samuel Taylor Coleridge's poem "The Rime of the Ancient Mariner," in which a dearth of drinkable water is linked to human beings' spiritual weakness and, ultimately, their redemption.

The environmental story thus featured not only sacrifice but also redemption in which readers could fulfill their emotional needs to feel virtuous by making an altruistic commitment to environmental values and initiatives. The spiritual journey of the environmental story line could take one of two paths: either as an individual or as a member of a group. The activist-recruit focalization emphasized individual action, whereas the organizer-colleague focalization emphasized joining with partners on the journey as a kind of pilgrimage; and the teacher-pupil focalization could involve either approach. Whether the approach was individualistic or collective, the environmental story engaged readers by offering a symbolic spiritual transformation that would make them feel more admirable, righteous, and virtuous because they demonstrated through action their commitment to environmental values.

The financial story line. If the environmental story concerned spiritual enlightenment, the financial story presented quite a contrast: economic enlightenment. Some organizations tried to create shared meanings and develop a collective understanding of and commitment to environmental initiatives by shifting attention to their financial impact. Texts whose primary intended audiences were hotel owners, franchisees, and managers often featured this story line. The actions expressed included selecting program options, running pilot studies, calculating their impact, and then, if they increased profits, implementing them fully. This story line used the salesperson-customer, cheerleader-fan, or teacher-pupil focalization pattern. The inferred reader as customer, fan, or pupil was motivated by obligation not to the environment but to the corporation: the fiduciary responsibility to make money for the business. The story line celebrated this action as ethical and proper, not as greedy or materialistic. The institutional pressure to "go green" was portrayed as an admirable, ethical motivator and as a positive economic force. In this story line economic values trumped environmental values.

The symbolism interwoven into the financial story line conveyed the themes of success and achievement. The American Hotel and Lodging Association's logo for its environmental program, for instance, featured a star, conveying the idea that hotel managers could be stars in their own organization if they used environmental programs to save money or establish new marketing opportunities. Success and achievement in the environmental story line were possible either individually or in groups. The salesperson-customer focalization emphasized individual action, whereas the cheerleader-fan focalization emphasized a team approach; again, the teacher-pupil focalization could involve either approach. In each case, the story showed how economic enlightenment—learning how to leverage environmental initiatives to enhance profit—could meet readers' emotional needs to feel appreciated by their organizations, recognized for their achievements, and successful in their work.

The service story line. Some texts avoided actions related to either the environment or to financial gain. The resulting story line shifted attention to service values: to customers, to employees, and to investors. The servant-guest and statesman-citizen focalizations created this type of narrative structure. The implied reader as guest could sit back and enjoy the responsiveness to his or her every wish. The implied reader as citizen could also rest easy knowing that the implied author as statesman had every company situation under control. In this story line, the main actions were performed by the implied author—the servant or statesman—who was doing whatever it took to provide outstanding service and meet the guest's or citizen's needs.

The symbolism associated with this story line built up the egos of the implied reader and thus fulfilled a need to feel important. By using children as symbols, this story line let readers see themselves as pure, carefree beings whose welfare was of utmost importance and who deserved only the best. This recognition could come to individuals as guests or to groups as citizens. In either case, however, the story reinforced the idea that in serving the environment, the implied author was serving the implied reader, whose needs were all important.

In summary, each story line had an underlying emotional dimension related to the symbolism interwoven into the story. The environmental story met readers' emotional needs to feel virtuous, the financial story met their needs to feel successful, and the service story met their needs to feel important.

Discrepancies between Storylines and Their Fabula

Having answered our first research question about how organizations used narrative texts to try to inculcate environmental values and promote environmental action, we turned to our second question, which focused on how such rhetorical efforts can fail. We wondered how contradictions and discrepancies in the story lines might undermine texts' persuasiveness. In this section we first explain concepts of narrative fidelity and probability, on which we based our analysis. Then we compare the story lines with the fabula: the universe of all possible elements that stories might have contained. The dichotomy between what a story includes and what it excludes can limit an organization's ability to build shared meanings and commitment among constituencies. We end by showing how unanticipated consequences complicated the situation.

Narrative fidelity and probability. To contrast the story lines with the fabula, we applied rhetorical concepts of narrative fidelity and probability, developed by Walter Fisher (1987) in his theory of the narrative paradigm. He conceptualized narrative as the master mode of discourse, which encompasses all others. The world, said Fisher (1987, 65), is "a set of stories that must be chosen among in order for us to live life in a process of continual re-creation." When people reason, they choose one story over another based on warrants expressed in any genre, including business genres such as those we analyzed in this study. Fisher said that as people reason, they use the tests of narrative probability and fidelity. "Probability" refers not to a mathematical concept but to internal coherence: whether the components of the story fit together consistently in a logical sequence. "Fidelity" refers to external correspondence: whether the story is consistent with a person's lived experience in the real world.

Like individuals, every organization has an ethos, which we define as an identity based on deeply held values and credibility demonstrated through action. The ethos of the organizations in our study partially depended of the fidelity and probability of the stories in their environmental texts. If the stories met these tests, then they would have a better chance of achieving their purposes: to inculcate values and increase constituencies' collective commitment to acting on those values. However, an organization's ethos can easily be compromised or subverted by contradictions within the story (failing to meet the test of probability) or discrepancies between the story and the fabula (failing to meet the test of fidelity). All three stories had such disconnects, and most were failures of fidelity, not probability. That is, the stories were internally consistent but conflicted with external situations and events that readers were likely to recognize. Although contradictions can sometimes enhance rather than disrupt efforts to gain support for organizational programs (Whittle, Mueller, and Mangan 2008), using intentional and strategic disconnects requires great caution, which was not apparent in these environmental narratives.

Flaws in the environmental story. The environmental story depicted the intended reader joining the environmental movement by making relatively simple sacrifices of personal effort or comfort but then gaining a major benefit: feeling virtuous and perhaps being recognized by others for this virtue. The actions occurred in a logical sequence and had no internal contradictions; thus, the test of probability was met. However, several external situations had the potential to diminish readers' belief in this story and thus cause the story to fail the test of fidelity. First, the story focused on relatively small ways to affect the environment, for instance, using fewer towels or different light bulbs, but did not mention the larger environmental impacts of hotels and especially resorts. Golf courses, ski resorts, theme parks, and other types of developments take land and resources that, if left in their natural state, would remain pristine beaches, wetland habitats, or forested mountains.

Second, many of the initiatives mentioned in the environmental story texts seemed superficial. One chain's hotels turned off some electricity, such as outdoor signs, and used candlelight in its restaurants—but only for one hour on one day. Another proudly announced in marketing materials that its front-desk computers were run by wind energy; in reality the hotel had a short-term contract for a tiny amount of wind-energy power compared to its overall energy consumption. Third, the environmental initiatives often diverted attention from the hotel business itself to distant locations, such as the Amazon rain forest. Altruism seemed more acceptable if related to the exotic and foreign than if applied to the company's own practices.

Fourth, many environmental initiatives shifted costs from the corporation to others. Some hotels solicited customers, clients, and employees to contribute money to a particular environmental cause. Other hotels encouraged employees to volunteer on their own time for fund raisers or activities such as beach clean-up days. One hotel's initiative to "Save the manatees" simply involved the hotel's gift shop selling stuffed manatees to customers. Business travelers were especially attuned to the fact that the money hotels saved through environmental initiatives went directly to company profits, not to environmental efforts or to customers through lower room rates.

All these discrepancies diminished the fidelity of the story and thus detracted from the organizations' ethos. In fact, the media raised questions about some environmental initiatives. When Marriott announced that saving part of the Brazilian rain forest was the centerpiece of its environmental strategy, media reports pointed out that the amount the corporation would donate, $2 million over three years, was tiny given its revenue; Marriott planned to ask its employees, customers, and clients to contribute the other $4 million it had promised.

Flaws in the financial story. The financial story depicted managers and companies testing various money-saving environmental initiatives, instituting them, attracting new customers who wanted to patronize green hotels, and as a result, saving money and increasing profits. The benefit for those who did so was success and recognition for their professional accomplishments. Again, the sequence of actions was logical, and the story met the test of probability. But this story, too, had discrepancies with the fabula: the full context. Capital and startup costs, including labor, were omitted because in many cases they would have been substantial. Retrofitting existing properties with energy-saving devices and building new properties that would meet U.S. Building Council standards would be costly, but the claimed payback times were often not proven. Texts directed at owners, investors, and franchisees often privileged the environmental story rather than the financial story, which was more often included in texts aimed at line managers who needed to show savings and profit from smaller operational ventures, especially those that shifted costs to customers and employees.

In addition, the financial story texts did not document claims about savings well, and some defied common sense. For instance, one savings calculator for managers inflated potential savings by saying that it took fifteen minutes on average to change one light bulb and that fluorescent bulbs lasted twenty times longer than incandescent ones. Estimates of how many guests participated in linen reuse programs ranged from 30 percent to 90 percent. Surveys of guests' preference for green hotels had slanted phrasing and no scientific sampling. The lack of documentation provided an easy reason for front-line managers not to believe the financial story and not to comply with its action requests. For these reasons the financial story did not meet the test of fidelity.

Flaws in the service story. The service story described how a hotel guest could just sit back and enjoy the exceptional service that employees would provide. The benefit was feeling important and honored. The story was appealing and logical, so it met the test of probability. However, many discrepancies undermined the story's fidelity to readers' experienced reality. The environmental programs, such as linen reuse, could reduce the perceived quality of the hotel and its price-value ratio. The move to fluorescent lights decreased task lighting that business travelers needed to work in their rooms; Project Planet noted this sensitivity in its guidelines. At the very time when hotels were trying to promote environmental programs as "good service," media exposés on such television programs as *20/20* and *Today* revealed bedbugs, semen-stained sheets, and other unsanitary conditions in luxury hotel rooms. YouTube disseminated these programs to even more audiences and also made available videos by individuals who had documented the lack of hotel sanitation standards. Trip Advisor, a travel site, created an annual list of the dirtiest hotels, and many bloggers added their comments. In short, external reports provided a broader picture that would make readers question the believability of a hotel's service story.

Unanticipated consequences. The environmental initiatives sometimes led to unanticipated consequences that never appeared in the stories. A sequence of events harmed labor relations and escalated customers' expectations, both of which proved costly. The linen reuse programs that the American Hotel and Lodging Association, the Green Hotels Association, and others began to promote in the mid 1990s reduced by up to 30 percent the time it took housekeepers to make up rooms. Nonunion hotels could realize this saving by hiring fewer housekeepers or reducing their hours. Unionized hotels, however, often had contract provisions that specified how many rooms per day each housekeeper would clean, so it was difficult for these hotels to realize the possible savings. An alternative use for the housekeepers' time arose when in 1999, Westin Hotels introduced the Heavenly Bed, an upgraded amenity that many hotels copied in the next few years. These beds featured thick mattresses, extra sheets, down comforters, duvet covers, and multiple pillows. In short, housekeepers changed fewer rooms' linen, but those that they did change took longer.

The work also was harder, partly because the new mattresses were heavy and unwieldy. Labor unions protested the increase in physical demands the new amenity put on housekeepers. One union's 2006 report, *Creating Luxury, Enduring Pain: How Hotel Work Is Hurting Housekeepers*, showed that the "amenity creep" had increased housekeepers' injury rate until it was almost double that of other hotel workers. A housekeeper who cleaned fifteen rooms with Hilton's Serenity Beds lifted over one thousand pounds of linen per day, according to the report. As with all amenities, hotel chains felt compelled to match their competitors, so by 2006, even moderately priced hotels installed the heavy luxury beds. An environmental initiative that seemed so simple—asking customers to reuse linen in order to help save the planet—led to the unanticipated consequences of injured employees, labor union backlash, and customers who came to expect luxury bedding as a norm, not a distinguishing amenity. Naturally, these elements of the fabula were omitted from the hotel's stories about the impact of environmental initiatives.

So, in summary, although the environmental story met readers' emotional need to feel virtuous, the financial story met their need to feel successful, and the service story met their need to feel important, these stories invited skepticism because of the omissions and the discrepancies with the larger universe of details about industry practices. All three stories failed the test of fidelity and thus potentially diminished the organizations' ethos.

NARRATIVE BALANCE AND ORGANIZATIONAL ETHOS

Narrative texts can contribute to or detract from organizational ethos. Although many of the texts we studied had narrative structures that introduced clear story lines, few intertwined multiple story lines or synthesized the environmental, financial, and service elements into one coherent story. Apparently, it was difficult to find a focalization perspective that would suit this rhetorical goal, even though the credibility of texts—and organizations—was at stake. A few texts, however, did try to achieve narrative balance. The 2008 social responsibility report issued by the InterContinental Hotel Group (IHG) illustrated this approach. Based in London, IHG is the world's largest hotel company in terms of number of rooms, over half a million plus another quarter million in the pipeline. The company has over four thousand hotels divided into seven brands, including InterContinental and Holiday Inns, located all over the world.

IHG's first corporate responsibility report, issued in 2008, combined all three stories, interweaving the environmental, financial, and service elements of the corporation's values. The environmental and financial stories predominated but were set in the context of a service story: corporate leaders serving employees and investors. By achieving some measure of balance among the stories, the text contributed to organizational ethos, shared meaning, and collective commitment to corporate environmental values and action.

IHG's environmental story. The IHG text told the environmental story through a series of short case studies that provided a social context as well as an individual call to action. The text focused squarely on the company itself, not distant parts of the environment, such as the Brazilian rain forest. Rather than highlighting landscapes or animal symbols, the text used charts and diagrams to explain the substance of the initiatives and to motivate action based on fact rather than emotion. The text discussed how the environment related to each of the company's four economic strategic priorities: brand performance, excellent hotel returns, market scale and knowledge, and aligned operations. Unlike many texts' environmental story, IHG's did not highlight superficial initiatives. For the renewable energy pilot, IHG's Willard InterContinental Hotel in Washington, D.C., was powered by 100 percent wind energy; a competitor, in contrast, bought a tiny amount of wind energy credits to power the front desk computers for a short time, more of a public relations gimmick than a real environmental action.

IHG's financial story. In telling the financial story, the IHG text emphasized the perspective of hotel general managers and showed how the corporation helped them institute environmental programs and translate results in both financial and environmental terms. The text created a clear picture of the goals, quoting the International Tourism Partnership's triple bottom line: balance among economic, social, and environmental performance. IHG talked in terms of "managing" costs, not necessarily "lowering" them. The IHG text limited claims, which heightened credibility. The report's letter from the CEO said that "we need a long-term commitment and strategy to deliver real benefit, not a quick-fix approach." IHG was clear that it tried to integrate the environmental and social goals with the economic ones. It did not claim to be a purely altruistic organization that was seeking to save the planet. The text acknowledged that some properties would take longer than others to integrate into environmental programs. By stating that the long-term benefits of responsible operations would outweigh costs, IHG indicated that the short-term benefits might not do so. After providing a chart that showed how much progress the company had made on its 2006 commitments, IHG stated that "we acknowledge that much still remains to be done." Humility was part of the organizational ethos created by the financial story.

IHG's service story. The IHG text's version of the service story showed that the company leaders were in command but were interested in input and participation from customers, employees, and the public. The text helped engage readers by interpreting technical data in everyday human terms. For instance, it said that $2.28 million in annual energy savings had the impact of removing 17,416 cars from highways. To meet the general managers' requests, the IHG text listed environmental data next to familiar equivalents that were meaningful to typical managers, employees, and customers. In one example, a hotel's consumption of 1,680 gigajoules of electricity was interpreted as the power that two hundred homes use in one month. This number was then further broken down in the amount per guest, in this case sixty street lights operated for one day. The change compared to the previous year was also explained in human terms, for example, a savings equivalent to the power that forty-four homes use in one month. Water data in kiloliters were translated into the number of Olympic swimming pools, minutes in the shower, or even toilet flushes.

The IHG text served readers by inviting them to participate in several ways. It described and illustrated an interactive website called the Innovation Hotel, which showcased creative ideas that would help hotels reduce their impact on the environment. Managers, employees, and customers could comment and vote on each innovation. The site showed specific changes the company had made because of participants' suggestions.

Through such efforts to create a broader, more encompassing narrative, organizations have the ability to enhance organizational ethos. Telling the whole story, rather than one small part of it, conveys respect for readers and a desire for an authentic relationship. The public pressure to "go green" sometimes conflicts with the financial pressure to increase profits. When a narrative integrates opposing forces from multiple story lines, however, readers are more likely to gain a sense that organizational decision making is based on a genuine sense of purpose, direction, and identity. Livesey (1999) pictured the rhetorical ambivalence that marked the discursive struggle in environmental-corporate partnership. The texts we studied show how this type of rhetorical ambivalence continues to create challenges.

CONCLUSION

When Bullis (1997) issued her challenge to business and management communication scholars to turn their attention to the natural environment, she argued that new theoretical approaches were needed to make these efforts succeed. Our study has introduced narratology as a new theoretical base and analytical method for such explorations. Our analysis has revealed how organizations in the lodging industry used a variety of author-reader focalization patterns in their texts to influence individual and group commitment to environmental values and action. These narrative patterns created environmental, financial, and service-oriented story lines that served contrasting rhetorical purposes. Symbolically, the environmental story met people's emotional needs to feel virtuous, the financial story met their needs to feel successful, and the service story met their needs to feel important. Some organizations, like InterContinental Hotel Group, achieved a narrative balance that contributed to a strong organizational ethos, identity built on consistent values and credible action. In other cases, however, persuasive efforts to gain commitment to environmental values and action were undermined by limited story lines containing inconsistencies and discrepancies. Especially problematic was the conflict between the expressed desire for financial gain and the need to project an image of environmental social responsibility. Lack of alignment between an organization's stories and the fabula from which they are drawn raises skepticism.

If ever there was a worldwide value, it is our collective responsibility to protect the natural resources on which we all depend. Yet, the global nature of environmental concern suggests two potential challenges in creating or strengthening organizational ethos in this regard. First, worldwide electronic access to information dramatically increases the potential to uncover discrepancies and omissions in organizational texts. People have become accustomed to investigate issues of significance and form independent opinions based on a variety of sources. Informed readers are likely to readily recognize the disconnects in texts that ultimately compromise an organization's ethos.

Second, the wide variety of constituencies with which organizations communicate presents a particular challenge when the goal is to create shared values about and understanding of environmental issues. Symbols can be powerful forces in advancing an organization's environmental goals, yet the risk of unintended interpretation is always present, especially in messages that evoke a strong emotional response. Organizations seeking to gain commitment to environmental values and action can increase the effectiveness of their appeals by understanding the impact symbols have on creating shared values and motivating action.

Regardless of their intentions, the stories organizations tell will be suspect—and ineffective—unless those organizations have built reputations for aligning action with espoused values. When readers perceive stories as mere fairy tales, organizational ethos is undermined and messages, "green" or otherwise, are unlikely to persuade constituencies to accept values and take action.

REFERENCES

American Hotel and Lodging Association. 2008. *2008 Lodging Industry Profile.* Washington, DC: Author.

Bakhtin, M. M. 1981. *The Dialogic Imagination.* Austin: University of Texas Press.

Bakhtin, M. M. 1986. *Speech Genres and Other Late Essays.* Austin: University of Texas Press.

Bal, M. 1997. *Narratology: Introduction to the Theory of Narrative,* 2nd ed. Toronto: University of Toronto Press.

Bansal, P., and K. Roth. 2000. Why Companies Go Green: A Model of Ecological Responsiveness. *Academy of Management Journal* 43: 717–48.

Bargiela-Chiappini, F., C. Nickerson, and B. Planken. 2007. *Business Discourse.* Basingstoke, England: Palgrave Macmillan.

Boje, D. M. 2001. *Narrative Methods for Organizational and Communication Research.* Thousand Oaks, CA: Sage.

Boje, D. M. 2008. Spin. In *The SAGE Handbook of New Approaches in Management and Organization*, eds. D. Barry and H. Hansen, 203–12. Los Angeles: Sage.

Boje, D. M., and G. A. Rosile. 2003. Life Imitates Art: Enron's Epic and Tragic Narration. *Management Communication Quarterly* 17: 85–125.

Booth, W. C. 1961. *The Rhetoric of Fiction.* Chicago: University of Chicago Press.

Bullis, C. 1997. Business Communication and the Natural Environment: Using Traditional and Contemporary Perspectives to Understand the Connections. *Journal of Business Communication* 34: 455–77.

Eco, U. 1984. *The Role of the Reader: Explorations in the Semiotics of Texts*. Bloomington: Indiana University Press.
Fineman, S. 1996. Emotional Subtexts in Corporate Greening. *Organization Studies* 17: 479–500.
Fisher, W. R. 1987. *Human Communication as Narration: Toward a Philosophy of Reason, Value, and Action*. Columbia, SC: University of South Carolina Press.
Fludernik, M. 2009. *An Introduction to Narratology*. London: Rouledge.
Genette, G. 1980. *Narrative Discourse: An Essay in Method*. Ithaca, NY: Cornell University Press.
Harris, L. C., and A. Crane. 2002. The Greening of Organizational Culture: Management Views on the Depth, Degree and Diffusion of Change. *Journal of Organizational Change Management* 15: 214–35.
Hartelius, E. J., and L. D. Browning. 2008. The Application of Rhetorical Theory in Managerial Research. *Management Communication Quarterly* 22: 13–39.
Iser, W. 1974. *The Implied Reader: Patterns of Communication in Prose Fiction from Bunyan to Beckett*. Baltimore: Johns Hopkins University Press.
Iser, W. 1978. *The Act of Reading: A Theory of Aesthetic Response*. Baltimore: Johns Hopkins University Press.
Jameson, D. A. 2000. Telling the Investment Story: A Narrative Analysis of Shareholder Reports. *Journal of Business Communication* 37: 7–38.
Jameson, D. A. 2001. Narrative Discourse and Management Action. *Journal of Business Communication* 38: 476–511.
Jameson, D. A. 2004. Conceptualizing the Reader-Writer Relationship in Business Prose. *Journal of Business Communication* 41: 227–64.
Johnson, D. B., and G. Macy. 2001. Using Environmental Paradigms to Understand and Change an Organization's Response to Stakeholders. *Journal of Organizational Change Management* 14: 314–35.
Kearns, M. 1978. *Rhetorical Narratology*. Lincoln: University of Nebraska Press.
Livesey, S. M. 1999. McDonald's and the Environmental Defense Fund: A Case Study of a Green Alliance. *Journal of Business Communication* 36: 5–39.
Livesey, S. M. 2001. Eco-identity as Discursive Struggle: Royal Dutch/Shell, Brent Spar, and Nigeria. *Journal of Business Communication* 38: 58–91.
Livesey, S. M. 2002. Global Warming Wars: Rhetorical and Discourse Analytical Approaches to ExxonMobil's Corporate Public Discourse. *Journal of Business Communication* 39: 117–48.
Sharma, S. 2000. Managerial Interpretations and Organizational Context as Predictors of Corporate Choice of Environmental Strategy. *Academy of Management Journal* 43: 681–98.
Slatoff, W. J. 1970. *With Respect to Readers: Dimensions of Literary Response*. Ithaca, NY: Cornell University Press.
Smith Travel Research, Inc. 2008. *The HOST Study*. Hendersonville, TN: Author.
Starkey, K., and A. Crane. 2003. Toward Green Narrative: Management and the Evolutionary Epic. *Academy of Management Review* 28: 220–37.

Tompkins, J. P., ed. 1980. *Reader-Response Criticism: From Formalism to Post-Structuralism*. Baltimore, MD: Johns Hopkins University Press.

Whittle, A., F. Mueller, and A. Mangan. 2008. In Search of Subtlety: Discursive Devices and Rhetorical Competence. *Management Communication Quarterly* 22: 99–122.

Conclusion

Robyn C. Walker and Jolanta Aritz

The purpose of this collection has been to bring together researchers doing work in the so-called areas of little *d* and big *D* discourse or business and organizational discourse. It has done so in a variety of ways, by providing theoretical illumination on how the approaches address differing levels of analysis that may overlap and intersect each other (Heracleous), by providing research that used methods and theoretical assumptions from both approaches (McClellan and Deetz; Fujio and Tanaka; Thomas and Stephens; Salge and Barrett; Ruiz-Garrido, Fortanet-Gómez, and Palmer-Silveira; Anderson; Jameson and Brownell; and Conley, Broome and Krawiec), and by showing how some situations that start with little *d* call forth and require big *D* analysis (Bargiela-Chiappini), regardless of their initial research intent.

Loizos Heracleous's chapter opened by providing four propositions intended to improve the clarity of theoretical exposition in the field, to address interrelated levels of analysis, and to potentially lead to more cumulative and integrated research in the field. Taken together, the four propositions offered by Heracleous shed light on the process of discursive reality construction and help to better situate the relationship between little *d* and big *D* discourses. For example, Proposition 1 (discourse can fruitfully be seen as situated symbolic action) lets us see that situated contexts are nested within organizational settings and thus can be studied at several levels.

These multiple levels of analysis are first, at the meta level of the ontology of discourse (the nature of discourse as situated symbolic action, informing the rest of the propositions); second, at the micro level of single texts, communicative actions, and individual communicative intent and cognition; third, at the meso level of discursive interaction and social construction of reality; and finally at the macro level of power, social context, and institutionalized meanings.

With this understanding as a backdrop, we might now see that little *d* discourses typically focus on the individual and meso levels of context, while much of big *D* discourse studies tend to investigate the institutional level.

Propositions 1, 2, and 3 underlie what is looked at by both little *d* and big *D* discourses and may be the focus of both research interests, while Proposition 4 is generally the interest solely of big *D* research, at least as the division between the two areas is currently understood. Through this exposition of theory, we can more clearly see the relationship of the two approaches, both in their commonalities and differences, among other things. But as other chapters in this collection show, the two distinctions sometimes overlap and can inform each other in complementary ways.

Heracleous recognizes this intersectionality and suggests it be leveraged through research that collects data at multiple levels of analysis. This type of multilevel research can help to address important research challenges, such as exploring both text and its context, or the roles and interrelations of both structure and agency.

This latter type of research was presented by McClellan and Deetz, who showed how the two fields—little *d* and big *D*—actually meet in their study of a planning session at a small college of art and design. Their starting point was critical discourse analysis—big *D* discourse—which typically embraces a concern for revealing hidden power relationships and a focus on language as a way to understand the complexities of organizational practices that marginalize the interests of some groups. They used the approach to look at an area typically of concern for little *d* researchers, local practices of talk. In doing so, they embraced the distinction between little *d* and big *D* discourses by claiming that their approach—politically attentive relational constructivist (PARC)—complicates this simple duality and engages the complexities of organizational talk by attending to the interrelationships among various meanings of organization and understandings of the self as expressed in different contexts and conversations of organizing practice. They claim that PARC attends to language as a relational *and* political process that constitutes experience.

Furthermore, they show how a PARC perspective can provide critical insight into the ways discursive formations become articulated, negotiated, and normalized. From this perspective, PARC can serve as another connection between the functions and focus of little *d* and big *D* perspectives. It does this by looking at three levels of analysis: understanding, critique, and transformation.

> Inspired by qualitative approaches that seek to develop understandings of organizational events as they occur in "natural" contexts (Lindof and Taylor 2002), our attention is directed toward understanding the organization as it is known in practice through interviews as well as exploration of organizational events and processes through participant observation. . . . *Critique* recognizes that social construction always occurs within relationships of power. . . . Critique helps expose the mechanisms through which relations of power

> are formed, reproduced, and maintained through discourses. Transformation involves reclaiming alternative meanings that have been marginalized by dominant, taken-for-granted ways of knowing an organization. The aim of this moment is to complicate the discourse and encourage discussion of alternative relational understandings in conversation. (Deetz and McClellan, 56)

Rather than engaging in critical approaches, such as critical discourse analysis, that typically attend to broader social processes or cultural practices that reinforce ideological meaning formations, a PARC approach attends to the conversations among stakeholders that simultaneously enable and constrain the understandings that guide organized life. Its area of study is thus the same as little *d* approaches. But its aim is to understand how change occurs, an area typically the focus of big *D* perspectives. "The aim of such an approach focuses not on critique of ideology but on revealing moments of meaning suppression in talk with the hope of finding opportunities for engaging in discursive transformations through moments of free and open conversation that questions the political formations of meaning and engenders new vocabularies of action motivated by alternative ways of knowing the organization and the self" (Deetz and McClellan, 77). The focus on little *d* data helps us to understand the process of big *D* concerns. From this perspective, big *D* concerns emerge from little *d* foci.

Their approach of negotiating these three moments of analysis also differs from the traditional discursive approaches that focused on developing deep insight or authoritative knowledge of the organization in that it aims to identify processes inherent in meaning construction that are treated as natural and invisible in organizational life and to then find ways of working with organizational members to engender alternative forms of interaction that might produce more productive and useful futures. They thus are interested in the possibility of transformation.

Bargiela-Chiappini provides another way to conceive of the intersection between little *d* and big *D* discourses in her discussion of Asian Business Discourses. According to Bargiela-Chiappini, in its current manifestation, Asian Business Discourse(s) concentrates on the analysis of pragmalinguistic aspects of (oral and written) communication in the workplace and their socioideological underpinnings. However, "in the context of a critical appraisal of specific epistemological and ontological positions within business discourse, the choice of the parenthetic plural form 'Asian Business Discourse(s)' (or ABDs for short) is significant [for] it encapsulates the tension between 'business discourse' as a European social epistemology (with methodological consequences), and the plurality of 'discourses' that are emerging from the distinct socio-historic business environments that compose the vast geo-political expanse known as 'Asia'" (Bargiela-Chiappini, 82). Bargiela-Chiappini argues that ABDs is an enterprise with Western antecedents but with increasingly localized expressions, which reflect the concerns and expectations of specific geopolitical and socioeconomic *locales*. This is where the traditional focus on language (little *d* discourse) begins to intersect with the traditional concerns of big *D* approaches, specifically, in regard to the problem of what language. That is, in actual workplaces, the problem of what language to use or to study, be it English, the native language or code-switching and code-mixing in multilingual workplaces, creates a problem that alters the focus on little *d* concerns to those of big *D*. According to Bargiela-Chiappini, "When linguistic preferences imposed by management clash with the employees' needs, expectations and effective practices, the financial and political consequences of corporate language policy become all too apparent" (97). With this move, business discourse—little *d*—makes the move to a big *D* perspective, whether intentional or not. The study of business discourse in Asian has by its very nature made little *d* approaches into big *D* ones.

Fujio and Tanaka pick up another thread of Bargiela-Chiappini's discussion to propose an analytical framework that builds on concepts developed by Japanese scholars as a first step toward a progressive "decolonization" of business discourse research epistemology and toward local control of socially situated inquiry. The findings of this study point to the interdependence of local interactional patterns and organizational discourse and challenge the solidity and homogeneity of management systems that are often taken for granted. The dynamics of what they term *harmonious disagreement* is a window on how a local discourse constructs companywide, team-oriented organizational systems and norms in Japanese companies. In other words, (Japanese) management systems do not preexist observable local business discourses. Instead, Fujio and Tanaka argue that such systems are being crafted by practitioners as instances of social reality. In this chapter, the authors showed how business participants effectively co-construct a localized discourse that reflects a continuous concern for the preservation of interactional "harmony," not as a value exclusive to Japan, but perhaps rather more as a response to ideological and social conditioning that promote hierarchy, status, and authority among the organizing principles of (corporate) life.

This intersection between language use and political consequences continues in Thomas and Stephens, as they look at public comments to a proposed change by the U.S. Coast Guard's Ninth District (USCG) to create a new government safety zone associated with a new live fire training policy for the Great Lakes. More specifically, they focus on discursive practices to understand how the power relations of the surrounding societal context are brought into the social space. In doing so, they combine little *d* discourse methods of analysis—coding of public comments for tone—with a second layer of analysis (as called for by Heracleous), a big *D* method of critical discourse analysis aimed at discovering themes, sources of power, and overarching frames used by the public and the Coast Guard. Their case presents a practical example that demonstrates the way in which political policy space can be opened, created, and shaped by a variety of actors, their use of discourse and the strategies inherent in discourse use. They thus not only show the intersection of big *d* and little *D* approaches to discourse but also continue the discussion of how discourse can create change.

Change is also the focus of Salge and Barrett, who looked at how an organization builds legitimacy for an initiative through the use of rhetoric or language. Quoting Berger and Luckmann (1996, 64), they maintain that "the edifice of legitimation is built upon language and uses language as its principal instrumentality" (178). Their findings contribute to the literature on organizational exploration and exploitation in the fields of organizational learning and strategic management. It demonstrates that a discursive perspective offers novel insights into the internal dynamics of exploration and exploitation. More specifically, they show that different types of change may affect the choice of strategic intent, beneficiary, and rationale in the language that is used by change agents. Furthermore, they show that change agents may also use differing persuasive appeals, theories of change, and legitimacy type depending upon the type of change being forwarded by organizational actors.

Ruiz-Garrido, Fortanet-Gómez, and Palmer-Silveira analyzed Chairman's Statements in annual reports to show how personal pronouns are used to establish a relationship between writer and reader and to some extent, to construct a corporate identity. Of all the studies presented here, it best exemplifies research from the little *d* tradition; although, it also transgresses to some extent into the social creation of reality realm in looking at constructions of relationships and identity through language use.

Anderson picked up on the topic of change as well as corporate identity in his study of meetings of a project team at a high-tech corporation in the western United States. As Anderson relates, old models of change assume that an organization is a stable, consistent, lasting, durable phenomenon and that change is the momentary disruption of that stability. Following this assumption, change management models, books, approaches, and hired consultants recommend that achieving change is best accomplished by "unfreezing" the current organization, making modifications, and then "refreezing" it into its new form (Lewin 1951). Discourse perspectives on change turn this assumption upside down, Anderson points out, to offer a view of organizational change as a discursive process in which language patterns help members to negotiate and alter underlying meanings. More specifically, organizational members draw upon previously agreed-upon patterns (structures) but also adapt them in creative ways, and it is this adaptation of previous conversations that form what we think of as organizational change (Anderson 2005).

Not only does Anderson demonstrate how a discourse perspective might add to our understandings of organizational change processes, he also shows how it can reshape our understanding of organizational identity. The concept of organizational identity has most often been defined as the aspects of an organization that remain relatively stable and constant over time. But a discourse perspective assumes that the element of stability that was proposed by earlier definitions of identity is an achievement derived as an outcome of interactions of organizational members. In this respect, identity is no longer a property of an organization as something it has; rather, identity is an accomplishment as an outcome of a collaborative social process. According to Anderson, the stability of an organizational identity actually exists as a result of the set of discursive patterns and choices that organizational members make to enact and jointly create it.

In his study, Anderson analyzed benchmarking discourse to assert that such discourse opens up a space for negotiating change by confronting organizational members' self-identity with that of another organization. The practice of benchmarking is thus a means by which organizational identity and stability are negotiated and constructed but which also provides an opportunity to categorize possible changes and brainstorm them in light of a newly learned language. His study thus shows us one more avenue for creating change.

Jameson and Brownell looked at narratives to learn how organizations use environmental texts to tell a story that will create shared meanings and develop a collective understanding of and commitment to environmental values and action. Because the success of such efforts is by no means assured, they also explored how contradictions and discrepancies might undermine the persuasiveness of environmental texts and thus diminish organizational ethos, defined as identity built on deeply held values and credibility demonstrated through action.

In their study, they identified seven focalizations through which organizations signaled different reasons to accept, believe, and act on environmental values. Each pattern built a different relationship between the implied author and implied reader and, by extension, between the organization and its intended audience. They then considered how the focalizations helped to construct larger story lines. Those narrative patterns created environmental, financial, and service-oriented story lines that served contrasting rhetorical purposes. Symbolically, the environmental story met people's emotional needs to feel virtuous, the financial story met their needs to feel successful, and the service story met their needs to feel important.

They found that organizations seeking to gain commitment to environmental values and action can increase the effectiveness of their appeals by understanding the impact symbols have on creating shared values and motivating action. For those stories to be effective, however, organizations must build reputations for aligning action with espoused values. When readers perceive stories as mere fairy tales, organizational ethos is undermined and messages, "green" or otherwise, are unlikely to persuade constituencies to accept values and take action.

From their study, we can see that processes of change and reality construction can be hampered by inattention to the creation of a corporate identity that aligns with the message of change. These studies thus interrogate and illustrate the iterative loop that forms the relationship not only between little *d* and big *D* discourses but among language use, change, and identity. The latter linkage is explained by the process of the creation of social reality, which is where this investigation started.

Conley, Broome, and Krawiec explored what corporate board members *say* about the significance of diversity on corporate boards to try to ascertain how they constructed a social reality around the notion of diversity. What they found is that their sample did not have a coherent narrative about the reason for or importance of diversity on corporate boards. Whether this has any connection to the relative lack of diversity on corporate boards in the United States will be have to be left to another study. But again, they show how the telling of stories can be critical to the creation of new social understandings within an organizational context.

In summary, the work in this collection has provided a lens through which we can better apprehend the multiple levels of analysis that might be applied to organizational research but also has provided a number of examples of how such multilevel analysis might be carried out and the results that come from such an understanding and approach. The results provide us greater understanding of the activities of social creation at play in organizations more generally but also enables us to see these how these activities produce or resist change and create or subvert organizational identities.

More than thirty years ago, Henry Mintzberg suggested that managerial work is too dynamic, fragmented, and unsystematic to fit within the conventionally understood (at that time) four functions of management—to plan, organize, coordinate, and control (Fairhurst 2007). His views were then attacked by those who said that managerial work is really mental work and the "observable behaviors, such as talking, reading and writing serve as inputs and outputs to neuropsychological activities" (Carroll and Gillen 1987, 43). Such an attack represented many in the United States, where a psychological lens and empiricist methods still predominate in the field of management

(Fairhurst 2007; Alversson and Sveningsson 2003; Conger 1998; Knights and Willmott 1992).

This collection provides more fodder for those who believe that the study of management could be dramatically deepened and widened by a whole-hearted embrace of the insight that might be delivered through discourse methods and approaches. That is, if we overlay Heracleous's model onto the psychological and empiricist methods that still predominate in the field of management, we can better see the levels of analysis that may be yet under-theorized and examined by these approaches and how discourse might add to our understanding in these areas in a complementary way. For example, the ontological field covered by Heracleous's Proposition 1 is largely assumed, ignored, or normalized in such studies. Even though the second level or the micro level of single texts, communicative actions, and individual communicative intent and cognition may be studied by those who look at leadership, teamwork, and negotiation, the actual practices involved in such activities might be better understood through discourse methodologies. Because of its concern with the social construction of reality, the meso level of analysis might also be largely overlooked by psychological and empirical approaches, while the same might be said for the macro level of power, social context, and institutionalized meanings. Because the ontological field is largely overlooked in the empiricist approach, the other levels of analysis that arise from that field may also be obscured.

Once these gaps have been exposed by applying Heracleous's model, it is clear how discourse methods and approaches can complement and enhance our current understandings and study of organizations.

But more than that, a discourse approach can call into question deeply held assumptions that underlie some of these approaches. In this collection, Deetz and McClellan speak specifically to this issue in their use of a phenomenological perspective to make this transition from psychology to language. Their PARC perspective is grounded in phenomenology and its presupposition that all experiences and things of the world are inseparable from the presubjective, preobjective relationships within the constitutive activities that brought them into being (Berger and Luckmann 1966; Deetz 2003). In other words, a PARC perspective recognizes discourse as a practice that calls forth the things of the world. This perspective embraces the notion that experiences and objects of the world are not "out there" as static, stable entities to be named by using language but rather, by using language to name the indetermined "things" of the world, the world becomes constituted through as a set of relational understandings enabled and enacted through discourse. From this perspective, language replaces consciousness as the site of experience production and communication replaces psychology as the focus of attention for understanding organizational life. It is thus potentially revolutionary in the way that we have understood organizations and in the way that we should be conducting our research within and about them.

Furthermore, many of the chapters in this collection focus on how change is brought into existence through language use or what might be thought of as the social creation of reality. Potentially, this foundational if not radical recognition could and should change the way we study and look at change within organizations and perhaps, even more broadly, within communities. As Anderson suggested in this collection, discourse perspectives on change radically disrupt the assumption that an organization is a relatively stable phenomenon to offer a view of organizational change as a discursive process where language patterns help members to negotiate and alter underlying meanings (Anderson 2005).

As displayed in the chapters in this volume, the notion of organizations as stable entities is clearly linked to the issue of organizational identity. Discourse perspectives provide an opportunity for understanding how organizational identities are created, negotiated, and resisted by different stakeholders. Such a perspective thus provides an opportunity to learn much more about not only processes of organizational change but also of organizational identity and to subsequently enhance our current understandings of these processes.

There are, of course, obstacles to such complementary work. While discussing future directions of business communication research in North America, Dulek and Graham (2009) critique the current state of interdisciplinary research for providing more lip service to the notion of interdisciplinarity. They are right to note that discourse scholars are not readily accepted into management theory and management researchers have tended to stay away from rhetorical theory and discourse studies. Yet, as this discussion as been aimed at showing, this constraint can be viewed as a significant opportunity that brings an extremely diverse knowledge base informed by different disciplines.

Some scholars have put forward the concept of multidisciplinarity as distinct from interdisciplinarity, whereby business and organizational discourse can be viewed as a separate and distinct discipline neither subordinate nor overshadowed by other disciplines that it draws on (Bargiela-Chiappini, Nickerson, and Planken 2007). Instead, the model of multidisciplinarity is seen as an opportunity to view business or organizational discourse as a separate discipline united by a shared interest in language as the vehicle of analysis of matters pertinent to organizational settings. We hope that this collection of works is another step forward in providing a forum for interdisciplinary researchers to share different methodologies that inform the area of inquiry—organizations, communities, and their actors—and moves the field of organizational and business communication forward in unique and complementary ways as a discipline in its own right that draws from such diverse fields as management, communication, linguistics, and anthropology.

REFERENCES

Alversson, M., and S. Sveningsson. 2003. Good Visions, Bad Micro-Management and Ugly Ambition: Contradictions of a (Non-)leadership in a Knowledge-Intensive Organization. *Organization Studies* 24: 961–88.

Anderson, D. L. 2005. "What You'll Say Is . . .": Represented Voice in Organizational Change Discourse. *Journal of Organizational Change Management* 18: 63–77.

Bargiela-Chiappini, F., C. Nickerson, and B. Planken. 2007. *Business Discourse*. New York, NY: Palgrave Macmillan.

Berger, P. L., and T. Luckmann. 1966. *The Social Construction of Reality: A Treatise in the Sociology of Knowledge*. New York: Anchor-Doubleday.

Carroll, S. J., and D. J. Gillen, D. 1987. Are Classical Management Functions Useful in Describing Managerial Work? *Academy of Management Review* 12: 38–51.

Conger, J. A. 1998. Qualitative Research as the Cornerstone Methodology for Understanding Leadership. *Leadership Quarterly* 9: 107–21.

Deetz, S. 2003. Reclaiming the Legacy of the Linguistic Turn. *Organization: The Interdisciplinary Journal of Organization, Theory, and Society* 10: 421–29.

Dulek, R. E., and M. B. Graham. 2009. Future Horizons: North America. In *The Handbook of Business Discourse*, ed. F. Bargiela-Chiappini. Edinburg: Edinburgh University Press.

Fairhurst, G. T. 2007. *Discursive Leadership: In Conversation with Leadership Psychology.* Los Angeles: Sage Publications.

Knights, D., and H. Willmott. 1992. Conceptualizing Leadership Processes: A Study of Senior Managers in a Financial Services Company. *Journal of Management Studies* 29: 761–82.

Lewin, K. 1951. *Field Theory in Social Science.* New York: Harper and Brothers.

Lindlof, T. R., and B. C. Taylor. 2002. *Qualitative Communication Research Methods*, 2nd ed.

Index

About the Editors and Contributors

Jolanta Aritz received her PhD in linguistics from the University of Southern California. She is associate professor of clinical management communication at the USC Marshall School of Business. She conducts research on small group communication, cross-cultural issues, leadership and business discourse and has published in the *Journal of Intercultural Communication Research, Journal of Business Communication,* and *Journal of Asian Pacific Communication.* Her collaborative interdisciplinary research project with Robyn Walker received a research grant from the USC Advancing Scholarship in the Humanities and Social Sciences Initiative. She teaches Advanced Business Writing, Communication Strategy for Business, Managing Communication in Organizations, and Communication for Doctoral Students at the Center for Management Communication at USC. She has been awarded multiple grants from the USC Fund for Innovative Undergraduate Teaching.

Robyn C. Walker has earned a bachelor's, master's, and doctoral degree in communication. She also has master's degrees in business administration and professional writing. She is the author of the textbook *Strategic Management Communication for Leaders (2nd edition)* and editor of *BCOM* (1st, 2nd, 3rd and 4th editions). She is editor of the *Journal of Business Communication* and teaches business writing and communication. Her research interests include place-based identity, intercultural group communication, and leadership communication. In collaboration with Professor Aritz, she has had articles published in the *Journal of Intercultural Communication Research, Journal of Asian Pacific Communication,* and *Journal of Business Communication.*

* * *

Donald L. Anderson, PhD, is the author of *Organization Development: The Process of Leading Organizational Change* (2nd ed., 2012) and the editor of *Cases and Exercises in Organization Development and Change* (2012). His studies of organizational discourse and change have appeared in publications such as the *Journal of Organizational Change Management*, *Gestion*, the *Journal of Business and Technical Communication*, and *Discourse Studies*. He is a practicing organization development consultant who has worked with Fortune 500 corporations, small businesses, and educational institutions. Dr. Anderson teaches at the University of Denver and is a member of the Academy of Management.

Francesca Bargiela-Chiappini has researched business discourse and intercultural communication for a number of years. Following recent collaboration with Asian colleagues, she is exploring the idea of a multicentered approach to the study of communication based on engagement with non-Western ontologies and epistemologies. She is honorary associate professor in the Centre for Applied Linguistics at the University of Warwick in England.

Michael Ian Barrett is professor of information systems and innovation studies at Judge Business School, University of Cambridge. His research interests include the role of discourse and social theory in studying IT enabled innovation. He is coeditor of a special issue of *MIS Quarterly* on Service Innovation in a Digital Age and is senior editor of *Information & Organization* and the *Journal of the Association of Information Systems*. He has published in a number of leading journals including *Information Systems Research, Academy of Management Journal,* and *Organization Science.*

Lissa L. Broome is the Wachovia Professor of Banking Law, directs the Center for Banking and Finance, and heads the Director Diversity Initiative (DDI) at UNC School of Law. She serves as the University's Faculty Athletics Representative. The DDI aims to increase the gender, racial, and ethnic diversity of public companies through an annual training program, a database of potential diverse directors, and periodic surveys of board diversity at the fifty largest NC companies. Broome is the coauthor of *Regulation of Bank Financial Service Activities* (with Jerry W. Markham). She holds a BS from the University of Illinois and a JD from Harvard Law School.

Judi Brownell is professor of organizational communication and dean of students at the School of Hotel Administration, Cornell University. She also has served as associate dean for academic affairs and as the director for graduate studies. Brownell teaches courses in organizational behavior and management communication and has designed and conducted training seminars for a wide range of hospitality, educational, high-technology, and other work organizations. Professor Brownell has international teaching experience and her online eCornell executive courses are used worldwide. She is author of several business and communication texts, including *Listening: Principles, Attitudes, and Skills* (2010).

John M. Conley is William Rand Kenan, Jr. Professor at the University of North Carolina School of Law. He is an anthropologist and lawyer, and his research has explored the language of law, business, and, most recently, science. He has written several books and numerous articles on the anthropological and linguistic study of the American legal system (with William O'Barr), the culture of business and finance, and the language and culture of biomedical research. His books include *Rules versus Relationships: The Ethnography of Legal Discourse* and *Just Words: Law, Language, and Power* (both with O'Barr).

Stanley Deetz, PhD, is professor, President's Teaching Scholar, and director of the Center for the Study of Conflict, Collaboration and Creative Governance at the University of Colorado at Boulder. He is author or coauthor of over 100 articles and several books including Leading Organizations through Transitions, Doing Critical Management Research, Transforming Communication-Transforming Business, and Democracy in an Age of Corporate Colonization. His current research focuses on intersector governance processes and designed interaction processes in relation to democracy, micropractices of power, and collaborative decision making. He was a Senior Fulbright Scholar and is a National Communication Association Distinguished Scholar and an International Communication Association Past-President and Fellow.

Inmaculada Fortanet-Gómez has a PhD in English philology from the Universitat de València. She is senior lecturer at Universitat Jaume I, where she teaches academic and business English as well as English language within the philology course of study. She participates in teacher training with courses on academic writing, conference presentations, and teaching in English and studies English and Content and Language Integrated Learning (CLIL) in university settings. She has published chapters and coedited several international volumes and has published in journals such as *English for Specific Purposes*, *English for Academic Purposes,* and *Discourse Studies*.

Misa Fujio is associate professor of business administration at Toyo University in Japan. She obtained a PhD from the University of Tokyo in applied linguistics. In addition to her research in this area, she has been conducting research in business communication based on her previous experiences working for American-based global companies. Her publications include "Silence during intercultural communication" (*Corporate Communications*) and *Communication Strategies in Action*. The strategies discussed in this publication were also broadcast in an NHK radio program, *The English Tidbits Club,* in which she appeared in 2009 and 2010.

Loizos Heracleous is chair of the Department of Strategy and Organization at Warwick Business School and associate fellow at Warwick and Green Templeton College at Oxford University. He earned his PhD at the University of Cambridge. His research interests revolve around organizational discourse, organizational aspects of strategy and corporate governance. He received three awards for his work from the Academy of Management and his research has been published in over 50 research papers, in journals that include the *Academy of Management Journal, Academy of Management Review, Harvard Business Review, Journal of Management Studies, Organization Studies and Human Relations*.

Daphne A. Jameson is professor of management communication at the School of Hotel Administration, Cornell University, where she has also been the director of graduate studies. She has served as president of the Association for Business Communication and won the Kitty O. Locker Outstanding Researcher Award in 2007. Her research uses literary theories and methods to explore business and technical discourse. She earned a PhD in English at the University of Illinois.

Kimberly D. Krawiec is the Kathrine Robison Everett Professor of Law at Duke University and teaches courses on corporate, securities, and derivatives law and taboo trades and forbidden markets. Her research interests include corporate board diversity, financial reform, corporate compliance systems, "rogue" trading, egg and sperm markets, surrogacy markets, and kidney allocation systems. Prior works on board diversity include articles in the *North Carolina Law Review* and *Seattle University Law Review*.

John G. McClellan, PhD, is assistant professor of communication at Boise State University. His research explores the discursive qualities of organizing with attention to issues of knowledge, identity, and collaborative change. His work appears in *The Handbook of Business Discourse, The Oxford Handbook of Critical Management Studies*, and *Reframing Difference in Organizational Communication Studies: Research, Pedagogy, and Practice.* With an interest in collaborative practices that might enable more sustainable and mutually beneficial ways of organizing, his work attends to discourses that simultaneously enable and constrain opportunities to transform the ways we understand and engage organizational life.

Juan Carlos Palmer-Silveira has a PhD in linguistics and lectures and carries out research at Universitat Jaume I. He is currently working in English for business communication (EBC) and ESP. He is the author of several books and articles published internationally, having coedited *Genre Studies in English for Academic Purposes* (1998) and *Intercultural and International Business Communication* (2006), among others. He is a funding member of the GRAPE research group.

Miguel F. Ruiz-Garrido, PhD, is a member of the research group GRAPE and associate professor at Universitat Jaume I (Castelló, Spain). He teaches English language, English for business communication, and English for nursing at different levels. His main research fields are English for professional and academic purposes. Within these fields he has coauthored *Hablar Inglés en la Universidad: Docencia e Investigación* (2008) and coedited *Intercultural and International Business Communication: Theory, Research and Teaching* (2006) and *English for Professional and Academic Purposes* (2010). He is currently coeditor-in-chief of the online international journal *Language Value*.

Torsten Oliver Salge is assistant professor for management and innovation at the Ruhr-University Bochum (RUB). He holds a PhD and an MPhil degree, both from the University of Cambridge. Prior to joining RUB, he was a postdoctoral research associate at the University of Cambridge. Moreover, he was a visiting scholar at the Universities of Oxford, Pennsylvania, Cambridge and Auckland. His research focuses on processes of learning and innovation with particular emphasis on public sector organizations and has been published in such outlets as the *Journal of Product Innovation Management* or the *Journal of Public Administration Research and Theory*.

Kimberlie Stephens is clinical assistant professor at the Annenberg School for Communication and Journalism at the University of Southern California in Los Angeles, CA. At Annenberg she teaches organizational communication and marketing research methods to graduate students in the Masters of Communication Management program, both on campus and online. Her research focuses on organizational strategic communication, social networks and interorganizational relationships. Dr. Stephens also earned her PhD from the USC Annenberg School.

Hiromasa Tanaka is dean of the International Studies Center and professor at the School of Humanities and Social Sciences at Meisei University in Tokyo. He received his Ed.D. in curriculum, instruction and technology in education from Temple University. His research interest are in the area of business discourse and critical pedagogy with a special focus on human resource development in multinational business corporations. Hiromasa was a managing consultant of SNNO Institute of Management. As a consultant, he participated in several corporate change initiatives and training curriculum development projects in Japan, Korea, China, Iran, Kazakhstan, Saudi-Arabia, Indonesia, and the United States,

Gail Fann Thomas completed an Ed.D. at Arizona State University in 1986. She is associate professor in the Graduate School of Business and Public Policy at the U.S. Naval Postgraduate School in Monterey, California, where she teaches managerial communication for MBA students and strategic communication for executives. Dr. Thomas conducts research on interorganizational collaboration, conflict management, and communication as it relates to strategy and organizational change efforts. She has published in several academic journals and coauthored a booklet on conflict management in team settings.

CPSIA information can be obtained at www.ICGtesting.com
Printed in the USA
BVOW060252131211

277962BV00003B/3/P

9 781611 474374